The
LOGIC OF BELIEF

An Introduction to the Philosophy of Religion

DAVID ELTON TRUEBLOOD

Professor of the Philosophy of Religion
Stanford University

----

*"The struggle between belief and unbelief is the only thing in
the memoirs of humanity worth considering."—Goethe*

HARPER & BROTHERS PUBLISHERS
New York and London

PREFACE

Every philosophical work must have a special emphasis, not only because the vastness of the field precludes equal treatment of all relevant topics, but also because each writer has his own convictions concerning what is important. In the following pages I have sought to present an introduction to the nature of belief in general and religious belief in particular, always from the point of view of the logician. An effort is made to deal objectively both with the reasons for belief and the difficulties of belief. The title chosen is intended to denote this emphasis. If the title is associated, in the reader's mind, with such similar ones as Balfour's *Foundations of Belief*, Newman's *Grammar of Assent*, and Gore's *Reconstruction of Belief*, I shall not be sorry.

Anyone who tries to think carefully on fundamental questions is keenly aware that he is sharing in a co-operative enterprise, and that his intellectual debts are legion. My greatest personal debts of this kind, I owe to two of my teachers, Dean Willard L. Sperry of Harvard, and Professor Arthur O. Lovejoy of Johns Hopkins, and to my former senior colleague, Professor Rufus M. Jones of Haverford. From Professor Jones I gained an abiding interest in religious experience as a revelation of the real world and from Dean Sperry I gained an admiration for "tough-mindedness" in theology. Professor Lovejoy confirmed my leanings in the direction of critical realism, encouraged me to submit all concepts to rigorous logical analysis, and opened my eyes to the metaphysical significance of time.

It is not surprising, with this background, that I should have been drawn to the writings of William Temple, now Archbishop of Canterbury, whose Gifford Lectures constitute one of the intellectual ornaments of our time. In Temple we find a thinker who combines a tough-minded epistemological realism with metaphysical idealism. The result may be called *dialectical realism*, and to this I subscribe. The reader will note that I refer more often to Dr. Temple's published work than to that of any other man.

It is my conviction that our intellectual labors can be far more valuable if we use the knowledge of the expert at whatever point our subject overlaps his. Those who are members of university faculties have a fortunate opportunity in this regard —an opportunity of which we do not avail ourselves sufficiently. On questions about *physics*, I have consulted Professor David L. Webster and Professor Paul Kirkpatrick. On questions about *biology*, I have consulted Professor Chauncey D. Leake. Similarly, Professor Calvin P. Stone has been consulted about *psychology*, Professor Warren D. Allen about *music*, and Hermann F. Fränkel has contributed a note on pre-Milesian philosophy. Other helpful readers have been Professors Frederick Anderson, Harold Chapman Brown and Henry Lanz. Some of these men take exception to some of the conclusions of this book, but their comments have been most valuable in regard to knowledge which only the expert possesses.

In Chapter XII I have used a few sentences from my larger studies on the subject of the chapter, *The Trustworthiness of Religious Experience* and *The Knowledge of God*. Otherwise all the material is now published for the first time.

D. E. T.

Stanford University

CONTENTS

INTRODUCTION

I. PHILOSOPHY, SCIENCE AND RELIGION 3

PART I. THE STRUCTURE OF BELIEF

II. BELIEF AND TRUTH 23
    A. Modes of Truth (Objective) 25
    B. Modes of Truth (Subjective) 33

III. THE NATURE OF EVIDENCE 37
    A. Proof 37
    B. Cumulative Evidence 41
    C. Scientific Method 43
    D. Analogy 47

IV. THE NECESSITY OF FAITH 51
    A. Difficulties of Knowledge 51
    B. The Argument for Realism 59
    C. Types of Agnosticism 62
    D. The Choice of Faiths 64

V. THE AUTHORITY OF DISCIPLINED INSIGHT 66
    A. The Inescapability of Authority 67
    B. The Personal Equation 72
    C. Disciplined Insight 75
    D. The Authority of the Amateur 79

PART II. TYPES OF BELIEF

VI. THE DEVELOPMENT OF THE NATURALISTIC CREED 87
    A. The Dialectical Movement of Intellectual History 87

B. Contemporary Naturalism   93
C. Details of the Naturalistic Creed   97

VII. THE INSUFFICIENCY OF THE NATURALIST CREED   103
A. The Unsatisfactory Account of Goodness   104
B. The Unsatisfactory Account of Truth   107
C. The Unsatisfactory Account of History   113
D. Transition   116

VIII. THEISTIC REALISM   118
A. Stability in Religion   118
B. Progress in Religion   120
C. The Place of World Religions   129
D. The Religion of Maturity   131

PART III. THE EVIDENCE FOR THEISTIC BELIEF

IX. THE EVIDENCE OF NATURE   143
A. The Existence of Science   144
B. The Fact of Evolution   148
C. The Second Law of Thermodynamics   154

X. THE EVIDENCE OF MORAL EXPERIENCE   160
A. The Phenomena of Conscience   161
B. The Objective Factor in Moral Experience   164
C. The Augustness of Ought   169
D. The Paradox of Freedom   172

XI. THE THEOLOGICAL SIGNIFICANCE OF AESTHETIC
EXPERIENCE   179
A. The Objectivity of Beauty   179
B. The Sense of Communication   187
C. The Aesthetic Argument   194

XII. THE EVIDENTIAL VALUE OF RELIGIOUS EXPERI-
ENCE   196
A. The Primary Datum of Religion   197
B. Normative Religious Experience   199
C. Subject and Object   203
D. The Tests of Veracity   206

XIII. THE APPEAL TO HISTORY   215
    A. The Witness of Historical Persons   215
    B. The Evidence of Historical Development   220

PART IV. DIFFICULTIES OF BELIEF

XIV. THE PROBLEM OF NATURAL SELECTION   229
    A. The Darwinian Hypothesis   230
    B. The Darwinian Controversy   234
    C. The Limits of Natural Selection   238

XV. THE PROBLEM OF WISH THINKING   248
    A. The Hypothesis of Projection   249
    B. Weaknesses of the Projection Theory   254

XVI. THE PROBLEM OF NATURAL LAW   261
    A. The Nature of the Difficulty   261
    B. Two Kinds of Order   265
    C. Examination of the Mechanical Theory of Law 269
    D. The Working Solution of the Problem   275

XVII. THE PROBLEM OF EVIL   280
    A. The Nature of the Problem   281
    B. Proposed Solutions of the Problem   284
    C. The Reduction of the Area of Difficulty   294

CONCLUSION

XVIII. THE BELIEF IN IMMORTALITY   307
    A. Empirical Evidence   310
    B. Intimations from the Nature of Mind   313
    C. The Corollary of Faith   319

SUGGESTIONS FOR READING   321

INDEX OF NAMES   337

INDEX OF SUBJECTS   341

ACKNOWLEDGMENTS

Acknowledgment is due to the following publishers who have granted permission to quote from copyrighted publications: to D. Appleton-Century Company for quotations from C. F. Russell's *Religion and Natural Law*; to Henry Holt & Company for a quotation from Patrick Geddes and J. Arthur Thomson's *Evolution*; to the Hogarth Press of Letchworth, Herts, England, for a brief quotation from Sigmund Freud's *The Future of an Illusion*; to Little, Brown & Company and the Atlantic Monthly Press for a quotation from Hans Zinsser's *As I Remember Him*; to the Macmillan Company for quotations from A. E. Taylor's *The Faith of a Moralist* and "The Vindication of Religion" in *Essays Catholic and Critical*, William Temple's *Nature, Man and God*, Alfred North Whitehead's *Science and the Modern World*, E. W. Barnes' *Scientific Theory and Religion*, and Rufus M. Jones' *Religious Foundations*; to the Oxford University Press for a quotation from Hartley Burr Alexander's *God and Man's Destiny*; to Prentice-Hall, Inc. for a quotation from W. P. Montague's *The Ways of Things*; to the Princeton University Press for quotations from Paul Elmer More's *The Sceptical Approach to Religion*; to Stanford University Press for quotations from G. A. Johnson Ross' *Behavior and Destiny*; the Yale University Press for quotations from William P. Montague's *Belief Unbound* and Charles A. Bennett's *The Dilemma of Religious Knowledge*; to L. J. Henderson for a quotation from his *The Fitness of the Environment*; and to the Clarendon Press, Oxford, for a quotation from Robert Bridges' Book III of *The Testament of Beauty*.

INTRODUCTION

CHAPTER I

PHILOSOPHY, SCIENCE AND RELIGION

"Religion, science and philosophy refer to the same world."
—E. S. BRIGHTMAN

Almost all the great philosophers, as well as many who would not label themselves with this slightly presumptuous title, have toyed with the question of man's precise mode of differentiation from other animals. Man is obviously different, but what is the crucial difference? What significant types of experience or modes of behavior do we find in human beings which we do not observe in other living organisms?

The answers to this question have been legion. It has been said that man is the only animal who laughs, the only one who weeps, the only one who prays, the only one who walks fully erect, the only one who makes pictures, the only one who reasons, the only one with a long infancy, the only one who uses tools, the only one who makes fires, the only one who can invent, the only one with a written language, the only one who is proud, the only one who can make progress, the only one who guides his own destiny, the only one who is penitent, and the only one who needs to be. The list could be continued much farther, and its very length gives vivid evidence of how keenly men of various periods have been interested in the problem.

These inquiries, some of which are playful, though not fully so, appear, at first, to have little in common and to lead nowhere, inasmuch as the answers are markedly diverse. But the most instructive fact about the entire enterprise is the fact that the question is persistently asked. Consideration of this fact leads to the conclusion that the question is more important than

any of its particular answers, inasmuch as the very existence of
the problem tells us something important about human life.
There is one conclusion to which all the facts point, and that is
that man is the animal who reflects, who asks apparently useless
questions, who is curious about matters far removed from those
concerned with food and shelter. Man cannot remain satisfied
with a world of *things*, but is driven on to probe its *meanings*.
One of his major needs is the need of understanding himself
and his place in an objective order. He is not satisfied merely to
act, but must know *why* he acts and whether he *ought* to act as
he does.

That man, whatever else he is, is a "metaphysical animal"[1]
is shown in many ways, one of these being the honor which
we accord to those who have tried to answer our perplexing
questions which, from a physical point of view, are unnecessary. Our most honored classics are, in large measure, just those
books which have dealt most successfully or most profoundly
with the spiritual life. Thus we honor the sacred scriptures of
various peoples, thus we prize the works of poets and philosophers and reprint them endlessly. We appear to be occupied
with mundane affairs, but actually we are willing to go to almost
any length to listen to those who give some evidence that they
are able to share some wisdom about the meaning of existence.
Unsatisfied in one way our metaphysical thirst inevitably seeks
satisfaction in another.[2]

Though there is a true sense in which the entire spiritual
life is a unit, in practical experience it tends to break up into

---

[1] Cf. Schopenhauer, "Er ist sonach ein animal metaphysicum."

[2] Contemporary evidence is afforded by the degree to which men whose
chief efforts have been devoted to natural science are turning to the consideration of broadly philosophical questions. This is true of physicists and
biologists alike. In a single recent number of the *Scientific Monthly* are the
following subjects of major articles: "A Physicist's View of Ethics," "Religio
Scientiae," and "Science and True Religion." An important part of the meeting of the American Philosophical Society in Philadelphia in December, 1940,
was devoted to a symposium on moral principles, chiefly from the point
of view of science.

separate and defined patterns of experience, concerned with special ways of seeking the fundamental ends of life. We are tempted to say that each form of the spiritual life seeks one of these fundamental ends. Thus we might say that science is that which seeks truth, art is that which seeks beauty, ethics is that which seeks goodness, and religion is that which seeks holiness. But such a division would be a gross misrepresentation, missing a large share of the richness of actual experience. Science is, of course, a search for truth, but philosophy is also, and certainly any religion worthy of attention claims with great vigor that it is true. It is noteworthy that so great a part of theological literature is concerned with the intellectual vindication of religion.

Most of the forms of the spiritual life have developed specialized professional practitioners. There have long been scientists, philosophers, artists, and priests or prophets. In each field there is a tendency for two groups to emerge, one concerned with the *study* of a field and the other with its *practice*. This is most striking in the pursuit of beauty, where there is a marked difference between the student of aesthetics who *examines* standards of beauty, and the artist or poet who seeks to *create* beauty. A poet, in the Greek use of the word, is a maker. The person, on the other hand, whose chief interest in beauty is theoretical, is more like a scientist. Aristotle pointed, in a memorable phrase, to the distinction between the scientist and the craftsman, by saying that the former develops skill "in the sphere of being" while the latter develops skill "in the sphere of coming to be."[3]

One of the distinctive marks of ethical experience is its failure to produce a class of professional practitioners corresponding to the artist in the realm of aesthetic experience. Most of those called moralists are really moral philosophers, concerned with the study of moral problems, but not claiming to be either better than others or more concerned with the pro-

---

[3] *Analytica Posteriora*, 100a.

duction of practical morality in the world. The more advanced men become in the moral sphere the less they claim to be good. The production of better moral conditions, furthermore, is the responsibility of all men and not of a specialized or separated class.

Our worst mistake, in considering the forms of the spiritual life, lies in the initial suggestion that they neatly divide the domain between them. As a matter of fact they overlap in various ways, and are not really correlative. For the most they do not *segment* experience. In a real sense, each includes or seeks to include everything, for the spiritual life is incurably totalitarian. The great leaders of religion have refused to admit a valid distinction between the areas of the secular and the sacred, but have maintained that everything has some possible religious significance.

In the same way, art recognizes no barriers. As art becomes more vigorous, it finds themes everywhere and discovers beauty in unconventional places; it is not confined to galleries and academies. In his justly famous Preface to *Lyrical Ballads* Wordsworth pointed out that poetry can, with dignity, use common themes with common words. The true poet writes not for a special class of men, but for man as man. "The Poet writes under one restriction only, namely, the necessity of giving immediate pleasure to a human Being possessed of that information which may be expected of him, not as a lawyer, a physician, a mariner, an astronomer, or a natural philosopher, but as a Man."[4] The artistic enterprise is not successful until beauty is both recognized and produced in every area of common life.

If this is true of art, it is even more true of morality. The good life consists not in performing one special class of actions, but in performing all actions well. There is nothing which we can do, say, or even think, which is totally devoid of ethical

---

[4] Preface to the second edition, Cf. *The Poetical Works of William Wordsworth*, Oxford edition, p. 938.

significance. This is true largely because of the way in which all lives are interdependent.

Not to be outdone by the other forms of the spiritual life, science reaches out and admits no barriers to its progress. Since science is a *method* of ascertaining truth, more than it is a body of doctrine, it may be extended in many ways. Thus we seek in modern civilization to make a scientific approach to social problems as well as to the problems of the natural order. More recently, an attempt has been made, in what is called empirical theology, to deal, in a fully scientific manner, with man's relationships to God.

Thus science, ethics, and religion are universal in scope and not guardians of divided realms. How, then, do they differ from philosophy? Chiefly in this, that philosophy seeks to envisage all things from the point of view of reflection, whereas other forms of the spirit envisage as much of reality as possible from the point of view of scientific method or aesthetic appreciation or moral significance or reverence. All seek to deal in some way or other with all of reality, but philosophy alone is vitally concerned with what is reality and what is only appearance. Thus, when we become critical and reflective, we can have a philosophy of art, a philosophy of science, and a philosophy of religion, to go along with ethics, which is the philosophy of conduct, and logic, which is the philosophy of philosophy.

It is desirable to consider in greater detail the difference between philosophy and religion, inasmuch as they are most easily confused in popular estimation. Sometimes the banal phrase "philosophy of life" comes to be practically a synonym for religion, and in some minds philosophy is supposed to be able to take the place of religion, with no consequent sense of loss. As a matter of fact the two approaches are widely different, in spite of the degree to which they deal with the same areas of experience. Both seek knowledge, but they seek it for different reasons. "Philosophy seeks knowledge for the sake of understanding, while Religion seeks knowledge for the sake of worship."[5]

Frequently, of course, both philosophy and religion are activities of the same person, and the individual can distinguish between his two ways of thinking and acting. As philosophers we look at individual facts of experience and they become question marks. We try to see what general conceptions we can form which will account for them. James Bissett Pratt is speaking for many of his fellow philosophers when he writes: "As I view it, the problem proposed to every philosopher might be worded thus: Given these and these facts, what hypothesis best unifies them and best illuminates the world we live in?"[6] As religious men we look at individual facts of experience and know that there is a deep sense in which they are already explained, for they are expressions of the mind of God. The more we know the intricacies of physics and chemistry, the more we understand the divine Mind which underlies these wonders.

This point of separation is made most clear by a consideration of the philosophy of religion. Here the method is the method of philosophy, but religion is the subject we explore. The philosophy of religion begins with experience, with the data of religion, as facts among other facts which we desire to understand. Having pointed carefully to the data, we next analyze them, and then we try to form an hypothesis which will account adequately for the data. Since that is the method of this book, it is a philosophy book. It is a book about religion, but it cannot rightly be called a religious book. The truly religious books are those which, like the great devotional classics, exemplify the devout spirit of religion as experienced. The books of the Bible are religious books, but they are not books about religion. In fact the very words "religion" and "religious" barely escaped entire absence from the Bible. It

---

[5] William Temple, *Nature, Man and God*, London, 1934, p. 30.
[6] James Bissett Pratt, *Naturalism*, New Haven, 1939, p. ix.

seems to have been left to the Greeks to invent the philosophy of religion.

Whereas the philosophy of religion begins with the data of experience and then seeks to account for these by means of an adequate hypothesis, making as few assumptions as possible, religion begins at the other end of the process. Religion begins with God as known and worshiped and explains the detailed facts of the world by reference to Him. If there is some interpretation of the facts which is incompatible with the central fact of God's revelation, religion is bound to reject such an interpretation or at least ask philosophy to investigate the validity of the interpretation in question. Thus philosophy may be of great use to religion, partly in giving intellectual support to faith, and partly in helping to eliminate whatever element of phantasy may have crept into religious faith. Religion may welcome the work of the reflective reason, but religion does not consist in intellectual assent to any or all conclusions of the reflective reason. Therefore a man may be a philosopher and not specifically religious in any practical sense at all. This is possible even when the name of God is frequently on his lips. It is thoroughly possible to use God as a necessary ingredient of a metaphysical structure, sometimes under the name of the Absolute, without the spirit of devotion which is the mark of religion everywhere. Such a use of the name of God is almost as far from religion as is the use of that name in heated arguments on religious subjects. Religious argumentation may be totally alien in spirit to religion itself. Archbishop Temple's genius for brilliant expression has seldom been better illustrated than in his remark: "The heart of Religion is not an opinion about God, such as Philosophy might reach as the conclusion of its argument; it is a personal relation with God."[7]

The characteristic features of religion which appear in various races and periods are four. In the first place there is a *belief*. Usually this belief refers to supernatural powers as their

[7] William Temple, *Nature, Man and God*, p. 54.

object, with the conviction that there is more to life than its mere material structure. In the second place there is a *cult*. This involves forms of public prayer and worship with varying degrees of ceremonialism. In the third place there is the resultant system of *moral practice*, involving codes of law seen as divinely given. For good or ill the practical lives of men are greatly altered by their religion. In the fourth place there is some *organization*, frequently with a professional priesthood and hierarchy. This is the church and it may be organized loosely or rigidly.

Though these features appear in most examples of what most people would call religion, we dare not suppose that religion is nothing but a combination of these. There is an *extra* which seems to be an irreducible factor and which makes religion unique among the forms of spiritual life. This extra is to be understood as a logical primitive, not to be explained as a mere combination of other factors. If it is a logical primitive, it is futile to hope that we can explain it fully by the use of other concepts, and, when we try to do so, we are committing what Professor G. E. Moore has so aptly called "the naturalistic fallacy."[8] When we try to explain religion as *nothing but* primitive fear plus priestcraft or *nothing but* a projection of childhood father idealizations we are committing this fallacy in a flagrant manner.

Even though we recognize religion as a logical primitive, and therefore not reducible to anything else, there are three important things which we can do in our effort to understand it. We can describe the unique mood which we call religious, showing what its kinships are. In the second place, we can show something of the manner in which the religious mood arises, and, third, we can show what its characteristic fruits are.

In describing the mood in question the following considerations are important. (a) *The mood is akin to poetry*. While it is obviously an overstatement to say with Matthew Arnold that

[8] Cf. G. E. Moore, *Principia Ethica*.

poetry and religion are the same, it is clear that the mood of prose is alien to religion. We cannot fail to be impressed with the fact that religious literature so often achieves poetic form. This is true not only of explicit poetry, like that of the Hebrew Psalms, but also of apparent prose like that of the parables of Jesus, filled with poetic imagery. It is perhaps inevitable that highly repeatable truth should take on poetic form since it would be intolerable to repeat it in less cryptic and moving ways. The Christian, in his effort to make a suitable testimony concerning what he knows of the love of God, breaks forth into hymns and songs, and even the modern Buddhist finds this practice worthy of imitation.

The poet sees an ordinary event, but he sees it as more than an event; it becomes for him a doorway revealing the hidden beauty or pathos of the world. Witness the reaction of Burns to the wreck of a mouse's nest or the reaction of Blake to the spectacle of the little lamb. Both those who enjoy poetry and those who produce poetry are able to see details as intimations of meaning much as the worshiper is able to find, in many areas, intimations of divine revelation. Arthur Clutton-Brock has interpreted the work of Blake as a poet in words that are strikingly suggestive of the life of devotion.

There is no other poet who has so great a fame based upon poems so short; and it was, no doubt, his faith, always present and acting in his mind, which enabled him to make short poems so large. He could see a world in a grain of sand, and Heaven in a wild flower; he could hold infinity in the palm of his hand and eternity in an hour, because individual things meant to him always the universal, in which he put his trust; and that is why we feel that universal in his little individual poems.[9]

This is a vivid and convincing way of saying that Blake was really a poet, for what Mr. Clutton-Brock mentions is what poets are always trying to do. This is why they exemplify

[9] Arthur Clutton-Brock, *Essays on Literature and Life*, New York, 1926, p. 64.

Shelley's saying that "imagination respects the similitude of things." Poets find all kinds of surprising similitudes because, to their sensitive minds, there is revealed a deep kinship between things. In like manner, the man of faith recognizes no creature as wholly alien to him, since all things owe their existence to a common Source.[10] For primitive peoples poetry is as natural as religion is, and it is only when we are removed from primitive spontaneity that we begin to question either their value or their validity.

(b) *The mood is akin to that of love.* More than one thoughtful student of religion has realized that the characteristic religious experience is more like falling in love than anything else we know in common life. The experience of falling in love is one in which one attachment heightens the emotional tone of all others. All aspects of life take on new meaning for the man in love. He does the same things which he did before, but nothing is really the same.

There are many levels on which life can be lived; we may merely go through the motions or we may thrill with a sense of life's meaning. There are some people who seem to have a special gift for high enthusiasm, with its constant escape from dullness, but all people who have caught something of the spirit of religion have this in a measure. This has been conspicuous in many who have not been fortunate in a worldly sense.

We shall have much to say later about the purely intellectual phases of religious faith, but we should be clear from the beginning that religion is never devoid of emotion any more than love is. It is not a defect of religion, but rather its glory, that it speaks always the language of feeling.

(c) *The mood is akin to that of loyalty.* The characteristic religious act is one in which a man gives himself, *without reservations,* to what he considers intrinsically worthy of his loyalty. The supreme trust which religion nourishes and expresses, is not an induction from tangible evidence, but some-

[10] Note George Fox's phrase, "unity with the creation."

thing which goes beyond evidence. It is not antirational, but it goes deeper than rationality. We are now aware that the saying of Job, "Though he slay me, yet will I trust him," is a mistranslation of the Hebrew, but the fact that this English expression has found a response in so many devout souls for so many generations is highly instructive, telling us something important about the mood which we call religious.

A thoroughgoing loyalty, which has a quasi-religious quality wherever found, is often observed among men, whether scientists, artists, or reformers, who are in conscious revolt against what they understand as religion. To give oneself loyally, and in complete trust, is to approach closely to the experience of worship, an experience sharply different from mere intellectual assent. Sometimes the religious man says "I believe," but far more often he says, "Into thy hands I commit my spirit."

(d) *The mood is akin to that of humility.* It may seem paradoxical to say that the religious spirit is marked by the sense of life enhancement which the lover knows, and at the same time, is marked by humility, but this is really not surprising. It is characteristic of the lover to know and to express his unworthiness, just as it is characteristic of the worshiper to know and express his sinfulness. There is an inevitable sense of contrast between the glory revealed and the feeble instrument who receives these impressions of glory. Thus the devout man makes confession an integral part of his prayer, while the prophet says, "Woe is me." We are assured that the publican who prayed "God be merciful to me a sinner" was closer to the Kingdom of God than was the proud Pharisee.

Sometimes the strange notion becomes current that religion encourages men to feel "good." As a matter of fact it does quite the opposite. It is easy to cite expressions from religions as far apart as Hinduism and Judaism to prove this point. It is, moreover, noteworthy that Jesus Christ, when he was addressed as Good Master, objected, saying, "Why callest thou me good? There is none good but God."

If we try to go beyond these four relevant kinships and to find one word which best tells what religion is about, that word is *reverence*. The mood of reverence is composed of apparent opposites, for the worshiper at once is filled with wonder at the Object of his adoration and yet he recognizes that this Object is not totally alien to him. Wonder and love, enhancement and humility, mingle together in unique ways. The experience thus described is more moving than mere knowledge and more intimate than mere wonder. Efforts at definition of religion have been even more barren and useless than most essays in definition, but, fortunately, there is little need for definition. The somewhat ostentatious collections of definitions of religion, sometimes found in psychologies of religion, lose much of their supposed value in view of the considerations urged by Professor Webb when he says,

I believe it would be as vain to demand a formal definition of Religion at the outset of our enquiry as it would be to demand a formal definition of Beauty at the outset of an investigation of an aesthetic problem. None such can be given which would explain to anyone altogether without experience of either what we mean by it; and probably none which could not immediately be countered by an admitted instance of Religion or of Beauty which obviously did not conform to our definition.[11]

The reason why definition is not needed is that the experience can be pointed to and recognized, inasmuch as no race is without it, and no individuals are untouched by it.

We may talk, if we like, about human life apart from the direct influence of religious experience, but the human life to which we thus refer is a fiction or, at best, an inference. We have no knowledge of such people in existence. All the peoples we know, or really know *about*, are peoples who feel in manifold ways the demands of a supernatural order on their

[11] C. C. J. Webb, *Religion and Theism*, New York, 1934, p. 12.

lives. No person in the Western world can escape, by an act of deliberate choice, the facts of Christianity. A person untouched by religious faith is like the "natural" child, living alone on an island, the contemplation of whom gave such enjoyment to certain intellectual leaders of the eighteenth century; he is a figment of the imagination. Since religion is thus universal in influence, an academic definition of it is unnecessary as well as futile.

When we seek to show how religion arises, we can hardly avoid the conclusion that it is "natural" and yet more than natural. It is natural in that it arises spontaneously, that it has apparently had an independent origin in various parts of our globe, and that it cannot be attributed to the machinations of priestcraft. But it is more than natural in the sense that, in all developed religion, there is conscious teaching. The idea of a merely natural religion is a convenient abstraction, useful in discussion, but we have never observed it in practice. Everywhere the spirit of devotion is artificially and consciously aroused or nourished. The difference between natural and revealed religion is slight, since it is natural for men to be aware of revelation, and revelation comes about in a multitude of natural ways.

It is also important to point out that religion arises in a nice combination of solitariness and community feeling. The lone individual may become a religious genius, but he has behind him the sense of sharing in the life of the group. Wholly solitary religion is as fictitious as wholly natural religion. Most men come to their deepened religious consciousness as they share in the worship of their fellows.

When we consider the characteristic fruits of religion we are in a world of wonder. The wonder lies not in the goodness of these results, for they are sometimes evil, but in intensity and extensity of the results. Religion does not always make life *better*, but not often does it fail to make life *different*. There is usually a sense of life enhancement and this is still the case when evil ends are pursued. It has often been observed that men fighting in battle with a religious cause as their cause are the most nearly invincible of men. Familiar evidence from long ago is provided by the Moslem sweep across North Africa and into Europe, but it is not necessary to go so far back in our history to find convincing evidence. The Nazi movement of our day has much of the spirit of a religion and, to an increasing degree, many of the external marks of a religion.[12] There is little doubt that many have experienced, in their fanatical devotion to a leader and to a cause, a species of "salvation." They have come to have a new quality in their lives, markedly in contrast to their former condition. The difference their religion makes may, in the end, be an evil difference, but it is a difference.

Though it is most important to make clear to ourselves the fact that religions may be harmful as well as beneficial, it would be untrue to suggest that the characteristic fruits, at least among the more developed religions, are preponderantly evil. Indeed, there are countless examples of lives in which the conscious acceptance of religious faith has brought reason and love, as well as courage and confidence. Often the insight of men has been markedly clarified, until they come to see as evil what formerly seemed harmless and they come to love as good what formerly they denounced or despised.

The Judeo-Christian tradition, which has been for sixteen centuries the dominant religion of the Western world, has never at any time been completely successful in altering the standards of men or dominating the course of events, so that our culture includes many vestiges that are distinctly sub-Christian in character, but, in spite of these facts, our spiritual heritage has been a social force of incalculable importance.

We are so prone to forget the roots of what we prize that we need words like the following to remind us:

[12] Witness the annual November celebration in Munich with use of processional, martyrology, and similar ritual.

There is nothing inevitable about those values which we do undoubtedly enjoy as members of a Christian civilization. We assume them as a matter of course and take them for granted; but you cannot have them forever or for long without the Christian faith as their presupposition and the Christian Society as their context and guarantee. Our civilization, in spite of all its blemishes and its many ghastly failures, is still a Christian civilization. Take away the Christianity and the civilization will not remain what you and I mean by civilization.[13]

It is our sorrow and our shame that nations long exposed to the Christian Gospel have engaged in recurrent wars of increasing bitterness and destructiveness, but it is part of the record that this same Gospel has made an increasing testimony to the iniquity of war. Shortly before the present conflict, Canon Quick said, with prophetic accuracy, "Unless the world becomes more Christian than it is, it will speedily become less moral than it has been." Much of the increasing sensitivity to the iniquity of poverty and of social insecurity is the direct product of religious insight. The work of Rauschenbusch and others of his type has borne fruit. In large measure our modern system of education, much of our conception of civil liberty, and many other features of Western civilization which we take for granted, would not be with us, at least not in their present form, if Christianity had not been exported into Europe. In the same fashion many of the features of life in India have been determined by the presence of the Hindu and Moslem faiths. Few men in our time have been more successful than has Professor Whitehead in showing convincingly the manner in which religious ideas find embodiment in cultural development.[14]

Not only does religion thus characteristically make a difference in the social and industrial order, but also it makes a great difference in the private lives of individual men. The

[13] J. S. Whale, *The Right to Believe*, New York, 1938, p. 55.
[14] Cf. Alfred North Whitehead, *Adventures of Ideas*.

testimony to this fact comes from believers and unbelievers alike. Even a thinker like Santayana, who rejects much of what we call reasonable religion, nevertheless sees its true nature and is grateful: "We must," he says, "rather thank it for the sensibility, the reverence, the speculative insight which it has introduced into the world."[15] There is a body of pragmatic evidence and it is this which is referred to by Professor Lyman when he speaks of "that aspect of religion in which it appears as an enlarger and quickener of life, as a source both of insight and of energy."[16]

The classic works of spiritual autobiography are full of evidence of the new quality of life which comes by religious faith.[17] John Bunyan may be taken as representative of the great company of devout souls who have been plagued by a sense of their own sin and unworthiness, and yet have known a creative and overwhelming joy to break through their sorrow. Testimonies like the following are central to Bunyan's reported experience:

But the next day at evening, being under many fears, I went to seek the Lord, and as I prayed, I cried, and my soul cried to him in these words, with strong cries: "O Lord, I beseech thee, show me that thou hast loved me with everlasting love." I had no sooner said it, but with sweetness this returned upon me, as an echo, or sounding again, "I have loved thee with an everlasting love." Now I went to bed in quiet; also when I awaked the next morning, it was fresh upon my soul; and I believed it.[18]

Perhaps the most remarkable of the fruits of religion is the joy of which so many millions have given evidence. Because of their faith, men have faced martyrdom with joy as well as high courage, giving their persecutors no satisfaction by their cring-

---

[15] George Santayana, *Reason in Religion,* p. 13.

[16] E. W. Lyman, *The Meaning and Truth of Religion,* New York, 1933, p. 10.

[17] St. Teresa impressed Matthew Arnold, not by her struggle, but by her gracious spontaneity.

[18] John Bunyan, *Grace Abounding to the Chief of Sinners,* Paragraph 190.

ing. But they have likewise faced with joy the far more prosaic events of common life, bursting out spontaneously in songs of praise for so great a salvation. St. Francis when he composed his "Canticle to the Sun" was standing in the main stream of religious experience. It seems natural to men and women to sing in worship and sometimes those who do not themselves sing aid those who do.[19]

The joy that comes from religion so impressed the biologist Romanes that this eventually became the crucial fact turning him from an unbeliever to a believer. Romanes tried very hard to be a consistent atheist, but, as he followed the method of science which first looks honestly at the facts, he found that he could not account for the amount of joy he observed except by means of the theistic hypothesis.[20]

It is a phenomenon with such a mood, arising in such a manner, and with such characteristic fruits that provides the subject matter of the philosophy of religion. That it is a subject matter important to the human race cannot be doubted. Considered merely as a social phenomenon of history it is worthy of careful study, but the claim it makes to be true in its affirmations about the nature of reality are far more important. These claims are so revolutionary for human life, if true, that no philosophy can afford to let them remain unanalyzed. To accept these claims uncritically is as unsatisfactory as to reject them uncritically. Both positions are narrowly dogmatic and fundamentally credulous. What is needed in all generations is the careful application of the philosophical method to the data provided by experience, to see whether they lead or do not lead to the substantiation of the central affirmations of all religion.

In one sense, the proper mood for such study is that of the detached observer, but, while we adopt this mood as long as

[19] Whittier, who did not sing in worship, wrote poems now used as hymns all over the world.

[20] Cf. G. J. Romanes, *Thoughts on Religion*. This is a posthumous work, edited by Charles Gore.

we can, we should know that the deepest secrets are never revealed in this way. It is not surprising that the deepest secrets in religion are reserved for the person who has gone beyond observation to participation, for this is true likewise of art and of love. Moreover, it is strictly true that much is revealed to babes that is hidden to the wise and prudent. Indeed this is one of the conclusions of disciplined philosophers as well as one of the paradoxes of the Gospel. It was that arch-philosopher of modern times, F. H. Bradley, who said, "Nothing justifies intellectual pride so little as philosophy."

PART I

THE STRUCTURE OF BELIEF

CHAPTER II

BELIEF AND TRUTH

"The truth (or falsity) of a proposition antedates the process by which it is verified (or refuted)." —W. P. MONTAGUE

———————————————————————————

Human beings are engaged very largely in the acceptance, development, verification, and promulgation of beliefs. Much of what we believe turns out to be false and some of what is false we discard. On the other hand, we come to accept as valid many beliefs which formerly we have rejected. Throughout our lives this process of acceptance and rejection, of testing and verification, goes forward. At one time we believe a disease is incurable; at another time we believe it is curable. At one time we believed we had knowledge of all of the planets which surround the sun; later we believed that our former judgment was incorrect. Sometimes, with new evidence, we return to beliefs, supposedly outmoded. Thus we have wavered on the question of the atmosphere of the planet Mars. We are always believing, and we are always subject to change in our belief. Much of this, whether in the history of mankind as a whole, or in the history of a separated individual, is the growth into maturity, according to which we discard first our childish beliefs, then discard our sophomoric beliefs, finally arriving at beliefs which are more likely to survive permanent criticism. But these, too, may be modified, if there is reason for their modification.

Beliefs refer to propositions and propositions are statements capable of being true or false.[1] They appear in the indicative

———

[1] The chief difference between belief and knowledge is that we can believe falsely, but cannot know falsely. Knowledge must be true knowledge. The best and fullest study of these matters is John Laird, *Knowledge, Belief and Opinion*, New York, 1930.

mood. These indicative propositions may be about a great variety of matters, as any ordinary conversation will show. We have beliefs about history, beliefs about the structure of material aggregates, beliefs about the future, beliefs about God, beliefs about what is beautiful or what we ought to do. Most of these beliefs we state categorically. We say "Columbus landed in the West Indies," "Water is composed of hydrogen and oxygen," "Rain is falling today," "There will be a snowstorm tomorrow," "God knows each individual," "Greek temples are more beautiful than Egyptian temples," "I ought to work rather than play tennis today." Each of these statements, similar to thousands we make every day, is elliptical in that the preliminary statement is omitted. We might reasonably preface each of these propositions by the words, "I believe," or "There seems to me good evidence that." Every proposition becomes in fact a judgment, and man is a creature greatly concerned with his own judgments. We take our judgments seriously and, foolish as we are, we are deeply interested in the correctness of our judgments.

The opinion is often voiced that, in matters of religious faith, the question of truth has no bearing. It is alleged that religious faith is to be judged solely by its utility, by the comfort it gives to distracted or broken individuals, by the motivation it provides in the creation of a civilization, by its function in helping to produce "social control." But religion has its supposedly good social effects only on one condition, the condition that it is *believed*. And it will not be believed if it is evidently false. If its claims are not based on truth, the day will ultimately arrive when this fact is known, and then, with disillusionment, will come the end of the desirable social function. Illusions are not effective when recognized as illusory.

Coleridge's famous aphorism is applicable here. "He, who begins by loving Christianity better than Truth, will proceed by loving his own Sect or church better than Christianity, and end in loving himself better than all."[2] In any case, insofar as we are reasonable, we welcome disillusionment. The conscious harboring of known illusions seems to most people to be monstrous or even pathological. Accordingly we welcome any help we can give one another in learning how to test our beliefs.

When we say we believe a proposition we mean that we think it is *true*. *Truth is correctness of judgment.* In order to understand better the ways in which valid belief is possible we need to consider somewhat carefully the meaning of truth and its modes.

A. MODES OF TRUTH (OBJECTIVE)

All judgments refer to an objective relation between the mind of the person who makes the judgment and what is actually the case. Here one terminus of the relation is fixed and the other terminus is subject to change. When we make judgments about Columbus, what actually transpired in the discovery of the American continents at the end of the fifteenth century is the stable factor. The opinion of men about these events is the changing factor. Whatever occurred is presumably not affected in the least by the accuracy or inaccuracy of our present knowledge of these historical events. If two scholars have different and diametrically opposed opinions about what happened, they cannot both have valid beliefs. New research may cause us to relinquish old hypotheses, but new research, if it is valuable, only brings us closer to what has been objectively the case all along.

A brilliant illustration of the way in which new research leads to a sharp reversal of belief is provided by the life of the renowned Richard Hooker, author of *The Laws of Ecclesiastical Polity*. The life of Hooker is of great importance, both because of the beauty of his character and the lucid expression of his thought. It is possible for the foremost modern Hooker scholar to say, "In the long and crowded roll of great English men

[2] Samuel Taylor Coleridge, *Aids to Reflection*, Aphorism XXV.

of letters there is no figure of greater significance to the instructed mind than Hooker." But it now appears that almost
all "instructed minds" have been in radical error, for three
centuries, in regard to certain features of the Hooker story.

Izaak Walton in his *Life of Hooker* produced an undoubted
classic. One of the most charming features of this classic is its
amusing references to Hooker's unhappy marriage and the difficult domestic conditions under which Hooker's masterpiece was
written. We have all felt sorry for the unworldly scholar from
Oxford who was so grateful to Mrs. Churchman for curing his
cold that he married her unlovely daughter Joan, and thereby
grew in patient humility.

Now Professor Sisson has been able to find documents of
the courts in the late sixteenth and early seventeenth centuries
to show that Walton's picture was almost entirely incorrect.
We now know that Walton's *Life*, charming as it is and presumably always will be, can no longer be regarded as history.
In fact, it now appears that the judicious Mr. Hooker, far from
making a poor marriage, made a most judicious one. His wife
was the daughter of a wealthy London merchant and brought
him a considerable dowry. His great book was written under
favorable circumstances and with abundant encouragement. His
widow did not connive at the destruction of his unprinted
manuscript. He left sufficient money at his death to make possible several Chancery suits.[3]

Instructed opinion about the great Mr. Hooker has assuredly
changed in the last few months, but this is by no means the
same as the statement that the *truth* about Mr. Hooker has
changed. It is likely that Sisson's judgments achieve a greater
degree of correctness than do those of Walton and thus the
modern scholar approximates the objective truth, which is independent of Walton, Sisson, and all the rest of us. In this case

[3] C. J. Sisson, *The Judicious Marriage of Mr. Hooker and the Birth of the
Laws of Ecclesiastical Polity*, Cambridge University Press, 1940.

it is the discovery of documents which makes possible the achievement of a higher degree of correctness.

Consideration of this illustration helps us to see *how superficial is the notion that the truth changes.* Indeed, this notion upon analysis turns out to be either a mere truism or patent foolishness. The truism is nothing more nor less than the fact that opinions change. This nobody doubts, and it is hard to think of a time when anyone did doubt it. The fact that opinions change is not exciting news. If the popular notion of changing truth refers to anything more than opinion it becomes patent foolishness because it leads to direct contradictions. If it is the "truth" about Mr. Hooker that has changed, then we must both think that Richard Hooker married Joan Churchman on February 13, 1588, and that he did not marry her on February 13, 1588. It was true at the time of Izaak Walton that Hooker's manuscripts were destroyed, but now it is not true. On this basis, it is difficult to assign any reasonable meaning to falsehood.

The notion that what is true for one person may not be true for another and that what is true now may not be true a century later is, of course, a popular version of pragmatism, one of the *many* pragmatisms which Professor Lovejoy has analyzed for us.[4] But this kind of pragmatism is self-defeating. If truth consists wholly of "working value," then this proposition itself has nothing but working value. It is not a mere definition for it makes a negative statement about the objective order. But there are many people in the modern world who do not find that the pragmatic denial of objective truth fits into their own experience, i.e., it does not have working value for them. Consequently, if we follow pragmatic principles, they are speaking the truth when they say the doctrine of pragmatism is not true.

The self-defeating character of popular pragmatism is even more clear when we consider the future. The doctrine holds that what is now true may not be true later, because, with new

situations, there may be a new working value. A Hulsean lecturer at Cambridge has shown what bearing this has on pragmatism's own doctrine:

The pragmatist is bound by his own theory to believe that the
time may come when it will no longer be found adequate to the
requirements of a wider experience to say that truth is relative. A
million years hence men may have discovered that the belief in an
absolute truth is the only belief about the nature of truth which
works. The pragmatists of those days, if any such there are, will
therefore be compelled to believe, on pragmatical grounds, that truth
is absolute. . . . If truth is absolute then, it must have been so
all the time.[5]

So far as meaningful propositions are concerned, there are,
objectively speaking, only two modes of truth and these are
truth and *falsity*. A meaningful proposition is either true or
false and it cannot be both.

Meaningless propositions constitute a special class and present considerable difficulty in logical analysis. If a proposition
is wholly lacking in meaning, we should not call it false any
more than we should call it true. It cannot be either in accordance with what is the case or in conflict, for it really says nothing. Perhaps the best illustrations of meaningless propositions
are to be found in political speeches, especially just prior to
general elections. It is possible that some of the most bitter
theological debates have been waged over propositions of this
kind.[6] Since the deliberate construction of meaningless proposition is a difficult feat, *The Hunting of the Snark* is rightly
judged a work of creative genius.

There is a tendency in modern life to avoid the sharp distinction between truth and falsity by the aid of devious and
confusing intellectual devices. Thus when we are discussing the
question of God's existence there are many who seek to avoid

[5] C. F. Russell, *Religion and Natural Law,* New York, 1924, p. 178.

[6] This is not to say that I accept the operational theory of meaning or that
I have any sympathy with the tendency, of which Stuart Chase is representative, to hold that almost all abstract words are meaningless.

a clear-cut judgment by saying, "God may exist for John, but not for Henry." This kind of statement is so common that it requires some analysis. What rational meaning can be given to the expression "exist for"? Perhaps it means that John has an idea of God and Henry has not. But if that is meant, why should the concept of existence be introduced at all? It is obviously true that men have different ideas of various kinds; what we want to know is whether these ideas refer to anything real, anything independent of the knowers. Of course John may have some knowledge that Henry does not have; he may have a more percipient mind, but in that case it is knowledge of something and if it is genuine knowledge it is knowledge of something which really is. Thus we are driven back to the concept of existence.

The logical result of the notion of something existing for one person and not for another would be a theory of the world in which all knowledge would refer merely to what is in the knower's mind. In that case not only would God, and the material order be mere ideas in his mind, but also Henry would be nothing but an idea in John's mind and John would be nothing but an idea in Henry's mind. We have not the disposition to argue with anyone who wants to travel that ancient road, but it is not a road that leads to any profitable destination. Certainly when men have worshiped God they have not supposed they were worshiping ideas in their own minds. These would not be worthy of worship. We are not doing a service either to faith or reason by failure to make a sharp distinction between truth and falsity.

One of the chief reasons for confusion about truth is the recognition that what is true in one place may not be true in another. Thus it may be said that such a proposition as "It rained today" is both true and false at the same time. There was rain in Ohio and there was not rain in California. Or perhaps it depends on what one means by rain. The answer to this objection consists in nothing more nor less than *precision*.

The proposition "It rained today" is true or false and not both, if we are clear on what we mean by rain, and if we define sharply our locality. If we do not do this we have not one proposition, but many. The proposition about rain in another state is a different proposition.

Herein lies the strength of the classical or Aristotelian logic. It teaches men how to avoid playing fast and loose with truth. Undoubtedly it fails to include much that is valid in our new ways of thinking,[7] but it teaches us sternly that some beliefs exclude other beliefs. It does not let us ease out of difficulties with weasel words. The traditional square of opposition may not be satisfactory in its analysis of universal propositions, but it is highly satisfactory in its insistence on genuine contradiction.

The A proposition is a universal affirmative, the E proposition is a universal negative, the I proposition is a particular affirmative and the O proposition is a particular negative. Now the chief point is that the diagonals represent genuine contradiction while the horizontal lines do not. The proposition "All men are mortal" is strictly contradicted by the proposition "Some men are immortal." If A is true, O is false, and, if O is true, A is false. The same relation obtains between E and I.[8] But A and E, while both could not be true, might both be false, and I and O, while both could not be false, might both be true.

We know that some propositions are false when we realize that contradictory statements are made on many subjects. One proposition is: "Prayer never makes a difference in the course of natural events." Another is: "Prayer sometimes makes a difference in the course of natural events." One or the other of these propositions is false.

It is no idle paradox to point out that we are more sure of

[7] Cf. George Boas, *Our New Ways of Thinking*.

[8] The familiar letters used to designate these propositions come from the vowels of *affirmo* and *nego*. Those not familiar with the traditional square can find one in any elementary logic textbook.

error than of anything else, for we imply it even by denying it. Either there is error or there is not. But if there is not, then those persons, who have believed there is, have been in error. It is really easier to be sure of falsehood than of truth, yet if there is falsehood there must be truth, for what can falsehood deviate from, if not the truth?

Furthermore we can be reasonably sure, in some cases, *which* propositions are false, and this is possible in respect to most primitive absurdities. Thus the proposition "The earth is flat" is almost certainly false and it was equally false when the majority of our ancestors believed it true.

Among propositions that are true, whether we are aware of their truth or not, there is an important difference between those which are "true but trivial" and those which are "true and important." Many of the trivial truths are essentially tautologies which no one doubts and about which no one greatly cares. The important truths are, for the most part, much more difficult to ascertain and far more exciting. Both kinds of propositions may be illustrated among those presented for religious belief. It is one of the merits of Professor Montague's remarkable little volume of Terry Lectures that he presented this difference with uncommon clarity.

Religion as we shall use the term is not a traffic with demons and the dark forces pertaining to them. The belief in such objects is almost certainly false and quite certainly without moral significance. Nor is religion merely a belief in an ultimate reality or in an ultimate ideal. These beliefs are worse than false; they are platitudes, truisms, that nobody will dispute. Religion as we shall conceive it is the acceptance neither of a primitive absurdity nor of a sophisticated truism, but of a momentous possibility—the possibility namely that what is highest in spirit is also deepest in nature, that the ideal and the real are at least to some extent identified, not merely evanescently in our own lives but enduringly in the universe itself.[9]

Here we have the three possibilities mentioned above, the

[9] William P. Montague, *Belief Unbound,* New Haven, 1930, p. 6.

false, the true but trivial, the true and important. We are most concerned about the propositions which are important *if true*, and what we want to know is whether they are really true. Our only interest in our own ideas is that they should be in conformity with what is objectively the case.

It is instructive in this connection to remind ourselves of the distinction so ably made by David Hume between the two fundamental kinds of object of human reason or inquiry, *Relations of Ideas* and *Matters of Fact*.

Of the first kind are the sciences of Geometry, Algebra and Arithmetic; and in short, every affirmation which is either intuitively or demonstrably certain. *That the square of the hypotenuse is equal to the square of the two sides* is a proposition which expresses a relationship between these figures. *That three times five is equal to the half of thirty,* expresses a relation between these numbers. Propositions of this kind are discoverable by the mere operation of thought, without dependence on what is anywhere existent in the universe. Though there never were a circle or triangle in nature, the truths demonstrated by Euclid would forever retain their certainty and evidence.

Matters of fact which are the second objects of human reason, are not ascertained in the same manner; nor is our evidence of their truth, however great, of a like nature with the foregoing. The contrary of every matter of fact is still possible.[10]

The truth which we seek in the spiritual life is truth in regard to Hume's second class of objects. The deepest difficulty with the ontological argument for God is not that the argument is invalid, for it can be so stated that it is not invalid, but rather that the Object at which we arrive is not really the Object which worship requires. What it proves is hardly worth the trouble. Actual religion is concerned wholly with *matters of fact* just as actual science is. The nature of God is not the same as the nature of a tree, inasmuch as God is not known by the physical senses and the tree is, but the question of truth is the

[10] David Hume, *An Enquiry Concerning Human Understanding,* Section II, Part I.

same in both cases. In both, the real question is the question of objective existence as a matter of fact.

B. Modes of Truth (Subjective)

It is sometimes said that propositions may be divided in three ways, false, true, and doubtful. But such a division confuses the objective and subjective modes of truth. Propositions may, indeed, be doubtful, but they are not doubtful in the same way that they are false. A particular proposition which is once false is eternally false, providing we are precise in its formulation, but a proposition which is once doubtful may cease to be doubtful, for doubt refers, not to the objective order, but to opinion in human minds.

The notion of degrees of objective truth makes little sense, but there are all degrees of doubt ranging from complete uncertainty at one extreme to complete certainty at the other. The matters about which men are necessarily doubtful are far in excess of those in which certainty is possible. Sometimes a distinction is made between certainty and certitude, the latter referring to human convictions and often in error, whereas the former refers to what is certain in and of itself. But it is doubtful if this distinction is helpful to the understanding. Though the truth of any proposition may be independent of our knowing, it is difficult to see how the certainty of a proposition could be independent of our knowing it, since it is *people* who are certain while it is propositions that are true.

We have the greatest certainty in regard to those objects of knowledge which Hume called *relations of ideas*. Granted the truth of premises in a valid syllogism, the conclusion follows in a manner to make us certain of it, but only because it is really involved in the premises. As Hume pointed out, the question of existence need not enter in such situations. The following, from Lewis Carroll, gives us a perfectly certain conclusion, though the individual premises do not refer to what is true in matters of fact:

    (1) All puddings are nice.
    (2) This dish is a pudding.
    (3) No nice things are wholesome.
    (4) Therefore, this dish is unwholesome.

It is doubtful if we ever have in the world complete certainty except in such a series as that given above. This certainty arises from our tacit acceptance of the principle of noncontradiction. Only by neglecting this principle can the fourth of Lewis Carroll's proposition be denied if the first three are accepted. Thus all certainty arises in conclusions that are fundamentally hypothetical. If some things are true, then other things are true, but this procedure postpones the prior question concerning the validity of the initial assumption.

We see now that there is a great difference in status between the propositions which Aristotelian logic has called universal and those which are called particular. The universals do not refer necessarily to existence, but are fundamentally matters of definition. To say "All men are mortal" is the same as to say "*If* there are men, they are mortal." Such a proposition need not be doubtful. If we find a two-legged rational animal who is not subject to death, we conclude that he is not a man, whatever his appearance. On the other hand, the proposition "Some men are mortal" refers to existence. It means that there are really creatures of a certain kind, and that they die.

Now useful and interesting as are the propositions which give us certainty by avoiding questions of fact, it is the propositions about which we may be doubtful which interest us most. To say that they are doubtful is to say that the question of impossibility does not enter. The only kind of genuine impossibility of which we know is that in which there is direct contradiction in terms. As we become more mature as a race we use the conception of impossibility less and less, confining ourselves to the humble task of learning what is and has been actual.

For the most part our doubtfulness is merely a measure of our own ignorance. Who really committed any particular crime is a fully determinate matter, but *we* are doubtful because our knowledge is slight and fragmentary. As our knowledge increases we become less doubtful until we approach what is called "moral certainty." This is the same as high probability, for probability, except as a study in pure mathematics with no necessary relation to actual events, is a measure of human ignorance. Augustus De Morgan defines probability as "the state of mind with respect to an assertion, a coming event, or any other matter on which absolute knowledge does not exist."[11] When we speak of what "probably" happened at the time of the birth of Christ we mean that we have more reason to believe one hypothesis than another.

We realize more fully the meaning of the statement that doubtfulness is only a measure of human ignorance when we point out, as did Bishop Butler, that, for an Infinite Intelligence there would be no such subjective mode at all. "For nothing," said Bishop Butler, "which is the possible object of knowledge, whether past, present, or future, can be probable to an Infinite Intelligence; since it cannot but be discerned absolutely as it is in itself—certainly true, or certainly false."[12]

The one class of knowledge in which it might reasonably be held that probability refers to events rather than to human inability is that in regard to the future. This is not a matter of ignorance unless we hold that the future somehow already *is*. But the point to make clear is that in matters of fact, we are as effectively removed from apodictic certainty as we are in matters of the future in which the calculus of probability is our only recourse, though the two forms of uncertainty arise from different reasons.

From these considerations there follows an interesting con-

[11] Augustus De Morgan, *Formal Logic*, p. 173.
[12] Joseph Butler, *The Analogy of Religion, Natural and Revealed*, Introduction.

clusion about the objects of religious knowledge. Not only are we concerned with *objective truth*, but we are likewise concerned with *matters of fact* and, accordingly, the subjective mode of religious truth is never that of complete certainty. Because we are seeking to know something which is both important and exciting, *if true,* the best we can have is high probability. There is always a chance we are wrong. Otherwise there would be no room for faith. Such a man as Newman may be more certain of God than of himself, but he has no right to claim *absolute* certainty. When we are talking about what is, we may always be in error, because our judgment is fallible and our means of knowledge are liable to error.

The existence of God cannot be demonstrated beyond a shadow of doubt for the simple reason that religious belief refers to something objectively real. When Kant pointed out the inability of the classic theistic proofs to give demonstrative evidence, he was not doing fundamental harm to religious belief, but rather helping, as others had helped, to set men free from a fantastic ideal of absolute certainty. Kant was, in this regard, supporting the conclusion, at which Bishop Butler arrived earlier in the same century, to the effect that "probability is the very guide of life." Since it is the guide of all actual life, we can expect, both in religion and in ethics, the same conception of the truth and the same dependence on presumptive evidence that we find in other matters.

CHAPTER III

THE NATURE OF EVIDENCE

*"If a man were now to deny that there is salt upon the table, you
could not reduce him to an absurdity."* —DR. JOHNSON

"We can demonstrate little outside mathematics."
—H. W. B. JOSEPH

If we think of truth as having an objective status and ourselves
as creatures who can approach it by intellectual effort, the
search for truth takes on an imperious quality. Since some opinions are undoubtedly nearer the truth than are other opinions,
it is our task to try to discover concrete ways in which opinions
can be improved. The improvement of opinion comes by the
accumulation and analysis of evidence. The ideal end of evidence is *proof.*

A. PROOF

There are few words in the language used more loosely than
the word "proof." We speak of many propositions as being
proved, when some analysis of the situation shows that the
situation leaves abundant room for doubt. Daily we discuss
hundreds of supposed "facts," but their factual character rests,
for the most part, on flimsy evidence. Frequently the negation
of a cherished belief can be upheld with a great show of argument. This is well illustrated by Doctor Johnson's celebrated
argument to the effect that the English military forces had not
really taken Canada from the French.

ï deny that Canada is taken, and I can support my denial by
pretty good arguments. The French are a much more numerous
people than we; and it is not likely that they would allow us to

take it. "But the ministry have assured us, in all the formality of the Gazette, that it is taken."—Very true. But the ministry have put us to an enormous expense by the war in America, and it is their interest to persuade us that we have got something for our money.—"But the fact is confirmed by thousands of men who were at the taking of it."—Ay, but these men have still more interest in deceiving us. They don't want that you should think the French have beat them, but that they have beat the French. Now suppose you should go over and find that it really is taken, that would only satisfy yourself; for when you come home, we will not believe you. We will say, you have been bribed.—Yet, Sir, notwithstanding all these plausible objections, we have no doubt that Canada is really ours. Such is the weight of common testimony. How much stronger are the evidences of the Christian religion.[1]

Just as it is possible to present reasons for doubting what all of us strongly believe, it is possible, as is sometimes humorously done, to uphold ridiculous conclusions by the use of evidence similar to that which is taken seriously in support of other beliefs. There is, for example, the story of the commission which traveled due north from a given point for five hundred miles and brought in the report that their findings indicated the existence of twenty hot dog stands to the mile all the way to the North Pole. Extrapolation may be, in some situations, the best method available, but it lays its users open to grave error.

It is easy to lampoon our most respected forms of evidence, and it is a beneficial undertaking, inasmuch as we tend to take our "proof" too seriously. The method of fair sampling, for example, can lead to some amusing conclusions. Thus, if we should happen upon the right numbers we could prove by this method that all numbers go into sixty without remainder. The evidence of this would be very great, greater indeed than is the evidence for many accepted conclusions, provided the numbers happened upon by judicious dipping here and there

[1] *The Life of Samuel Johnson*, by James Boswell, Modern Library, pp. 259-260.

were 2, 3, 4, 5, 6, 10, 12, 15, 20, and 30. This is not unreasonable sampling.

Most of the objects, of which we speak familiarly and often,
have never come within the range of our sensory perception.
For example there is hardly anyone who has seen his own
brain, yet each speaks familiarly of this organ and does not
doubt its existence. All of our knowledge of historical events
and most of our knowledge of contemporary events is at second or third hand. Not many persons have seen their grandparents' grandparents. We usually consider that the best evidence is documentary evidence, but it is not hard to imagine
a literary hoax, and more than one has, in fact, been perpe-
trated. A really successful forgery would not, of course, be
detected, and some such there have doubtless been.

Sometimes our belief that propositions are proved rests on
little more than a pathetic faith in the printed word. This is
what gives point to the joke about the purveyor of patent medi-
cines who shouts, "Don't take my word for it; don't take anybody's word for it; read what it says on the bottle and see for
yourself."[2]

Even direct experience is by no means sufficient to dispel all
reasonable doubt, since our sensory organs frequently lead us
into error. Not only are illusions the stock in trade of the con-
juror, but they also appear in ordinary life. Many court trials
have involved contradictory evidence from persons of good
faith, reporting on the basis of immediate experience. The
difficulty of trustworthy testimony from direct experience can
be shown also in psychological experiments. There are many
situations in which people "see" what is not there to be seen.

The only proof which is logically coercive is that which depends on strict deduction. We say it is demonstrably true that,
if "a" is the ancestor of "b" and "b" is the ancestor of "c,"

[2] An extreme instance of the unreliability of the printed word occurred in
the author's own experience when he read, in a reputable daily newspaper,
of his own death.

then "a" is the ancestor of "c." If either x or y is true then we know for certain that the proposition to the effect that both x and y are false is itself false. But this kind of certainty is bought at a great price, the price of tautology. The conclusion says in one way what the premises have already said in another way. This is not to say that such deductive reasoning is fruitless. As a practical matter we can, by such means, arrive at conclusions which are true, but which do not appear to be true, without the deduction. An interesting example is the statement that at least two persons in New York City have the same number of hairs on their heads. This, which seems at first beyond valid proof, seems adequately proved when we call to attention two other propositions, viz.:

No human head is large enough to have more than five million hairs.

There are more than five million persons in New York.[3]

This kind of proof, with which we are most familiar in mathematics, is of the "If-then" variety. *If* the premises are true *then* the conclusions are true. It gives certainty *within the system*, but it rests ultimately on primitive propositions, which we may call postulates or axioms according to our taste. The whole of our logical structure, by means of which we try to find our way through the baffling data of the world, depends upon principles which cannot be proved since they are necessarily assumed. The chief of these is the law of noncontradiction. Much of the charm of *Alice in Wonderland* lies in the fact that this masterpiece presents a world in which this primitive assumption of noncontradiction is not made.

Though we should be foolish to despise the kind of certainty which strict deduction provides, we are well aware that most of the problems which face us in the world cannot be solved in this way. The validity of the syllogism does not relieve us of the necessity of finding out whether the premises are in accord-

[3] This illustration is given in *An Introduction to Logic and Scientific Method*, by Morris R. Cohen and Ernest Nagel, New York, 1934, p. 6.

ance with the truth, and this must be done by the slow process of the accumulation of evidence. The more we go beyond vagueness to precision, the more difficult this becomes. Indeed, we may be justified in the observation that the more precise a proposition is, the less probability there is of its truth. We are more likely to be wrong if we say John Smith was born at a certain address in a certain city of Maryland, than if we say he was born in North America. Intelligent students have long recognized the validity of this principle and make use of it in written examinations. By avoiding refinements in the answer, the chance of making obvious blunders is diminished accordingly. Nevertheless it is precision we want in real life, and there seems no easy way to secure it.

B. CUMULATIVE EVIDENCE

The chief way in which we approach certainty as a limit is by the discovery of *converging* lines of evidence. Any single piece of evidence must be respected, but the chance of avoiding error is vastly increased if there is support from independent sources. The difference between one line of evidence and two or three, pointing in the same direction, is tremendous. This is the point of Butler's famous aphorism, "For probable proofs, by being added, not only *increase* the evidence but *multiply* it."[4]

Consider, for example, a particular crime in which a child is stolen for ransom. Later a man is accused of the crime and stands trial. Usually there is not one *single* line of evidence which is sufficient to constitute proof, even in the vague way we use this concept in ordinary speech. The child's nurse may identify the man, but, as was noted above, persons under severe emotional strain are not reliable in regard to their sensory impressions. The man may be caught with the child in his possession, but this is not sufficient since he may be, wittingly or unwittingly, shielding the kidnaper. Most men, even of poor reputation, would pick up a lone child, found by the roadside.

[4] Joseph Butler, *The Analogy of Religion,* Part II, Chapter VII.

The man may confess that he has committed the crime, but that alone is not enough, since men have confessed crimes they have not committed, and this they have done for a variety of reasons. At least there has been such good evidence against confessions that the confessions have been generally doubted.

Each *single* bit of evidence is, as we have seen, inconclusive. Always there is another valid conclusion. We cannot *prove* that no two men have the same fingerprints. What is important is to find converging lines of evidence, and find so many that the result is not in practical doubt, even if there remains an iota of theoretical doubt.

The point to note is that this difficulty of simple proof, with the attendant necessity of cumulative evidence, applies to everything we know in the realm of matters of fact. It applies to evidence for the existence of God, to evidence for the existence of atoms, to evidence for the existence of historical characters. This needs to be stressed, because it is so often overlooked. One of the most common of popular errors appears in this connection when we face religious knowledge. There are many who lightly reject belief in God because, they say, the existence of God cannot be "proved," by which they mean that there is no single, obvious, incontrovertible line of evidence for God's existence. The appropriate retort is to ask what matter of fact there is in the world for which there is some *single, obvious* and *incontrovertible* line of evidence. We are saying nothing derogatory about religious knowledge when we say it is a matter of high probability, for this is true of all matters of fact. There is no valid excuse for the inconsistency which rejects belief in one field because absolute certainty is lacking, and is credulous in other fields where it is equally lacking.

But what about scientific method? Does not this give us a superior kind of evidence which is logically coercive of belief? The popular opinion seems to be that what is "proved scientifically" is really proved.

C. SCIENTIFIC METHOD

Though "scientific" is, in popular estimation, a blessed word, almost a sacred word, there is nothing fundamental to scientific method that is not a refinement of the common sense used for centuries by all kinds of persons. It is generally agreed that scientific method involves four steps: *observation, hypothesis, implication,* and *verification.* Though we sometimes call this the inductive method, it is obviously far more, inasmuch as the third step is strictly deductive.

The modern man is grateful for the careful application of this method of refined common sense to various problems, and there would seem to be no type of problem to which it cannot be applied. There seems no reason, for example, why this method may not be applied to religious experience as well as to experience of the physical order.[5] What wc have called natural science is not science, *par excellence,* but only one branch of science. The methods of observation and verification differ according to the type of experience studied, each field requiring its own type of intellectual acumen. A good scientist is not merely one who does painstaking research, but, far more, one who has the imagination to construct experiments which will be as nearly crucial as experiments can be.

Since the climax of the scientific method is verification, we need to inquire into this step with especial care, to learn whether a superior kind of certainty is achieved. The essence of verification is the testing of an hypothesis to see whether the effects, which ought to appear if the hypothesis is true, actually do appear. This conception of verification, which has received its most important consideration in the thought of John Stuart Mill, is the heart of what is called the experimental method. Mill emphasized the procedure according to which we observed what happens in circumstances to which

[5] I have tried to apply it to religious experience in two books, *The Trust-worthiness of Religious Experience,* and *The Knowledge of God.*

the hypothesis applies, deliberately instituting such circumstances if need be. Since this procedure seems to be so reasonable and so harmless, many are surprised when they are made to realize that this principle of verification depends upon a long-recognized logical fallacy.

The fallacy inherent in the process of verification has been known for many years as "the affirmation of the consequent." The logical form is:

> a implies b
> b is true
> Therefore, a is true.

This might be illustrated as follows:

> If John was in the wreck he must have bruises.
> John has bruises on his body.
> Therefore, John was in the wreck.

Stated thus baldly the verification in regard to John's participation is obviously fallacious. The bruised man may have been in the wreck and he may not, for there are many ways of getting bruises. Before the evidence is really convincing one must show that there is no other way in which the bruises could have come in this particular instance, but that is a long, difficult, and circuitous task. Professor Joseph the celebrated Oxford logician has pointed out that the fallacy here is the same as the failure to recognize the plurality of causes. Different causes may produce the same effect, and different theories may have the same implications. "A theory whose consequences conflict with the facts cannot be true;" concludes Professor Joseph, "but so long as there may be more theories than one giving the same consequences, the agreement of the facts with one of them furnishes no ground for choosing between it and the others."[6]

When we try to argue back from the implicate to the implicant we are acting on the supposition that universal affirma-

[6] H. W. B. Joseph, *An Introduction to Logic,* Oxford, 1916, p. 523.

tive propositions can be converted simply, and it is common knowledge that such conversion is not valid. Though all men are mortal, it does not follow that all mortals are men. In fact, they are not. Rain implies wet ground, but wet ground does not imply rain. There are other reasons for wet ground.

Since verification is based on a logical fallacy, how is it possible for scientific method, which so stresses verification, to give the help it clearly gives in the refinement of opinion in such a way that it approximates the truth? The answer is that *we overcome the fallacy in great measure by committing it in a refined fashion, many times instead of once.* This is not a gratuitous paradox, but a principle of profound importance. We find many and intricate results which ought to appear if our hypothesis is true and we check them one by one. The logical form comes to be not merely:

$$a \text{ implies } b$$

with the subsequent verification of b, but rather

$$a \text{ implies } b, b^1, b^2, b^3, b^4, b^5, \text{ etc.}$$

Then we check or verify as many of these complicated resultants as we can, to see whether they are, in fact, found. If all are found, the process is still the affirmation of the consequent, but by affirming so many we have a situation in which only a miracle of coincidence would be the alternative to the validity of our induction. Thus we are back with our principle of cumulative evidence, which is based ultimately on the primitive assumption that this is the kind of world in which the miracle of coincidence does not normally occur.

All the fundamental features of verification are so well illustrated in the question of the existence of atoms that the following statement from Professor David L. Webster[7] may be reprinted, with profit, at this point:

[7] David L. Webster is Professor of Physics at Stanford University. The paragraphs quoted appeared first as a footnote to *The Knowledge of God*, New York, 1939, pp. 188, 189.

In this sort of verification the repetition of the fallacy must be of the right kind. This may be illustrated by the case of atoms. The first piece of evidence to be discovered for them was the fact that the hypothesis of their existence explained an important law of chemistry, namely the law that in any compound the elements occur in certain fixed proportions. This fact led Dalton, at the opening of the nineteenth century, to state his belief in atoms. The law of fixed proportions was verified anew with the analysis of each new compound, but still for about half the century most scientists remained skeptical about atoms. Their skepticism was the correct attitude for that time, because, if there had been a mistake in the theory that atoms were the cause of the fixed proportions, the mistake would have applied to each new compound as well as to the old ones. This sort of repetition in committing a possible fallacy is useless.

On the other hand, near the middle of the century it was found that the hypothesis of the existence of atoms explained also phenomena of a very different sort, namely the changes of pressure of gases, such as the steam in the cylinder of an engine; and soon explanations of other radically different phenomena were added to its list of achievements. If there had been a mistake about the explanation of the fixed proportions in chemistry, that mistake would not have been likely to apply also in the steam engine. The steam engine would have needed a new mistake independent of the first and pointing also to atoms only by coincidence. Such a coincidence, like doublets in throwing a pair of dice, would have been remarkable, but not extraordinary.

As more phenomena pointed to atoms, however, the belief that such mistakes had occurred came to require a coincidence like that of many throws of the dice, all showing the same number. The required coincidence was soon extraordinary and eventually incredible. It is now so very incredible that all reputable scientists find it far easier to believe in atoms, in fact so far easier that they now regard the hypothesis of atoms as an established fact.

Those who use scientific method most, do not ordinarily have for it the superstitious reverence felt by so much of the public, but rather recognize that it is the best way we have, though admittedly far from perfect. The classic statement on this subject is from one of the greatest men in the entire history of science, Sir Isaac Newton:

And although the arguing from experiments and observations by induction be no demonstration of general conclusions yet it is the best way of arguing which the nature of things admits of, and may be looked upon as so much the stronger, by how much the induction is more general.

The conclusion to which we are led in regard to scientific method is that it is a good method, but not a method which is foolproof or productive of absolute certainty in any realm. We freely admit that science does not give us the kind of logical necessity which we find in mathematics, but we are satisfied without it. We are willing to go on with high probability as the guide of life, but it is important that we should know what we are doing in that case. Scientific knowledge is not fundamentally different from other knowledge; it is merely the most careful kind of knowledge about matters of fact which mortals know how to achieve.

D. ANALOGY

It is not always realized how widely we are dependent upon analogy for any growth in our knowledge of the world and its ingredients. It is not uncommon for many persons to reject an argument, not because it is based on a poor analogy, but because it is based on *any* analogy. In view of this popular opinion we are fortunate in having available, splendid modern discussions of the necessary use of analogy in all disciplined thought. Among the most careful writers on the subject are J. Maynard Keynes in his *A Treatise on Probability* and L. Susan Stebbing in her *A Modern Introduction to Logic*. Both of these scholars have shown that analogy is necessarily involved in all induction. Mr. Keynes goes so far as to say, "Scientific method, indeed, is mainly devoted to discovering means of so heightening the known analogy that we may dispense as far as possible with the methods of pure induction."[8]

The only way in which we can begin to find order, in the vast storehouse of data we call the world, is to find *resemblances*. Fortunately the world includes a great many groups of objects which logicians have called "natural kinds." The finding of natural kinds, the *classing* of objects together on the basis of resemblance is the first step in scientific observation. Even induction by simple enumeration is not possible unless the instances enumerated have common properties. There is no point in investigating the color of crows unless crows are somehow alike, and enough alike so that we know *which* birds to observe.

Science is more than classification, but it necessarily involves classification, since otherwise each individual piece of information would stand alone and meaningless. The class names which we call common nouns are useful precisely because certain properties are often found together. It is because of a known positive analogy between many objects in a class that we feel justified in going on to any kind of generalization. And, unless we go on to some kind of generalization, we make no progress at all, but confine ourselves to the fruitless task of complete enumeration. We are interested in prediction, in conclusions, and these get all their cogency from the principle of analogy. The only justification for the conclusion that diabetes can be controlled by the use of insulin is the reasonable analogy between the few men and women who have been observed in this connection and the many men and women who have not been so observed.

The disdain which many suppose they have for analogy arises from the use of the argument from analogy in an illegitimate way. It is always illegitimate if the resemblance noted is not *relevant* to the conclusion based upon it, and this is often the case. To argue that there are living creatures on the other planets, merely because these planets revolve around the same

[8] J. Maynard Keynes, *A Treatise on Probability*, p. 241.

sun, would be an extreme example of irrelevant resemblance. What is far more important is to find resemblances in atmosphere, in temperature, and in the external marks which living creatures sometimes produce. This last consideration is the explanation of the great importance that has been attached to the alleged "canals" on the planet Mars.

Since analogy cannot be avoided if we are to have any induction at all, i.e., any reasonable extension of belief beyond the paltry area with which we are intimately acquainted, a great part of our task consists in the refinement of analogy so that we discover truly relevant analogies. "To determine what is relevant and what is not relevant," says Miss Stebbing, "is to employ scientific method."[9] But here again we are dependent, not on some mechanical procedure, but on the good sense of the particular man whom we call a scientist. But there is one rule that is genuinely helpful, "The more we can increase the total known analogy, the more likelihood there is that we shall increase the number of important properties that it contains."[10]

In addition, it is worth while to mention one warning. That is, that the more precise we are in regard to the inferred properties, the less likely is the conclusion to be true. It is more likely that Mars contains "men" than that it contains "white men six feet tall," and both types of inhabitants are far less likely to exist than is "some form of life." Similarly, if we argue from what purpose means in men to what the evidences of purpose must mean in the external world, we are on far more firm ground if we assert that there is Mind back of nature than if we assert that God is like men. We are relatively safe with analogical reasoning if we seek to increase the comprehensiveness of the implying properties and seek at the same time, to decrease the precision of the implied properties.

We shall find in the study of belief about the fundamental nature of the world, which occupies so large a place in religious

[9] L. Susan Stebbing, *A Modern Introduction to Logic*, p. 251.
[10] *Ibid.*, p. 253.

knowledge, that analogy is bound to be used. But in using analogy we should guard against the supposition that we are using a second-best method or something peculiar to religion. When we recognize that the most painstaking empirical inference of any science is pervaded by analogical factors, we need not hesitate to include these same factors in our inferences about the universe and about God. Since analogy is unavoidable, the effort of the reasonable person is directed to its wise and careful use, rejecting the substitution of metaphors for evidence.

The conclusion we reach from many different lines of approach is that nothing in this world is logically coercive. Deductive systems rest upon postulates, and inductive systems rest upon analogy which, when sufficiently refined, gives nothing more than high probability. All we can do for any man is to show what the evidence is, and let the evidence do the convincing. If it is not convincing, there is nothing more that we can do. Logical processes merely present reasoning in clear form, and if a person, noting this form, says he does not see, there is no more that we can do. At least there is no more at the time. Often all we can do is to wait.

CHAPTER IV

THE NECESSITY OF FAITH

"It must certainly be allowed that nature has kept us at a great distance from all her secrets, and has afforded us only the knowledge of a few superficial qualities of objects." —DAVID HUME

"I know in part." —ST. PAUL

Man's claim to have genuine knowledge seems very simple and reasonable until we begin to examine it, and then it is recognized as being full of mystery. What we habitually claim is that we are so made that we are able to have true awareness of natures other than our own, to understand them as they are in themselves, and to understand something of the relationship both of them and of ourselves to the Whole of which all are parts. Men never claim to know the Whole, but they do claim to know *things*, other *persons*, *values* and even *God*. But what right have we to suppose that we know *anything*?

A. DIFFICULTIES OF KNOWLEDGE

As we study carefully our relationship to the world, parts of which we claim to know, we begin to see that there is a real sense in which we are imprisoned. All we have is our own sensations, our own impressions, our own thoughts. How do we get outside this circle of our own experiences to a real knowledge of the external world? It is a common practice for those who are at pains to deny the knowledge of God to point out that all reported experiences of God are merely experiences *within* the minds of men. How then can we assert religious knowledge? But it should be obvious that the same kind of reasoning applies to every conceivable item of alleged knowledge. The knowledge of God is, in this regard, in no worse and in no better situation, than is the knowledge of "physical objects" or of other persons. If anyone wants to be a complete subjectivist in regard to knowledge, that is his privilege, but we can, at least, ask him to have a decent respect for consistency. He cannot keep our intellectual respect if he plays fast and loose with his subjectivism.

As we analyze the apparently simple relation called knowledge, we find that there are three distinct leaps in the process, leaps of which we are not normally conscious because we make them habitually.

(1) The first leap is that by which we infer any external world at all. How can I be absolutely certain that the impressions I feel come from some source external to my own consciousness? The only reasonable answer is that I *cannot be certain of this*. Since some of the qualities which I normally attribute to an external source are shown, upon analysis, to be purely subjective, how do I know that any of the qualities I observe are anything else than subjective? How do I know that these green trees, these thinking human beings, and the entire external world are not the imaginary figures of my dream? Probably the best evidence that we cannot be certain of the external source of our impressions is that we cannot give the consistent subjectivist a wholly convincing answer to his arguments. He cannot be dislodged by argument, though he may, indeed, share the perplexity of Alice concerning "Which dreamed it?" Every good subjectivist should ponder the following contribution to philosophy:

Now, Kitty, let's consider who it was that dreamed it all. This is a serious question, my dear, and you should not go on licking your paw like that—as if Dinah hadn't washed you this morning! You see, Kitty, it *must* have been either me or the Red King. He was part of my dream, of course—but then I was part of his dream, too! Was it the Red King, Kitty? You were his wife, my dear, so you ought to know—oh, Kitty, *do* help to settle it! I'm sure your paw can wait.

But perhaps there really wasn't a Red King at all. Whenever we believe in a Red King or in any external object of knowledge, we are crossing a chasm. What we are pleased to call the "real world" seems to account fairly well for our impressions, as we shall see later, but a superior intelligence might be able to formulate any number of hypotheses which would account for our impressions equally well. Of course we all believe in the existence of the "real world," but it is a wholesome exercise in humility to try to understand why we believe in it. We make the leap chiefly as a matter of sheer faith. This is true whether we are scientists or philosophers or men of common sense, for we are all on the same ground in this important regard. Balfour's account of why we assume the reality of knowledge is hard to improve:

If we do so, it is not, as the candid reader will be prepared to admit, because such a conclusion is justified by such premises, but because we are predisposed to a conclusion of this kind by those instinctive beliefs which, in unreflective moments, the philosopher shares with the savage. In such moments all men conceive themselves (by hypothesis erroneously) as having direct experiences of an independent material universe.[1]

In a brilliantly written chapter called "The Cartesian Faux-Pas" Archbishop Temple has shown how a great part of modern reflective thought has been vitiated by the original position of Descartes that the mind deals only with its own ideas. If our own ideas are all that we really know in the beginning, then our own ideas are all we really know in the end, and Descartes crosses the chasm from the self to the objects of knowledge by a purely artificial construction. If we are going to have faith in the end we may as well have it in the beginning. And, as a matter of fact, we do have it in the beginning in an

[1] Arthur Balfour, *The Foundations of Belief*, eighth edition, p. 128.

inexpugnable manner. No man really doubts the external world any more than he doubts his own existence.[2] We can *imagine* ourselves doubting it, but we do not actually go beneath the fundamental subject-object relationship which is the essential element in all knowledge. "What Descartes indulged in his stove was purely academic doubt;" writes Temple, "he was really as sure of the stove as of himself."[3]

Our faith in actual objects of actual knowledge may be sheer animal faith, but it is not a faith which is expelled by any increase in sophistication. What all men really depend on, in this matter, is what Professor Lovejoy has called the "spontaneous creed of the natural man." Philosophical realism of some sort is an instinctive faith, neither produced nor destroyed by argument, resting on assumptions which no man can prove and which no man really doubts.[4]

(2) The second leap is that by which physical stimuli pass over into conscious experience. There is a vast and fundamental difference between "ether waves" and the experience of sound or the experience of sight as the case may be. We ordinarily denote this difference by saying the waves are physical events whereas the experiences are mental events. On the one hand is the realm of things and on the other is the realm of thoughts. The sound waves have length and can be measured accurately by a number of intricate mechanical devices. Some of these devices are not fundamentally dissimilar to those found in the inner ear. Different parts of the intricate apparatus appear to be sensitive to different vibrations and send "messages" accordingly to the brain. But somehow or somewhere the most profound transformation takes place and there comes to be a reality which

[2] No doubt most readers agree with Professor Lovejoy when he says, "The occasional lovers of philosophic paradox who have professed such disbelief seem to me merely to display an unconvincing affectation."—*Contemporary American Philosophy*, Volume II, p. 96.

[3] William Temple, *Nature, Man and God*, London, 1934, p. 66.

[4] A. O. Lovejoy, *The Revolt Against Dualism*, New York, 1930, pp. 11-15. Professor Lovejoy presents five items in the epistemological creed of the natural man.

has modes of behavior utterly different from the modes of behavior observable in physical objects. It follows a different set of laws. How different the two realms are was stated brilliantly by Blaise Pascal when he said, "All bodies, the firmament, the stars, the earth and its kingdoms, are not equal to the lowest mind; for mind knows all these and itself; and these bodies nothing."

In the realm of physical objects, the presence of an object in one place means that it is not also in another, and when anything is shared there is less for the original owner. This is not at all true in the realm of conscious experience. When two share an experience there is not less for each, but rather more. Moreover such concepts as location and length or weight have no meaning at all when applied to mental events. They may be used in describing the "scraping of horses' tails on catgut," but they cannot reasonably be used in describing what happens when great music is understood and appreciated. To seek the experience of music by the concepts which apply to material aggregates is to hunt the Snark itself.

You may seek it with thimbles—and seek it with care.
You may hunt it with forks and hope; You may threaten its life with a railway-share;
You may charm it with smiles and soap.

The trouble is that when you find it, you will learn to your amazement, that it is really not a Snark at all, but a Boojum instead.

Our sense organs are wonderful mechanisms, but they are only transmitters. The increasing knowledge about the cunning devices of these transmitters does nothing whatever to dispel the mystery of the change which occurs when nerve impulses produce conscious sensations.

Since this mystery is better expressed by poetry than by prose we are wise to be unusually attentive when the late poet laureate of England addresses himself to this theme:

> Tho' measure true
> every wave-length of ether or air that reacheth sense,
> there the hunt checketh, and her keen hounds are at
>   fault;
> for when the waves have passed the gates of ear and eye
> all scent is lost: suddenly escaped the visibles are
> changed to invisible; the fine measured motions to
> immeasurable emotion; the cyphered fractions to a
> living joy that man feeleth to shrive his soul.[5]

The leap of thought which is demanded by the transition from physical stimuli to inner experience is made more difficult, rather than less difficult, by the advance of scientific opinions. The world in which science asks us to believe is not only unlike our experience, it is also unlike our sensory stimuli. It is not the world we see, which seems, for the most part, made up of solid things, but a world chiefly empty, with the emptiness partially relieved by rapidly moving electrons and protons. No doubt the reasons for believing in the existence of this strange world of the physicist are excellent ones, but they are not the reasons of ordinary empiricism. The world does not *look* and *feel* and *taste* the way modern science says it is. Balfour's statement of this predicament is worth repeating here:

For, consider what kind of a world it is in which we are asked to believe—a world which so far as most people are concerned, can only be at all adequately conceived in terms of the visual sense, but which in its true reality possesses neither of the qualities characteristically associated with the visual sense, namely, illumination and colour. A world which is half like our ideas of it and half unlike them.[6]

Thus we have not only the paradox according to which physical stimuli can arouse what is more than physical, but also the paradox that these same stimuli reveal to us a world which is fundamentally different from the picture they reveal. Even

---

[5] Robert Bridges, *The Testament of Beauty*, Book III, lines 766-773.
[6] Balfour, *op. cit.*, pp. 129, 130.

the regularity of nature, on which we depend so largely in our scientific knowledge is largely a fiction so far as experience, and experience alone, is concerned. Regularity there no doubt is, but what our senses give us is a rapidly moving and highly confusing set of different pictures. Even the most careful experiments conducted by the most careful investigators do not show identical results. The plain lesson taught by personal observation is not the regularity, but the irregularity of nature.

(3) A third leap involved in knowledge is that which makes possible public or communicable knowledge. The difficulties inherent in the communication of knowledge seem to be insuperable, and yet we all believe that it is actually communicated. Poets and mystics have long maintained that their experiences are ineffable, but is not *every* experience ineffable? How do I know that you see what I see? As a matter of fact, we probably do not see the same scene. No matter how close together we are, each has a slightly different perspective. Even in a single community there are so many different types of training and antecedent experience that there are vast differences of appreciation. This is well illustrated in any visit to an art gallery. Our social knowledge is based, not on identity of experiences, but on differences in experience.

Now, if each human experience differs from every other human experience, are we not imprisoned in regard to relation to one another just as we are imprisoned in relation to the external world? We appeal wistfully to one another but we can do little more.

We can make signs to one another, in the hope that these signs will be intelligently interpreted, but we cannot in the last degree transfer our perceptions from mind to mind. In a matter seemingly so simple as indication of the primary qualities of the senses, of colour, form, sound, smell, touch, temperature, we know full well that our whole social attitude is one of question and trust, not one of necessitated social experience. We say, Look, do you not see?

Sniff, can you smell it? . . . This present glory of the meadow prismatic with its dews, fragrant, fresh, illumined, I and my companions may exclaim over in choric delight, but no one of us can ever in remotest measure be certain that the object of his delight is present and understood by any of his fellows. Indeed, what possible assurance is there that what is green for me may at all be so for another, in a world where each is colour-blind to the perceptions of every other? or fragrant or fresh where all disputing of tastes is footless? or illumined where all light is inward? The community wherein we believe we share a world of common sense is sustained wholly by faith in one another's intuitions.[7]

All this leads to a radical change in our popular and uncritical understanding of the relationship which exists between knowledge and faith. The ordinary view is that knowledge comes first and faith afterward. We know all that can be known and then we press on into the unknown with the eye of faith. But the truth lies in the precise opposite of all this. *Faith precedes knowledge* and makes knowledge possible. Apart from faith, defined as "conviction apart from or in excess of proof," we are shut up within the confines of our own minds, separated from any possible knowledge of the world or of other minds with whom we can share our knowledge. Knowledge comes when the original *sensa* are interpreted and organized by epistemological faith. Upon such faith rest not only the lofty creeds of ethics and religion, but also the maxims of daily life.[8]

The fact that the supreme act of instinctive faith by which we break out of the prison of our subjective selves is quite unshaken by any argumentations does not mean that it is a faith wholly independent of reasonable thought. Though we should still be philosophical realists, even if we could not argue for realism, it may be noted that argument helps to sustain our instinctive faith which is at the basis of knowledge.

[7] Hartley Burr Alexander, *God and Man's Destiny*, pp. 194-196.
[8] Lord Balfour argued this point so well that the argument needs no repetition.

B. THE ARGUMENT FOR REALISM

By realism we mean that theory of the world which holds that there are objects of knowledge which actually enjoy independent existence. There are many differences among realists, but this is their common faith. All agree that the knower may be deluded and that objects are understood by the knower in the light of his own particular limitations, but they insist that there is something waiting to be known. There are objects which would exist even if they were not known by ourselves or any other mind and which, accordingly, are more than ideas in the mind of the subject who is the alleged knower. The realist insists, in short, that there are existences which are not relative to the cognitive situation, though eventually they may become so. There are, he believes, flowers that bloom unseen.

This faith is to be defended, first, by removing certain intellectual barriers and, second, by positive considerations. The chief intellectual barrier is the notion that an event can be wholly "accounted for" in terms of subjective factors. But this turns out to be nothing but a superstition or a prejudice. How could the existence of subjective factors amount to a denial of the existence of objective factors? I have an idea of a tree, it is true, and this undoubtedly helps me in giving patterned order to the visual sensations which appear, but it is not clear why this eliminates the possibility that there is also something outside my window which gives rise to these curious sensations. I may come to the time of prayer with an idea of God, but this alone is not sufficient to show that the experience of prayer is purely illusory with no objective revelation of God. In both cases there are, of course, subjective factors, since that is merely another way of saying that we are bound to receive all messages, whatever their origin, by means of our own human faculties. And it is a *non sequitur* to make the recognition of subjective causes the equivalent of a rejection of the existence of objective causes.

The chief source of confusion on this important point has been a poor understanding of the notion of cause. In uncritical thought, there is the widespread notion that there is a single cause for every event. Thus we ask, "What caused John's illness?" and we are satisfied when we are given the name of a germ. But an illness has *many* causes, most of them exceedingly complex.[9] That the germ alone is insufficient is evident from the fact that germs are often present without the appropriate symptoms of illness. The general condition of the human organism, the weather conditions, and many other conditions constitute together the complex "cause" of an illness. *The point is that the discovery of one cause does not entail the elimination of others.* The experience of light may be caused by the fact that I open my eyes, but it may, *at the same time,* be caused by the fact that there is sunshine. It seems clear that the same principles apply equally to physical knowledge and to religious knowledge. In either case objective status may be lacking, but the existence of subjective conditions is not sufficient to show that this is the case. The fact that we know with the mind does not mean that we cannot know what is outside the mind. If we thus rid our minds of the notion of causal simplicity we are prepared to receive the positive arguments for realism. These arguments may be many, but three stand out in sharp relief.

(1) There is a great difference between what we know as perceptual and nonperceptual experience. Objects which seem to be perceptual have about them a strength, a vividness, a permanence, and a commanding quality which are not involved in the experience which we recognize as imaginative or hallucinatory. This is not explained on the subjectivist hypothesis, but is fully reasonable if there are real objects which help to produce genuine perceptions.

(2) Many of the objects of the external world give evidence of their own continuity even when not observed by our own

---

[9] Professor Joseph calls this the doctrine of the Composition of Causes. Cf. *An Introduction to Logic,* p. 492n.

minds. Thus a fire which is left burning in a house, where no one is, seems to have been going on during our absence because the fuel is partially burned. There is succession in nature whether we think about it or not. How can we account for the filling in of these gaps between subjective experience other than by an external physical order independent of us?

(3) There is fundamental agreement as between many observers in regard to what is experienced. This does not mean that there is never any difference about the external world, supposing there is an external world, but it does mean that the amount of agreement is so great that it is hard to explain by the miracle of coincidence. There is thus good reason to suppose that there is an actual world which makes possible public experience.

It is important to insist that the pan-subjectivist is faced with a tremendous miracle. It is true, as we noted above, that no two perceptions are identical, and yet they have so much in common that they must be explained by reference to a common source.

The reasonable conclusion is that our ideas, in spite of the fact that they are and must be subjective, have or can have *objective reference*. They have objective reference because they refer to objects and they partake of the nature of truth when they grasp the character of these objects correctly. Such a statement is epistemological rather than ontological. That is, it says nothing whatever about the constitution of objects. God, according to what most men of recent centuries have believed, is spiritual in nature. To say that God exists really, and therefore is not merely a projection of our own minds, is to say that He is an object or that He has objective status, and to say that a stone really exists is to say that it likewise is an object. The notion that only physical things can be objective is, of course, sheer prejudice, with no evidence to support it.

Though we cannot escape from the circle of our subjective ideas, we can find *within these* an order which is indicative of what lies beyond that order. Ideas of imagination and ideas of perception are both ideas, but we can compare them in such a way as to learn much. Thus experience, in spite of its fallacious tendencies, provides the tests of its own reliability. Otherwise we should have no tests, for we cannot get outside experience. When I "see" a stove in a darkened room and seek to test the validity of this experience, all I can do is to add another experience, namely, I reach out to see what comes by the sense of touch.[10] Qualitatively the two experiences are on the same level. We wish we might have some external standard of veracity, but, since we do not have it, we follow the more humble means of comparing and contrasting the various items in our experience, to learn which, among them, are trustworthy and which are untrustworthy.

Though our outlook is thus circumscribed, and our efforts are severely limited, there is good evidence that *we really do have some knowledge*. There is excellent reason to believe that we know, through idea, something which is not an idea, namely, a situation. We never know fully, and we never know beyond a shadow of doubt, but we are creatures who can *know in part*.

C. TYPES OF AGNOSTICISM

Agnosticism, rightly conceived, is a wonderfully wholesome position for a human being to adopt. It is most salutary to realize how little we know and how few of our convictions, whether in science or in common sense, can be upheld by a strict logical process. We need to be agnostics first and then there is some chance of arriving at a sensible system of belief. So long as we are cocksure we are not likely to learn.

It was such a mood of humility which Thomas Huxley and some of his followers sought to make common in the latter part of the nineteenth century. The golden text of the entire movement is found in the words "Sit down before fact as a little child." It is the agnosticism in line with this advice which

---

[10] The reaching out is itself only another experience. Thus an operational theory of knowledge does not avoid the predicament as stated.

ought to become universal. What it means is the rejection of prejudice, of doctrinaire positions taken in advance of the evidence. The entire paragraph in which Huxley's aphorism first appeared is helpful in this connection.

Science seems to me to teach in the highest and strongest manner the great truth which is embodied in the Christian conception of entire surrender to the will of God. Sit down before fact as a little child, be prepared to give up every preconceived notion, follow humbly wherever and to whatever abysses nature leads, or you shall learn nothing. I have only begun to learn content and peace of mind since I have resolved at all risks to do this.[11]

This kind of agnosticism, in the experience of Huxley's contemporary and fellow scientist George John Romanes, produced an openness to new truth that led eventually to positive religious belief. Romanes, for whom the famous lectureship was afterward named, began his public life as a convinced atheist and upheld his conviction by the anonymous publication of *Thoughts on Theism*. But in his effort to be a good agnostic his thought continued to grow. He could not ignore the fact that millions of persons had claimed and continued to claim genuine experience of fellowship with the Living God. They might be justified in this claim, and they might not be justified, but a good agnostic could not decide in advance; he could only study the facts as given.

Pure agnostics ought to investigate the religious consciousness of Christians as a phenomenon which may possibly be what Christians themselves believe it to be.[12]

By such patient and open-minded investigation, with the attendant elimination of pride, Romanes was led to reverse his position. When he died at the height of his powers, aged forty-six, he left the notes for his unfinished book which was published as *Thoughts on Religion*, and which showed him to be

[11] *Life and Letters of Thomas H. Huxley*, New York, 1901, p. 235.
[12] G. J. Romanes, *Thoughts on Religion*.

a convinced theist. Faithful to what seemed to him the spirit of science, his agnosticism became the gateway to that limitation on complete agnosticism which is called belief.

Sometimes those who call themselves agnostics uphold a far less defensible faith.[13] There are some who, impressed by an analysis of the conditions of knowledge, decide that knowledge is impossible. When they call themselves agnostics they go beyond the humility involved in "We *do not* know" to the dogmatism involved in "We *cannot* know." This last is wholly indefensible, because it asserts a really incredible kind of knowledge. We should need to know much more than we now know to be sure that it is impossible for the nature of the real world to be revealed to mortals. Moreover, the proposition is self-contradictory. Agnosticism is necessarily a limited creed, since, if it goes beyond a certain stage, it is self-defeating. The true position seems to lie neither in complete Gnosticism nor in complete agnosticism, but in the conviction that we have partial and fragmentary knowledge which can be improved by means at our command. This leaves room for a difference between the blind searchings of the savage mind and the disciplined searchings of the scientific mind. Both are based on faith and both are surrounded by vast areas that are unknown, but the edge of the darkness can be pushed back, at least a short distance. The skeptic and the agnostic are useful members of society because they aid in the avoidance of dogmatism.

D. The Choice of Faiths

We have seen above that faith is unavoidable in the various fields of human endeavor. There is no genuine certainty anywhere in the world of reason, for even that of mathematics depends upon postulates. We have pointed out the faith inherent in the scientific enterprise, chiefly an undemonstrable belief in the regularity and essential uniformity of nature. We have

---

[13] This has led to the practical elimination of the term agnosticism from our contemporary philosophical vocabulary.

shown, also, the kinds of faith which are involved in all speculation about reality. Other areas than those of science and philosophy could have been included in this survey, since it is obvious that the physician, the businessman, and the statesman depend likewise on faith every day of their lives.

It is well known that there is faith in religion and sometimes it is uncritically supposed that it is found nowhere else.[14] Moreover it is sometimes suggested that reliance on faith indicates some kind of intellectual weakness. We now have abundant reason to see that this is not the case, since faith is what makes knowledge possible. But to say that we are forced to depend on faith is not to say that one faith is as good as another. All faith is suprarational, but it need not be irrational or antirational. A great part of the discipline of philosophy is concerned with discrimination between competing faiths.

Having determined that faith is inescapable the great question becomes, "*Which* faith?" The very effort to formulate a faith is a valuable exercise and points in the direction of the answer to our question. We may agree with T. S. Eliot that "It is better to be stupid in a faith, even in a stupid faith, than to be stupid and believe nothing," but we want to avoid all the stupidity we can.

[14] Though there is faith in science and faith in religion, it is important to note that the two kinds of faith have distinct differences. The faith of science is largely dependence on law, whereas the faith of religion is characteristically trust in a person or persons. Cf. Charles Bennett, *The Dilemma of Religious Knowledge.*

CHAPTER V

THE AUTHORITY OF DISCIPLINED INSIGHT

"Testimony has great weight, and casts the balance."
—DOCTOR JOHNSON

As we seek to determine which items of faith are reasonable and therefore acceptable, we naturally ask which are most in accordance with the facts or most faithful to experience. But this inquiry only leads to another, for men are by no means agreed concerning what the facts are in any important field and they do not report the same experiences. What some call facts others call fictions and what seem to some men to be veridical experiences seem to other men to be hallucinations or illusions.

Our dependence on facts turns out to be somewhat pathetic, since we do not know any facts at all except as they are involved in the experience of men. This is part of what was meant in Chapter IV by saying every proposition is really a judgment. When a man says "King Charles the First was executed," he means "*I believe* King Charles the First was executed." Our dependence appears to be on facts, but it is really a dependence on men. Most *cognoscenda*, "things to be known if possible," are outside our bodies. Most of what we believe about the external world is received at second hand and rests on the prior belief that some men are more trustworthy reporters than others. We believe that the first white man to reach the North Pole was Admiral Peary rather than Dr. Cook, but our chief reasons for this belief depend upon information about the character of these two men.

The area of immediate experience open to any individual is extremely slight—a mere slit in the world's expanse. Thus to say that we shall believe only what we know directly at first hand is to reduce our belief in a fantastic manner. All history would be thereby eliminated and we should be confined to the *specious present*. A life so ordered would be intellectually poverty-stricken, if, indeed, it were possible at all. Intellectual self-sufficiency, like economic self-sufficiency, is only possible at a level of existence too low to be attractive.

A. THE INESCAPABILITY OF AUTHORITY

The conclusion to be reached, in view of our individual mental poverty is that we cannot avoid reliance on some sort of authority. Because sense experience is so open to error and because our reflections on our experience may be fragmentary or uncritical, we need to listen to those qualified to know. Characteristically our reliance is on the authority of the expert who may be defined as the man whom there is reason to trust. In all matters in which judgments of great difficulty are demanded, it is clearly more reasonable to trust the insight of a few persons than to submit the decision to the many:

Shall we submit our standards of aesthetic, scientific, educational, and philosophical values to a plebiscite? Shall we take a popular vote on Darwinism, the Kantian philosophy, or the Celtic movement in literature?[1]

In all these abstruse subjects we need something in the nature of a supreme court of learning and this is what we have in a rough manner. The periodic meetings of the learned societies and of the professional societies point in this direction. The authoritative value of the French Academy and of the Royal Society in Great Britain has been tremendous. The Harvard College tercentenary meetings were rightly considered a "supreme court of learning" and other anniversary celebrations at other academic centers have much of the same flavor. Moreover, every university is authoritative insofar as it is a

[1] Joseph A. Leighton, *The Field of Philosophy,* New York, 1923, p. 9.

community of learned men, helping and criticizing one another. President Conant expressed the academic ideal when he said on the first day of the Harvard Tercentenary, "Not the scholar but the community of scholars."[2]

Perhaps the experts never fully agree, but they check each other's excesses, corroborate each other's discoveries, and help the laymen to know something about the facts by agreement on some points. The best reason for believing the atomic theory is not that most people have tested it—which they have not—but that the relatively few who have studied it carefully are in substantial agreement.

Herein lies the great importance of those arrangements which help us to know who the few are. The Nobel prizes and various lesser prizes are of value in this regard. One who gets such a prize has been able to win the high regard of various kinds of fellow experts and we can rest assured concerning his competence. Honorary degrees, when they are not debased by commercial motives on the part of the donor, also help to build up the *complex system of reasonable trust*. In fact an honorary degree is the chief method of showing approval that democratic America has developed. And the value of the degree depends on the esteem in which the granting institution is held. Thus intricately is the authoritative pattern woven.

One of the most interesting modern examples of the systematic and deliberate use of this principle is afforded by the management of the London *Times*. The transfer of common shares, except in one instance, cannot be made without the approval of a committee whose members are the Speaker of the House of Commons, the Governor of the Bank of England, the Warden of All Souls College, Oxford, the Master of the Rolls, the Lord Chief Justice, and the Headmaster of Eton College. An unusual effort has been made to secure the services of those whose judgment may be trusted not to let the management of the newspaper fall into unworthy hands. For this purpose it is

[2] *The Tercentenary of Harvard College,* Cambridge, 1937, p. 101.

far better to appoint holders of positions than individual men, because there has already been a long sifting process before a man holds such a position. The holder of the position speaks with authority because he presumably has the support of his institution.

Not only are we dependent upon authority in affairs of national importance, and in abstruse intellectual matters, but almost equally so in the affairs of everyday life. We submit ourselves and our loved ones to the authority of the physician, and when his opinion differs from ours on some crucial point we recognize that he is more likely to be correct than we are. Of course he may not be correct, but the evidence is weighted in his direction.

When we submit ourselves to authority we need not submit ourselves blindly. We have a right to inspect the credentials of the alleged expert, for these credentials can be understood by the layman. Let us consider the choice of a dentist. We want to employ a dentist with technical skill and high moral character. The latter is especially important, because we could be duped so easily, and more easily by a man with good technical skill than by a man without it. I am at the dentist's mercy for two reasons: first, I do not have an intimate knowledge of the correct procedure, and, second, I cannot see what is being done. It is clear, therefore, that in making my selection, I am seeking primarily one whom I can trust, both in regard to skill and good faith. Since I cannot be my own dentist I am forced to trust the expert, first making an adequate effort to be sure he is an expert. This I shall learn chiefly by his standing in the opinion of his fellow experts. Is he allowed to belong to his professional society? Does he have diplomas showing satisfactory training in reputable institutions? These pertinent questions refer to an interlocking system of authority with a wholesome tension between parts. There are checks and balances of many kinds, of which the crediting agencies of educational institutions provide one example.

Similar conditions exist in all professional arrangements. A professional man is one whom we trust because of training and connections which justify our trust. Though what are called professions illustrate the principle of dependence upon authority in a marked degree, something of the same kind, though in lesser degree, appears from the top to the bottom of an ordered society. Familiar illustrations of the everyday application of the principle of authority are the use of the Union label and the Good Housekeeping label. The reliance upon authority is a forced option, since the alternative of my reliance on the opinion of the accredited expert is reliance upon my own uninstructed opinion.

There are two popular errors concerning authority which such considerations should serve to correct. The first is the notion that authority is chiefly to be found in religion. Authority has a place in religion, not because religion is different from other human pursuits, but because it is like them. The more we deal with intangibles of any kind, that is to say, with really important matters, the more we are forced to rely on authority to a great degree, for there is no simple rule of thumb to which we can appeal. There is a strong tendency to suppose that there is no more reason to listen to one man than another in spiritual matters, because the subjects considered are notoriously incapable of proof. The proper conclusion to be drawn, however, is the precise opposite of this. It is *because* the subjects are incapable of proof that we need to avail ourselves of superior wisdom.

The fact that sensitive religious men in all faiths have set great store by religious literary monuments is not hard to understand. We turn to the Hebrew prophets because they were men of undoubted genius in the spiritual life, just as we turn to Bach or Mozart, undoubted geniuses in musical production. We *may* consider our own religious opinions better than the opinions of the major prophets, and we *may* consider our own musical opinions better than those of the classical composers, but the chance that we are correct in this kind of judgment is not great. Those who do not like Shakespeare are advised to consider what is wrong with themselves.

Devout men have turned to the classical expressions of religious experience with reverence and hope, precisely because they have had a salutary humility. We know nothing of an *infallible authority*, just as we know nothing of *absolute certainty*, for these seem to be denied to mortals, but we do know that there are some whom it is sensible to trust above ourselves. Any man who has begun to understand the weakness of individualism knows that he needs something to buttress his feeble little life. The long experience of the church is more likely to lead to correct answers than is the experience of the lone individual. Sometimes the rebel against authority is a prophet, but far more often he is merely a fool. We are not justified in converting the proposition, "All prophets have been misunderstood" into "All who have been misunderstood have been prophets."

It makes a good deal of difference what our standard of spiritual authority is and how we accept it, whether critically or uncritically, but some standard there must be. This is recognized not merely by the so-called authoritarian or Catholic churches, but also by small independent groups. It is doubtful, for instance, if any religious group has so stressed the principle of authority as has the Religious Society of Friends. This became explicit as early as 1674 when Robert Barclay published his *The Anarchy of the Ranters*. Quakers early learned to check their own "leadings" by submitting them to the group inspiration of the local "meeting." When we realize this, we see that Sabatier's famous title *Religions of Authority and the Religion of the Spirit* is not wholly satisfactory. The disjunction is not as sharp as Sabatier supposed.

The dependence on authority is not confined to religion and is not even found chiefly in religion, but appears wherever men are humble about their own opinions, aware of the complexity of life, and eager to know about difficult matters. The interest which thoughtful men take in literary and artistic criticism is further evidence that this is the case. We do not bow down slavishly to the critics, but we pay attention to the critics; in other words, we regard them as authorities.

The second popular error about authority which calls for correction is the notion that authority and reason are somehow rival ways of coming to know the truth. Even some reputable books on philosophy, like Montague's *Ways of Knowing*, encourage this idea by the arrangement of their chapters. The reader gets the notion that reason is one way of knowing the truth, whereas authority is another. But the analysis of the question, as we have considered it, has already shown that dependence upon authority is itself the path of reason.

When we rely on authority we are, in most cases, doing the most reasonable thing we can do. It is far more reasonable for me to rely on the opinion of Mr. Milliken in regard to cosmic rays than it is to rely on my own unaided and highly amateurish efforts.[3] The point is that when we rely on authority we are not, *for that reason,* guilty of credulity. *There is a reason for our reliance.* We trust the men and institutions presenting the most reason for being trusted. We must use reason to determine *which* authority to follow, just as we use reason to determine *which* faith to adopt.

B. THE PERSONAL EQUATION

We often say that we wish to eliminate the personal equation in various human enterprises. We mean by this that we want something which is independent of the opinions of men. We like those games in which a clear-cut decision by means of a

[3] There is a philosophical discipline strictly correlative to the training in scientific method which makes us trust the scientist. A brilliant exposition of philosophic method is given by Arthur O. Lovejoy in his essay, "The Meaning of Romanticism for the Historian of Ideas," *Journal of the History of Ideas,* June, 1941, Volume II, pp. 262-270.

score is possible, as against those in which the outcome is decided by a board of judges.

But the more we try to eliminate the rôle played by men in our understanding of the nature of the world the more we come to realize that we are thoroughly unsuccessful. Even measurement is not a foolproof and fully objective procedure, inasmuch as it is men who do the measuring, and when we try to be really accurate we find a striking lack of entire agreement. Frequently several measurements are taken and the one finally chosen may not be identical with any one actually reported since it is a mean. It is obvious that some men are far more trustworthy than others in accurate measurement.

It might be supposed that, if there were any one way in which the personal equation could be eliminated it would be in following scientific method. Yet reflection shows that every step of scientific method involves a dependence on the informed judgment of men, so that, unless able men carry on the research, the results are not trustworthy. The method cannot dispense with human wisdom and genius. Let us see how each step involves the human factor in a marked way.

In the first place, it takes special ability to *observe* intelligently. Any layman who has taken a cross-country walk with a skilled geologist knows how inadequate the layman's observation is. There are many things obvious to the trained man which the layman actually does not "see." This is even more marked in looking through a microscope or telescope. The instrument may be properly in focus and the conditions of illumination may be right, but the amateur sees only a blur.

In the second place, the construction of a fruitful hypothesis depends on human genius to an unusual degree. Hypotheses do not make themselves. They often seem commonplace to later observers, but the original insight is far from commonplace. The invention of an hypothesis which, if sustained, may bring order into an otherwise confused mass of data, is fundamentally similar to the work of a poet or a prophet.[4] We have an abundant autobiographical literature, showing how the happy flash comes in an unpredictable manner and at an unpredictable time, but usually after the problem to be solved has been wrestled with long and patiently, and sometimes temporarily put aside.

In the third place, the task of seeing what is implied in an hypothesis, and thus to prepare the way for verification, is a matter of intellectual labor which depends for its success, not merely on the nature of external events, but on the quality of the person who performs the labor. It is at this point, as we saw above, that the purely deductive element of scientific method is involved.

Finally, in the fourth place, verification, itself, is a matter of personal ability. What is chiefly needed is persons who can construct novel and "crucial" experiments in order to test the results to see whether what is implied really occurs. But even if it does occur, the original contention is not proved, since there might be more theories than one leading to the same consequences. If we find more and more "predicted consequences" which actually occur, we decide that the theory is substantiated, but it is by no means *proved*. When does this point of practical substantiation occur? For this we have no rule, but must depend on the good sense of men. Professor Joseph has stated this point with admirable clarity as follows:

In such matters we must consider what is called the weight of the evidence for a theory that is not rigorously proved. But no one has shown how weight of evidence can be mechanically estimated; the wisest men, and best acquainted with the matter in hand, are oftenest right.[5]

As we reach the higher levels of science we find that our dependence on personal trustworthiness becomes more impor-

---

[4] Poincaré has been particularly convincing on this point. Cf. *Science and Method*.

[5] H. W. B. Joseph, *An Introduction to Logic*, pp. 523, 524.

tant than in the elementary branches, for the simple reason that the number who can follow their alleged results critically is small. Since dependence on men is so great and so pervasive of our experience, we need to learn all we can about what it is that makes men trustworthy guides to their fellows.

C. DISCIPLINED INSIGHT

When we begin to inquire into the conditions of intellectual trustworthiness we are led to consider the rôle of logic. Is there not some system of logic which men can learn and then, after that, can be depended upon, since they will be guided by their logical method to correct conclusions?

It must be admitted that men have long sought such a method and sometimes some men have supposed they have found it, but they have not been permanently convincing. The traditional logic is a marvelous instrument, by no means to be despised, but knowledge of it does not help very much in practical life. A man cannot reasonably say, "Now here is a problem to be solved. Since I know logic I shall use a logical method of solving it." The chief difficulty is that the traditional logic is so largely mathematical and, like mathematics, is abstract, whereas real life is always concrete. Valid syllogisms are valid because they deal with abstract and unchanging relations, but no man orders his life syllogistically.

Traditional logic is concerned with necessary inference, and the key to necessary inference is the universal. We need to talk about all triangles and some triangles, about all men and some men. This is all very well in mathematics, but it does not apply to life. In actual experience we have not the certainty involved in universals, but tendencies. We cannot say truly that all soldiers are brave. Research would probably indicate a curve of bravery among soldiers like the curve of intelligence among students. We can learn about these matters, but there is no foolproof way. Neither Aristotelian logic nor modern scientific method can show a man how to find the truth unless he is a man of insight. This line of thought is leading to a sharp reversal of what is popularly supposed to be the rôle of logic in human experience. We see it now, not so much as a *tool* as *a preparatory discipline*.

In the end there is no appeal beyond the actual apprehensions of men. That is our supreme court. It was the great merit of the Cartesian revolution in philosophy that it showed the defects and inapplicability of the Scholastic logic and encouraged men to depend on the "natural light" of the mind. But this merit need not make us rest satisfied that one intuition is as good as another. Truths that are self-evident are not, for that reason, self-evident to everybody. There are many things which are self-evident to the master which are not self-evident to the pupil. We cannot, in the end, go beyond the intuitions of men, whether in science, ethics, or religion, but these intuitions are only reliable when they are the apprehensions of disciplined minds.

This suggests that the function of logic, any kind of logic, is not so much to guide our mental operations *after we have "observed,"* but rather to sharpen our minds in advance so that we shall see what there is to see. According to this conception what we need is not a method to follow, but a discipline to increase our sensitivity, to sharpen our awareness, to make us recognize the truth when we see it. This makes the biographies and autobiographies of persons of recognized insight extremely important reading. How did men like Pascal and Newton and Darwin achieve the ability to see what others could not see while looking at the same general scenes? If we could know that, we should be well on our way.

One thing is clear, and that is that the insight comes at the end of a process of experience in a certain field, not at the beginning. When we recognize this we are returning to the doctrine taught by Aristotle at the end of his *Posterior Analytics*, a doctrine which seems to be the final wisdom of his logical inquiries. Curiously enough, when we refer to Aristotle's logic we usually include only the first part of his ambitious work. The *Prior Analytics* give rules for inference from established knowledge. The *Posterior Analytics* do something better, they deal with the attainment of real and valid knowledge. The last pages not only show the importance of intuition, but show how intuition comes.

So out of sense-perception comes to be what we call memory, and out of frequently repeated memories of the same things develops experience; for a number of memories constitute a single experience. From experience again . . . originate the skill of the craftsman and the knowledge of the man of science, skill in the sphere of coming to be and science in the sphere of being.[6]

Not only is judgment made dependable by anterior discipline, but it must be the *appropriate* discipline. The training by experience upon which we rightly depend must be relevant to the problem at hand before it has value. Thus a good judge of English poetry may not be any judge at all when a nice problem in the age of rock formations is presented. It is a common experience in public life for men who have achieved eminence in one field to begin to dogmatize about some wholly alien field, and thereby make themselves ridiculous. Men in biology are frequently mere tyros in ethics, but quite unaware that this is the case. Natural scientists are more likely to expect attention outside their own fields than are scholars in the humanities, because those outside natural science are well aware that it is a specialized field, made so by the intricacy of the apparatus, if for no other reason.

This point needs to be stressed because it is often overlooked in the field of religious experience. A distinguished chemist asserts that he does not believe in God—that throughout his life he has never had any sense of the reality of the presence of God. Many are impressed by this. Here was a highly intelligent person with a finely trained mind and the negative evidence provided by his testimony must be given considerable weight.

[6] *Analytica Posteriora*, 100a.

But wait a moment. Are we so sure? Before we give this testimony *any weight at all* we need to know much more. Did the scholar in question submit himself at all to the kind of situation in which he could expect to be aware of God's presence if God really is? This scholar would not have expected an opinion in chemistry to be worthy of attention unless the person announcing the opinion had undertaken a great deal of training in chemistry. All great things are hard, and there seems no reason to suppose that it would be easier to know God than to know the laws and elements of His creation. Of course the hypothetical scholar in question may have been a man who engaged in the discipline of his devotional life as assiduously as he engaged in the sharpening of his judgment as a chemist, for the two are compatible, and, if he did, his words demand respect, but the point is, that if he did not, his opinion is *wholly lacking in value*.

Emphasis on the importance of disciplined insight as the best approach to truth enlarges our conception of the meaning and function of logic. Logic comes to be that kind of training which best opens the "eye of the soul." There are some modern persons who suppose they can dispense with logic. Sometimes they say of a proposition, "It is logical, but we cannot accept it." If they mean that they are willing to act in unreasonable ways, it is difficult to see what standard they uphold. If we cease to think accurately we merely think badly, and there seems no escape from logic in the broad sense. What those who make such remarks probably intend to convey, however, is the conviction that life is too rich and varied to be forced into the forms of a purely subsumptive system. The world is far more than applied mathematics. This is clearly true, and means that we must make our logic a more inclusive discipline. But some such discipline there must be if the intuitions of man's mind are to be trusted.

What we have just said bears directly on the question of authority. The authority we can trust best is that of disciplined insight with experience of an appropriate kind. If we can find, in any field, men who fulfill these conditions and if there is substantial agreement in their independent judgments we have as good an indication of what is true as men are likely to find in this world.

D. THE AUTHORITY OF THE AMATEUR

Though what has been said above applies to religious experience as it applies to ethical, aesthetic, and scientific experience, there is a unique aspect of religious authority that should be indicated. This unique aspect appears in the paradox that, so far as religion is concerned, *the expert is the amateur*. A great part of the Bible was written by men whom we must call laymen. The first of those amazing men whom we call the writing prophets, and who have set their mark on the subsequent course of events in a remarkable way, was not a religious professional at all, but a simple herdsman, and this was his boast: "I was no prophet, neither was I a prophet's son; but I was an herdsman, and a gatherer of sycamore fruit: And the Lord took me as I followed the flock, and the Lord said unto me, Go, prophesy unto my people Israel."[7] In many of the books of the Bible there is evidence of open conflict between those whose words we now revere and the official custodians of religion at the time, i.e., the priests.

This lay tradition has been maintained to a large extent in Christianity and is also exemplified in non-Christian faiths. The priests become authoritarians, but the "authorities" to whom they appeal are largely amateurs. Names such as St. Francis and George Fox come readily to mind in this connection. The professional observer in science is far more likely to be dependable than the nonprofessional observer, but it is otherwise in religion. In religion there is something about professionalism which dulls the sensitive spirit. It is largely on this account that the word "religionist" is almost a term of abuse. In

[7] Amos, 7:14, 15.

generation after generation it seems necessary, if religion is to continue its vitality, that there be an upsurge of lay religion, challenging conventional and professionalized faith.

The fact that the person of religious authority is the amateur is a matter of far-reaching significance. It means, for one thing, that the appropriate discipline requisite for religious insight and experience is something within the reach of all, and not something necessarily confined to the few, as in so many human undertakings. This is why religion is profoundly democratic. In the nature of the case there are not many scientists and not many physicians, but there are hundreds of millions of men and women who participate in religious faith. This does not mean that the kind of discipline requisite for the knowledge of God is any easier than the discipline requisite for scientific knowledge, but it does mean that it is a discipline within the capacity of normal human beings, regardless of race, education, or standards of culture. It is interesting to note that the slogan "Every man his own physician" is a ridiculous slogan, but the slogan "The priesthood of the believer" surprises no one.

Some recognition of the democratic nature of religious insight, coupled with the popular prejudice in favor of scientific knowledge, has led many to suppose in our day that the notion of the authority of the expert, although wholly tenable in science, is not tenable in religion. The popular statement is that science is a matter of fact, whereas religion is a matter of opinion, in which one man's conviction is no better than any other. What we have seen about the importance of the personal equation makes this largely nonsense. Once the principle of authority is accepted, there is no reason to make exceptions to it. This is the point of the following passage from one of the letters of Cardinal Newman to William Froude:

You say that an ordinary man would think it his duty to listen to any great mechanical philosopher who should bring reasons for even so great a paradox as the possibility of perpetual motion; why should such personal reverence be reserved for mechanicians alone? Why not for theologians?[8]

The point at which we should question Cardinal Newman is in his reference to theologians. Many of those of accepted authority in the religious life have not been theologians. The Cardinal's statement would be unexceptionable if we should substitute the word "saints" for the word theologians. By a saint we here mean one who has lived a pure and selfless life. The prime requirement for spiritual competence is tenderness of spirit. Sometimes a professional theologian has also been recognized as a saint, but the combination is difficult. Newman came closer to it than most.

Religious insight does not come to the unprepared, but the preparation is different from other preparation. In large measure it consists of an elimination of our own conceit, of intellectual pride, which are enormous barriers. The only way to enter into the Kingdom of the Truth is to become as a little child. There are many things which are hid from the wise and prudent and yet revealed unto babes. Pascal and Voltaire may have been equally well endowed intellectually, but Pascal had this kind of preparation for religious insight, whereas Voltaire did not. Accordingly, their conclusions are not worthy of equal attention.

Cocksureness is as effective an hindrance to spiritual sight as is dirt on the glass a hindrance to microscopic sight. There is much more to be said about the discipline appropriate to religion, but the point to make now is that it is open to the rank and file. There is nothing the clergyman can know which the layman cannot know. Clergymen are not more adept than others at the art of worship and may be less so. There is no secret or esoteric knowledge in religion that is hard to understand. Religion has no professional secrets.

A second important result of the fact that the religious expert

[8] Gordon Harper, *Cardinal Newman and William Froude*, Baltimore, 1933, p. 206.

is the amateur is that religious authority is always in high tension. Since there is no secret knowledge, it is the privilege and duty of the lone individual to challenge the "authorities." He may have as good a right to be heard as anyone. The common man cannot reasonably challenge the experts of California Institute of Technology on the subject of cosmic rays, since the person without years of technical training cannot even understand the symbols used, but a herdsman can reasonably challenge a priest or group of priests, since each man may have the direct knowledge of God in his own experience. The heart of religion, we must remember, is not an *information about God*, but *experience of God*.

The established authority must forever be checked by the judgment of the individual and by new groups. Where there is a clear conflict between the judgment of the individual and the group judgment (which is authoritative in that it is more likely to be right) the individual is wise to put the burden of proof upon himself. But, if after careful consideration in all humility, the heretical person is convinced that the way opened to him is divinely appointed, he must go forward in it. The maintenance of this tension between private religious insight and authority is most wholesome, avoiding on the one hand the stagnation which mere authoritarianism produces, and, on the other, the confusion of mere individualism.

The essential nature of religious authority explains, in large measure, the otherwise amazing respect felt for Jesus of Nazareth all over the world and for so many centuries. He was a carpenter, He challenged the professional religionists, He was disciplined by silence and by the spirit of the little child. Here is all we need, and men recognize it when they see it. To put great faith in what He taught, not in slavish obedience, but in the conviction that He is more likely to be right than we are, appears, in the light of our reflections in this chapter, as a most reasonable procedure. It would be irrational to do otherwise.

Such a consideration means that we begin our study of the

central faith of religion with a rational prejudice in favor of positive belief. This is true, not only because of the authority of Jesus, but likewise because of the authority of millions of devout persons of high and low degree who have corroborated the same testimony. But we do not rest here. Admittedly the case for the objective reality of God is good from the start, but this does not relieve us from the necessity of rigorous logical inquiry. Our exactingness ought to increase with the increase of the importance of the affirmations put forward. In philosophy and religion we ought to be, not less critical of our conclusions, but more.

PART II

TYPES OF BELIEF

CHAPTER VI

THE DEVELOPMENT OF THE NATURALISTIC CREED

"Now most of the earliest philosophers regarded principles of a material kind as the only principles of all things." —ARISTOTLE

The number of serious beliefs about the nature of reality is really not great. In all times and places the same fundamental answers to the riddle of existence are given. All the major metaphysical types of our times may be matched by similar types in ancient Greece, the chief novelty we introduce being that of ingenious combinations, some of which are of doubtful consistency.

Not only do the same fundamental types continually reappear, but also they tend to reappear in a certain sequence, both in the life of a people and the life of the individual thinker. Each stage has its merits, but each stage has its difficulties as well. It is highly important that we know what the fundamental types of belief have been, in order that each person may be more intelligent about his own beliefs.

A. THE DIALECTICAL MOVEMENT OF INTELLECTUAL HISTORY

The first fundamental answer to the riddle of existence, being at once the first form of philosophy and the earliest religion, may be suitably named *naïve spiritualism*. Whether we call it a religion or a philosophy makes little difference, for the two were long interfused and have only been separated by reflective thought. The first fundamental belief was spiritualism, because there was an habitual tendency to make reference to divine powers and it was naïve because the action of these powers was assumed uncritically. This period must have lasted for many thousands of years and, in any case, it was incalculably longer than the succeeding periods have been.

We do not know, and probably we shall never know, when this naïve spiritualism first became the practical faith of men. Perhaps it was when they *became* men, inasmuch as we should hardly call creatures men, whatever their physical form, if they were utterly insensitive to the things for which naïve spiritualism stands. Sometime, long, long ago, our rude ancestors began to believe in the existence of invisible powers and to order their lives accordingly. This occurred not only among the ancestors of white men, but likewise among the ancestors of black, brown, and yellow men. Illustrations of fetishism, of totemism, and of taboo can be drawn from cultures far removed from one another geographically and, so far as we are able to ascertain, independent of one another, as regards cultural borrowing.

Naïve spiritualism finds no fundamental defect in magic, but actually introduces some of the spirit of magic into prayer. It has no real objection to the anthropomorphism which sometimes identifies the invisible spirits with beings of human shape. The problem of evil does not, on this level, seem highly perplexing. Such a world view, though it involves important theoretical assumptions and belief, does not often make these explicit; it is concerned almost wholly with the practical orientation of life to the spiritual powers. Thus there are many prayers, much incantation, and great ceremonies concerned with birth, adolescence, marriage, victory, penance, and death. In many of these the community as a whole is involved.[1]

This world view may truly be said to have been practically universal throughout most of the career of mankind. Any serious challenge to it is a relatively modern innovation. In its

[1] One of the best descriptions of this naïve spiritualism is that of W. E. Hocking in *Types of Philosophy*, 1929, pp. 28, 29.

naïve form spiritualism continues in many parts of the human race to the present time. Even among those supposedly devoted to the advanced religions, this naïve spiritualism is not far below the surface and is often demonstrated. This is clear in the supposed Christianity of the South American Indians, but we need not go that far to find it. The way in which prayer tends to slip back into magic formulae is a case in point. Naïve spiritualism is the faith of the childhood of the race, and man is a creature with a long infancy.

In view of the nature and quality of man's rational powers, it was inevitable that eventually this well-nigh universal faith should be challenged. As men's critical powers began to emerge into maturity it was wholly natural that some adventurous spirits should ask whether the invisible spirits really existed, whether prayers made any difference, and whether ceremonies were anything other than self-deluding acts. It has, therefore, been normal for a second type of belief to succeed the first and to appear as its negation. This second type of belief may conveniently be called *naïve naturalism*. It has arisen as an historical phenomenon in different cultures at different times, but with features so similar that a normal type can be described. Moreover, it appears not only as an historical phenomenon at particular junctures of time, but also as a normal reaction in the later adolescence or early maturity of many individual persons. This kind of recapitulation is beyond doubt and is, indeed, so common as to affect our language. The use of the word "sophomoric" arises from the recurrence of this phenomenon generation after generation.

Perhaps the most striking historical example of the rise of naïve naturalism out of naïve spiritualism is that provided by the Milesian School of Greek philosophy. The intellectual movement represented by the Milesians is usually accounted the beginning of European philosophy and histories of philosophy usually deal with it in their first chapters. Actually it was far from the beginning of European philosophy. At best it belongs

to the second chapter and the first chapter is a very long one.[2]
This first chapter should be devoted to the world view native
to the Greek mind, which found its finest expression in Hesiod
and the Homeric poems. There were many pre-Socratics, and
the ones we usually designate by that name were chiefly those
who were in revolt in some sense against the dominant spiritualistic world view.

The point to make clear is that if the faith in the Olympian
deities was naïve and uncritical, the belief we call naturalism
was almost equally so. Thales and his immediate successors,
important as they were as intellectual pioneers, introduced in
an extreme form the oversimplification which has been the
chief error of naturalistic philosophers in all subsequent generations. To say that everything is made of water, as Thales
supposedly did, is only a bit more extreme than to say everything, including the thoughts of those who propound the theory,
is really reducible to mechanics.

There is little doubt that Thales, Anaximander, and Anaximenes were great and courageous men. They were men of
quick and restless imagination, and it is not surprising that they,
in their conscious opposition to the received spiritualistic world
view, went over to the opposite extreme. Moreover, they had
something to show for their intellectual labor. It is a credible
tradition that Thales predicted successfully the eclipse of the
sun which occurred in 585 B.C. and the members of the school
seem to have been good political prophets as well, pointing out
the danger of the selfish, and eventually fatal, policy of isolation which Miletus was following.

[2] Professor Hermann Fränkel furnishes the following note: The traditional
view ignores Hesiod's profound and subtle speculations on the universe and
its basic constituents, on the gods and the other powers controlling nature
and life, on man and his position in the world, and on all kinds of social
relations; just as it ignores the fact that before, during, and after the age
of the Milesians, Greek poets discussed religion and ethics in a truly philosophical spirit. Frequently the so-called natural philosophers merely applied
to nature ideas originally evolved in moral speculations. This is only natural
since Greek philosophy tended to interpret all nature, including the "inanimate," in terms of the highest form of life: the human.

When we call the philosophy of the Milesians naturalism we mean that they sought to explain the natural world from within itself as a self-sufficient system. This tendency seems to have been more explicit in Anaximander (610-546 B.C.) than in his famous teacher. The fragments of his teaching which have been preserved and the comments provided by later Greek thinkers suggest that he explained the apparent novelties which come in the course of history as nothing but combinations or separations of parts already in existence. This has been the heart of naturalism ever since, which may be termed, in brief, "the philosophy of nothing but."

It was an easy step from this early Milesian naturalism to the wholly mechanical scheme of the first atomists, Leucippus and Democritus. The only surviving fragment of Leucippus is "Nothing happens without a cause, but all for a specific reason and under the pressure of necessity." This fragment indicates no real divergence from the spiritualistic hypothesis in its more advanced and orderly forms, except that it leaves no place for freedom of thought, but the general opinion is that Leucippus, like Democritus, arrived at a materialist conclusion.

So influential was the naturalistic bias of these pioneers, whether of the colonies or of the homeland, that they seem to have provided the literate public with the stereotyped conception of what a philosopher was. Thus Aristophanes makes fun of Socrates and ascribes to him doctrines which are consistent with the teachings of the Milesians or the atomists, but are not substantiated by anything we learn about Socrates from the men who undertook seriously to perpetuate his memory, i.e., Xenophon and Plato. The idea seems to be that, since Socrates was a philosopher, he was, for that reason, a naturalist. Of course this was an injustice to the Pythagoreans and Eleatics, as well as many of the Sophists, but their doctrines, being closer to the naïve spiritualism which was the general background of all people, were not so striking or shocking as were the naturalistic doctrines.

If naïve spiritualism was the thesis and naïve naturalism was the antithesis, the Socratic tradition was the synthesis. It is to be noted that we may expect the synthesis to restate the fundamental position of the thesis, but in a critical and sophisticated manner, taking advantage of the negative contributions of the antithesis. The Socratic-Platonic-Aristotelian intellectual succession represented the effort of wholly civilized and mature minds to understand the world in its complexity. They could not be satisfied with the superstitious, anthropomorphic, and fantastic theories of the long generations of uncritical men, but neither could they be satisfied with a materialistic system which sought to reduce the higher aspects of experience to lower and simpler constituents. In other words, they took *mind* seriously and could not rest until they had a conception of the universe which, while orderly, placed mental reality at the heart of things. There is, indeed, a natural order and it becomes a suitable field of scientific investigation, but it is not understandable without reference to another type of order which is its ultimate ground. This, which has come to be looked upon as The Great Tradition, reaffirms the long uncriticized view that the world is the theater of spiritual powers, but it likewise reaffirms the naturalistic contention that the events of the tangible world are not subject to caprice.

This Socratic-Platonic-Aristotelian tradition has become, in large measure, the dominant world view of the Western world. Found easily adaptable to the Christian Gospel, it has been taught, with minor variations, in all the succeeding centuries. It has provided much of the philosophical background of theism and has been the faith of most men who are unsatisfied either with simple spiritualism or simple naturalism.

The history of Greek philosophy is important, partly because it is the history of all philosophy in prototype. In many subsequent generations there has been the same dialectical movement, with a naturalistic revolt against simple faith and this revolt followed by a reasoned or critical faith. The whole

process has been illustrated on an advanced level in the philosophical history of the West during the last fifty years. First
we find an orthodox academic philosophy usually called
idealism. The revolt against this was the simple *realism* which
its critics came to call *naïve realism*. This, in turn, has been
replaced, in large measure, by some form of *critical realism*,
which reasserts many of the basic insights of idealism, but re-
nounces subjectivism. This is fundamentally a movement in the
direction of intellectual maturity, and is chiefly found among
professional philosophers.

B. CONTEMPORARY NATURALISM

Whatever be the present position of academic philosophers,
there is little doubt that a naïve form of naturalism is the
dominant metaphysics of our Western culture just now, so far as
the rank and file of literate persons is concerned. Popularly, at
least, we are in the second dialectical stage, and not primarily
in the first or third, though there are some in both of these. We
find the dominant thought represented by the evident majority
of university undergraduates and among a highly vocal proportion of their teachers.

This contemporary naturalism is, for the most part, not a
self-conscious metaphysic and is seldom explicitly defended in
books. It is, instead, part of the temper of the age and far more
important for the history of the human race than if it were to
be found chiefly in books. This current naturalism does not appear to those who accept it as something derived specifically from
Greek naturalism nor as having any special connection with the
fashionable materialism of the eighteenth century. It appears
rather to be a view which is obviously inspired by the facts of
nature which are learned by the methods of natural science.

This contemporary naturalism deserves to be called naïve
naturalism just as that of the early period of Greek philosophy
does, but for an added reason. This reason is that the current
naturalism is very largely accepted by those who do not realize

that it is a philosophy; they do not know that it is thoroughly possible, with intellectual integrity, to accept the methods and conclusions of modern science and yet espouse a world view which is sharply at variance with that which is currently popular.

Before describing in detail this naturalism, it may be well to show why it arises. There are at least four separate reasons for its popular acceptance. (1) The first of these is the success of the scientific method. By means of the scientific method, especially as applied to physical things, men have been able to change the face of the earth to a remarkable degree in the last three hundred years. Here is a kind of learning in which we escape idle theorizing and show tangible results. Men who are scientifically trained can produce machines which fly when they are needed and bridges which stand when they are constructed.[3] Is it not evident that a view of the world most harmonious with this scientific work must be a true one? Where did men ever get by all their talk about Platonic ideas? But when they were willing to deal with the tangible and the measurable they really did get somewhere.

Even in spite of the misgivings of the skeptically minded, when they observe the most obvious results of scientific advance in the form of bombed cities, it remains true that the prestige of science is today deservedly great and that any philosophy which really could be shown to be implicit in it would have a great initial advantage in the form of presumptive evidence. But the claim that naturalism is implicit in natural science, often assumed without argument, is far from self-evident and requires careful analysis.

(2) The second reason for the wide acceptance of contemporary naturalism is the distrust of authority. Rightly or wrongly, authority as a means of discovering truth is in disrepute, that is, it is in disrepute theoretically, for in practice it is more popular than ever. The authority of some distinguished

[3] Actually, of course, this kind of success is far from universal. Witness the fall of the Narrows Bridge near Tacoma, Washington.

scientists is accepted unquestionably by millions who have no means of testing for themselves the scientific beliefs they ingenuously hold.

We shall have occasion later to investigate more fully this inconsistency between theory and practice, but it is sufficient at this point to show that the modern naturalistic mentality believes that the way of authority is somehow indissolubly bound up with a theistic interpretation of the universe. Thus the supposed rejection of authority and the substitution of verified experience is thought to entail the rejection of any spiritualism, whether naïve or critical. The fact that this process is full of intellectual confusion does not, as yet, render it uninfluential in leading many in the direction of some naturalistic creed.

(3) A third reason for the present dominance of naïve naturalism is the wide acceptance of evolution as an explanatory principle. This is not the same influence as that deriving from natural science, inasmuch as evolutionary theory is much older than modern science. Something of this nature was actually suggested by Anaximander in the sixth century B.C. Moreover, evolution is far more of a philosophical concept than a strictly scientific one. The notion that all life has been derived from a single unicellular organism is an interesting and useful concept, but it is purely speculative and lies in an area in which scientific demonstration is entirely out of the question. It may be a reasonable faith, but nothing more.

Though there are many evolutionary theories, some of them mutually inconsistent, it is the special theory associated with the name of Charles Darwin that has most caught the popular imagination. This is popularly supposed to show, beyond reasonable doubt, that all the changes of species, throughout all time, have come about purely by *natural selection*, i.e., with no instrumentality of mind or purpose. The very title of Darwin's most famous book is highly influential in this regard. If the change in species has come "naturally," does it not seem reasonable that all other developments whether of solar systems or the lives of men have come about in the same way? Thus reference to a divine Mind is not so much refuted as rendered unnecessary, and by the principle of parsimony we do not multiply explanations beyond what is necessarily required.

(4) A fourth reason for the popular acceptance of naïve naturalism is found in a peculiarly modern form of the desire for simplification. The desire for simplification has been with us for centuries, leading to various forms of monism, but it now appears especially in the tendency to inquire into origins and to be satisfied that an explanation is reached when these are known. Thus we investigate the history of morals and we find, supposedly, that in the beginning morality was nothing but a set of taboos or fear of tribal chieftains. We conclude that all morality, even its developed form, is *really* nothing but taboos and has no objective validity. Or we investigate the history of religion and conclude that it arose out of primitive fears of the unknown. Consequently the religion of civilized men is really nothing but superstitious fears. By the same argument science could be reduced to primitive magic.

The absurdity of this procedure of thought has long been obvious and has been called, for several years, the "genetic fallacy." It has been recognized by careful thinkers, from Aristotle on, that the true character of anything may be known by what it develops *into* rather than what it develops *out of*. It is quite as *reasonable* to understand a seed in terms of a tree, as to explain a tree in terms of the seed. But there are many forms in which its fallacious character is not apparent. One of these is the tendency to reduce all higher manifestations of life to their simpler and more primitive constituents. Since, in the evolutionary process, matter probably came before life, it is matter which is the fundamentally real. Therefore, life, if it were fully known would be nothing but matter. The prejudice in favor of the primitive or the original affects many of the sciences. There is, for example, a tendency to view psychology as nothing but a branch of biology, and similarly a tendency to interpret biology as mechanics.

C. Details of the Naturalistic Creed

Given these influences, what are the main features of the naturalist creed of our time? It is desirable to present this without caricature, to describe not some figure made of straw, but a system of belief which its millions of upholders would recognize and accept as their own. We must remember that this system, uncritical as it may appear to be upon analysis, arises from a praiseworthy motive—the attempt to face the world honestly, rejecting the will-to-believe, and refusing to balk at the ugly facts of the world. Great numbers have come to the conclusion that any alternative philosophy is the product of "wish thinking" and this they honestly renounce.

The system of belief about to be described we call "naturalism" for the good historic reason that this use of the word has been so adopted by many eminent philosophers in the recent past. Important among these are James Ward and Lord Balfour. Of course such a use of a word never satisfies everybody and all people are at liberty to make new definitions of words if they like, providing they warn their readers that they are doing so. There is nothing sacred or even permanent about the meaning of words.

Professor James Bissett Pratt has recently produced a book called *Naturalism*, but the naturalism of which he speaks is far from identical with that herein described and likewise different from that criticized by Ward, Balfour, and their contemporaries. Professor Pratt seems to be moved by the laudable motive to rescue something fine from its ignoble associations and accordingly he presents naturalism in a splendid light. But, in order to accomplish this, it is necessary for him to so define naturalism as to be practically identical with common honesty or with any good philosophy. "The one characteristic common to all the naturalistic systems," he writes, "is the persistent attempt to find out, by all the resources of empirical fact and unprejudiced logic, the truth about the world we live in."[4] We can be grateful to Professor Pratt for this excellent statement of purpose. If this be naturalism, let us all be as naturalistic as possible. What sincere searcher after truth is to be ruled out? Certainly not those who have supposed themselves to be the critics and opponents of naturalism.[5]

What we propose to do is to give naturalism a meaning which is not synonymous with philosophy in general and, on the other hand, is not so specialized a view that there will be few to accept it as their own. We repeat that the naturalism so described is fundamentally naïve in that most of its philosophical implications are unexplored by its numerous adherents. The chief elements of this naturalistic creed are five:

(a) *Renunciation of the contrast between the natural and the supernatural.* There is only one order with which we are obliged to reckon and that is the natural order. The fundamental explanation of the world is to be found in it and not outside it. This rules out creation as a meaningful concept. The world had no Creator for it has always been, in one form or another, and it explains itself. The world is fundamentally monistic. There is only one set of laws and these are operative

---

[4] James Bissett Pratt, *Naturalism,* New Haven, 1939, p. 17.
[5] The practice of describing one's own position in words to which no thoughtful person could take exception is not a new practice. Professor Wallace, the great contemporary of Charles Darwin, said, in defense of naturalism, "Its faults spring from a creditable motive. It is the desire to be honest, to say only what you can prove, to require thorough continuity and consistency in the whole realm of accepted truths." In similar vein Thomas Huxley defined agnosticism as consisting essentially "in the application of a single principle, which is the fundamental axiom of modern science. Positively, this principle may be thus expressed: in matters of the intellect, follow your reason as far as it will take you, without regard to any other consideration. And negatively: in matters of the intellect, do not pretend that conclusions are certain which are not demonstrated or demonstrable." As Andrew Seth pointed out, all of us should seek service under the agnostic flag, on this basis, since agnosticism, so defined, is another name for intellectual honesty. Cf. A. Seth, *Man's Place in the Cosmos,* New York, 1897, p. 293. Professor Seth's entire study of the use of the word "naturalism," with especial reference to its use by Arthur Balfour, is illuminating

everywhere. Man is altogether part of nature, one of the animals, distinguishd by a large brain and a fully erect posture. God, if he exists at all, which is doubtful, is merely the power immanent in this world. There is no actual transcendence, and the notion of God as personal is a pure projection based on human vanity.

(b) *Belief that the essential order of the world is mechanical.* There is causation everywhere, but all this causation is of the type recognized in physics. Among the best illustrations of such causation are those afforded by astronomy. When a planet moves in a certain way this movement can be fully accounted for in terms of mass and motion of it and other heavenly objects in its vicinity. All this can be made extremely definite and precise. Mystery is removed. Other objects such as living bodies, including those with minds, are really moved in the same way. The only reason they do not appear to follow strictly mechanical laws is that we have not probed deeply enough. When we know more than we now know this will be seen to be the case. Mechanical laws are the laws of the entire universe.

(c) *All actions are determined by prior conditions.* Since causal sequence is found everywhere and since this causation is mechanical, freedom is a false notion. The planet is not free to choose its path. The billiard ball is not free to choose its devious progress on the table. In fact, with a little care we should be able to anticipate the entire course which the ball follows. Given a knowledge of the size of the table, the location of obstructions, as well as the power and direction of the initial blow we should be able to tell when the ball would stop and where. Certainly we are highly accurate in predicting eclipses. And the practical ability to predict is the best evidence of determinism. Why should we not be able to do this for the entire course of events, including human events? If we could know the precise structure of all the brains of all people, as well as the nature of natural resources, we should be able to predict accurately the outcome, not only of any current war, but of all future wars. Of course we cannot do this, but the difficulty lies not in the nature of events; it lies in our failure to grasp so much detail. The problem of prediction is, therefore, merely the problem of human ignorance and nothing more. Thus every act of every man is part of an unalterable system of events and the conviction we have concerning choice of ends is merely a pleasing delusion.

(d) *The behavior of men is not qualitatively different from that of lower animals and can be understood in the same way.* Whatever we do is the direct result of a combination of physical factors, those within the organism and those operating from outside. What a man thinks makes no real difference in the course of events since his very thought is nothing but a concomitant of a physical sequence. These physical sequences can be studied especially in the form of conditioned responses. Though the conditioned response is clearest in lower animals, the principle applies equally to men. Its adequacy is, of course, disguised by man's complexity of nervous structure, but it is there all the same.

One of the curious features of this part of the naturalistic creed is the way in which an extreme form of behaviorism is rejected in name, but accepted in principle. For the heart of behaviorism consists in this, that it elects to deal with man and man's "mind" as though there were no qualitative distinction between him and the lower animals. His speech and self-conscious thought are therefore minimized, inasmuch as they cannot be discovered or seriously studied in other organisms. The very word "behavior" is chosen as against "action" because it is less likely to suggest something different from what occurs in a physical system, physically determined.

(e) *All values are purely subjective.* Man is so constituted that he has preferences, both in art and in social behavior, but these preferences refer to nothing having any objective status. I think one thing is right and you think another is right, but there is no way to argue the matter, since we are merely talking about our private inclinations. By conditioning it would be possible to alter entirely a person's conception of what is beautiful and the same could be done in regard to what is considered good. Our sense of values is produced by purely natural causes in the first place, and later is determined by cultural upbringing. Therefore one conception of what is right is quite as good as another. A good illustration of this part of the naturalistic creed is provided by one of the letters from young collegians which the *Atlantic Monthly* received in response to an article by Arnold Whitridge called "Where Do You Stand?" and which were printed as providing case material for "our time." One young man wrote: "In college I studied some psychology, and the first lesson I learned was that there is no right or wrong to human behavior. Do you think the Germans don't think they are in the right?"[6]

That this young man represents a very large section of his generation can hardly be doubted. That there is no objectivity in ethics, that to ask whether an act is *really* right is like asking whether the eyes of a dragon in a dream are *really* green— these are part of the unexamined creed of millions of literate persons who hold these convictions not tentatively, but certainly.

Here, then, are five items in a creed: *monism, mechanism, determinism, behaviorism, subjectivism.* These are supposed to go together to form a consistent system and make up what many proudly claim as their "philosophy of life." It is to this composite that we are applying the term *naïve naturalism.* Perhaps there is a more appropriate term, but it is not readily suggested. *Positivism* has been suggested, but it is inadequate for two reasons. In the first place, the positive philosophy of Auguste Comte (1798-1857) while he was, of course, being metaphysical in his rejection of the possibility of metaphysics, placed his chief emphasis on limitation of method. The positive stage of knowledge, he held, is descriptive rather than ex-

[6] "Undergraduates and the War," by Paul P. Cram, *The Atlantic Monthly,* October, 1940, Volume 166, p. 412.

planatory. Whether this method can actually be followed is doubtful, but in any case it is not the method followed in the creed we have outlined. There is much in it which goes beyond simple description to genuine speculation. A second reason for not using the term positivism is that this word continues to have an outlandish sound to English speaking persons. The noun seems to have almost no connection with the common meaning of the adjective. It is so clearly a manufactured word and needs elaborate explanation whereas naturalism does not.

In conclusion it is useful to point out again that the name is not really important, but the ideas are. These ideas which are now so widespread as to be practically dominant and, in some minds, hardly subject to debate, represent what is essentially a faith by which men are trying to live.

Instead of accepting this creed supinely, thus substituting a new orthodoxy for an old one, it is desirable that we should consider it critically or even skeptically. Is it really more adequate than the naïve spiritualism which it has so largely displaced? To such an inquiry we turn in the next chapter.

CHAPTER VII

THE INSUFFICIENCY OF THE NATURALIST CREED

"Critical scepticism is the leading remedy indicated for this mood of dogmatic serenity."
—LORD BALFOUR

The test of the adequacy of any world view is to be found in its capacity to make an intelligible account of the various kinds of experience which the world has to show. The most effective fashion of refuting a metaphysical position is to show what the position entails, and, if it entails something in obvious conflict with indubitable aspects of experience, the original position is rightly considered a false one. A convenient illustration of this is the case against philosophical subjectivism. The really damning argument against subjective idealism is the fact that it entails solipsism. The person who chooses to believe that all of his experiences refer to ideas in his own mind, and not to anything beyond his mind, cannot be dislodged from his position, but it can be shown that he has no reason, on this basis, to assume the existence of other persons with whom to argue the point. Such is the importance, in the search for truth, of the principle of implication. It is in this way that the philosophical inadequacy of the naturalistic creed, outlined in Chapter VI, may be indicated.

What we must ask ourselves is this: *Do we know anything to be true which is inconsistent with what is logically implied in the hypothesis of the complete mechanical determination of all changes that occur in bodies?* If we do, then the hypothesis must be given up as an adequate account of the nature of reality. Reflection reveals three such difficulties which the naturalistic hypothesis faces, difficulties so great as to discredit the claims commonly made by its upholders. One of the difficulties is concerned with *morals*, another with *knowledge*, and a third with *history*. Naturalism cannot reasonably show how these are possible.

A. THE UNSATISFACTORY ACCOUNT OF GOODNESS

A great part of the life of man is concerned with ethical judgments. We read history, and, as we do so, we distribute praise and blame. We are greatly concerned that our own actions should be such as to be considered praiseworthy in the eyes of an unprejudiced observer. We are conscious of experiences, and these among the most important in our lives, in which we make difficult moral decisions, sometimes at great cost to our personal comfort or worldly success. When we fail to do so we condemn ourselves. We are frequently covered with shame, condemning our failures to live up to the highest we have known. By our remorse we clearly imply that a genuine decision was made, but also that it was made wrongly.

In all of this we are conscious of one area of experience which is sharply different from all others. When we condemn our own actions we maintain that there was something which we *ought* to have done and which we did not do. This, by common speech, we put in a class by itself. To say "I ought to do this" is not the same as to say "it is to my advantage" or "it is prudent" or "it is customary" or "it is commanded by the state" or "I desire it." In fact we habitually decide between what we think we ought to do and all these others. Frequently there is a clash between them. It may be customary for condemned men to run away if they can, but Socrates stays because he senses a difference between what is moral and what is customary. The martyr distinguishes between what the crowd commands and what seems to him to be right.

So pervasive and far-reaching is this experience of moral endeavor or moral failure, as the case may be, that it becomes the deepest source of satisfaction and interest in literature. The most moving scene which the world has to show is the scene of genuine moral struggle. Thousands of pieces of great literature, with their uncounted millions of readers, bear witness to this fact.

But if the naturalistic creed is a true one, all this bother about moral excellence is arrant nonsense. Moreover it is all meaningless. If all events, including the events in human lives, are inevitable results of a mechanical process, what is the point in making moral judgments at all? The action of the "good" man who saves the homeless at risk to himself is nothing but the inevitable result of the working of physical elements following mechanical laws. His action is no more moral than is the action of water going over a waterfall. The water cannot do otherwise than it does; the man cannot do otherwise than he does. Not only is our praise a bit silly, but even this silly praise is the inevitable result of the formation of our bodies and their physical environment so that we cannot do other than praise what deserves no praise. Furthermore, on this basis, there is no moral difference between the man who risks his life in relief in a bombed city and the man who accentuates the bombing by turning traitor to his country.

We can go further than this in showing what naturalism entails. All that we call moral is, of course, nothing but the inevitable result of natural selection. In this process some accidental variations were successful in that they had survival value. That, supposedly, is why man is so pugnacious. And altruistic tendencies supposedly have had survival value because they have aided *groups* in surviving. But there are many kinds of tendencies which aid in the survival of both individuals and groups, providing they are carried out to a sufficient degree. The ruthless destruction of one's enemies may be a highly successful exercise, providing it is done intelligently and not in an amateurish manner. If goodness retains any meaning at all, in the naturalistic scheme, it means adaptive behavior and evil means maladaptive behavior. Even this does not make much sense, since, if each organism is forced by its heredity and environment to do what it does, *whether* any behavior will be adaptive or maladaptive, is already determined.

The important point is that the extreme tyrant is following a type of life that is wonderfully well adapted to our present competitive order. The most ferocious tyrant is thus the best man. He is most successful in the struggle for existence and he does not weaken his "goodness" by any compromises with tenderness.

This has not been the doctrine of those usually accounted our most sensitive persons. Many of these, far from admitting for a moment that survival and moral excellence are synonymous, have stoutly maintained that there are many conditions under which it is not worth while to live, and this applies to the groups as well as to the individual. They have held, both in theory and in practice, that there are many things much more worth prizing than the life of the body or material success of any kind. Of course they may all have been deluded, but it is doubtful if the most convinced naturalist wants to live in a world devoid of such persons.

On the naturalistic theory of the world, this moral revolt of man is a meaningless affair. Is not an interest in honesty merely a purposeless product of the evolutionary process, fundamentally like the bull's combativeness and destined to be obliterated unless it aids in survival? Why should the naturalist be concerned about the intrusion into a mechanical system of moral ideas which sit in judgment on the system? They have no more validity than has the hare's timidity. The way in which the conscience distinguishes between virtue and success, the way in which it condemns what it cannot approve, all this is a ludicrous spectacle if we are dealing merely with one natural phenomenon, as purposeless, as "accidental" as any other. In short, on the naturalistic basis, the moral and spiritual life is wholly unintelligible.

Naïve naturalism, if logically and rigorously applied, not only fails to account for the very existence of the moral life, but actually hinders the promotion of that life. It is generally supposed that the proportion of good and evil in the world can be materially affected by human action. This, indeed, is the premise of most of our human efforts at betterment in social, political, or economic organization. But men and women really convinced of the truth of the naturalistic creed would not be influenced by such foolishness. They would realize that all their actions are completely determined by past events of a mechanical kind, they would know that conscious endeavor could not possibly make any difference, and they would know, furthermore, that even the goals supposedly aimed at were nothing but the products of the struggle for survival, having no authority of their own.

There are few, indeed, who are willing to go this far, but this is the distance they would go if they were to follow their naturalistic creed in its implications. That people are unwilling to do so, that they try to keep what they admire in a system inconsistent with naturalism, even while they suppose themselves to be adherents of the naturalistic creed, is a damning piece of evidence against the tenability of that creed. This is bad enough, but we do not stop here. Not only is naïve naturalism inconsistent with moral excellence; it is likewise inconsistent with the existence of knowledge.

B. The Unsatisfactory Account of Truth

Naturalism may not claim to be right or good, but it does claim to be true. This, indeed, is its boast. It is claimed that the principles of naturalism are accepted, as against more comforting doctrines, because we as men are interested in what is true and will espouse it at whatever cost. There is at least one virtue which the naturalist prizes, perhaps inconsistently, and that is intellectual honesty.

But the naturalistic creed makes truth or true knowledge

meaningless. Let us see how this is done. The standard unit of behavior is the conditioned response. Responses may be simple or complex, but they follow the same general laws. When a dog presents the behavior known as salivation, we can account for this behavior by a full consideration of the parts involved. The parts involved can be set in motion by appropriate stimuli, the appropriateness depending upon the physical constitution of the body called the dog and the disposition of the body's parts. These have already been modified by past stimuli and the re-actions of the body to them. Here we have a system, which, if known, can give us reactions according to order.

There is no difference in principle between the dog's saliva-tion and the dog's barking or anything else, except that some actions may be more complex than others. By the same token there is no difference in principle, so the naturalistic creed main-tains, between the barking of the dog and the crying, eating, or speaking of a man. As it is commonly stated, there is no difference of kind, but only a difference of degree. In the man the body is more complex, and the past stimuli have been more numerous, but again the response is the necessary result. If we really knew all the neural and muscular factors and the history of former conditioning, we should not need to appeal to such mythical factors as desire, thought, and purpose. It is the movements of bodies that count and that can be studied as other physical objects are studied, by what they do. The move-ments of the larynx, which we call speech, are as much parts of a complex mechanical order as is the salivation of the dog. Given all the physical constituents, these laryngeal movements could be predicted accurately by any competent observer. And thought, unless it is incipient laryngeal motion, is nothing at all, according to naturalistic theory. Naturalism cannot consist-ently consider, as belonging to reality, that which has no weight or motion.

But if thought *is* laryngeal motion, it is sheer nonsense to speak of thinking *truly*. A man thinks as his conditioning makes him think, and that is the end of the matter. I write as I do now and I think as I think now because of the stimuli and my physical constitution, which produce reactions called thinking or writing. And likewise the naturalistic philosopher thinks and writes as he does for the same reason. It then becomes ridiculous to say that one system is more true than another for each is what it must be. It makes no more sense, then, to call a thought true than to call a rain cloud true. The rain cloud is produced by a set of physical causes and cannot be other than it is. If all movements of bodies are equally necessary, they cannot be discriminated as true and false. Even my act of discrimination is another necessitated event and no more significant than any other. As Professor Joseph has pithily remarked, "It seems as nonsensical to call a movement true as a flavour purple or a sound avaricious."[1]

All that a naturalistic author can logically maintain is that his books are the necessary outcome of a complex physical system. But, by the same argument, the books of his critics have exactly the same kind of background. There is then no way to distinguish between genuine and spurious knowledge. But naturalism cannot claim to be true and, at the same time, entail a situation in which there is no difference between truth and falsehood. A lie is as much determined as anything else.

At this point the convinced naturalist may counter by saying he does not take his naturalism in the extreme form of behaviorism which holds that thought *is* motion. He admits that there may be thought in the ordinary sense of the word, but nevertheless this immaterial something is the *effect* of bodily movement. I can have something nonphysical called knowledge, but this is a necessary result of states of the brain. It is quite clear, however, that such a compromise does not make naturalism more acceptable to reason. Is not the thought called error also a necessary result of states of the brain? The state of the brain is the necessary result of other bodily states and we are

[1] H. W. B. Joseph, *Some Problems in Ethics*, Oxford, 1931, p. 14.

right back in our closed system. If I judge that my thought is knowledge and not error, judging, as we say, by comparison with the facts, this new thought or judgment is merely a result of another state of the brain and in no way superior to the former thoughts in this regard.

The climax of this criticism of naturalism, in its radical and revealing form, is that it provides no intelligible theory of error. It holds that error occurs and is, indeed, extremely common, inasmuch as so many people have not become convinced naturalists, but it does not tell us how error is possible, how error can be detected or even what error is. Certainly there is no valid appeal to logical principles, for thought, we must remember, is either the impotent epiphenomenon or nothing but contractions of the voice muscles. In either case the erroneous conclusion is as much necessitated as the correct one. A conclusion cannot help being in accordance with physical fact, for it is nothing but a link in a chain of physical fact.

Of course, if naturalism is accepted, what I have written in the above paragraph, on what seems to me a really conclusive argument against the common form of naturalism, is nothing but another necessary product. I could not do otherwise than carry out the mechanical process of my bodily movements. And if you, the reader, consider my arguments sound or unsound, as the case may be, your conclusions, likewise, have nothing to do with the truth, but are determined as is the movement of the weather vane, and not otherwise. But herein lies the obvious inadequacy of the system which involves such paradoxical conclusions. *That which undermines everything undermines nothing, for it has already undermined itself.*

Why should men construct a system so patently self-defeating? The chief reason seems to be a desire for neatness and order. We can observe a machine as a closed system with great success. So much goes in and so much comes out. We can describe what it *does* and we do not need to complicate our examinations by such mysterious notions as purpose and consciousness. The desire is the desire to avoid the mysterious, but it is a fair question whether this end is achieved.

Explanation in terms of purposive activity is eschewed because of its supposed mystery, but mechanical determination is not less mysterious. What does it mean for energy to be transferred from one physical body to another? Actually the only kind of initiation of action with which we are really acquainted is that which goes on in our own bodies when we transform intention into actuality. There seems no evident reason for seeking to explain the familiar by reference to the fundamentally unfamiliar and unknown.

The inadequacy of naturalism is not recognized by the lovers of philosophical neatness, because they are so often blind to the metaphysical implications of the system they espouse. Far from noting the metaphysical implications of their system they claim it has none. Naturalism, they suppose, is merely the scientific view of the world, with no metaphysical nonsense, and with all the success of modern science giving it intellectual prestige.

One of the many philosophical debts which the modern scholar owes to Professor A. O. Lovejoy arises from this keen critic's exposure of metaphysical assumptions in systems supposedly innocent of metaphysics and proud of it. A striking example of such exposure is seen in Professor Lovejoy's paper, "The Paradox of the Thinking Behaviorist."[2]

Professor Lovejoy's method of criticism is not to point to some fact or experience which the behaviorist denies, but to one which the behaviorist admits to be a fact.

. . . Now, such a fact can very easily be pointed out. It is the fact that the behavioristic psychologist himself exists. For a behavioristic psychologist (a) is a human organism, (b) whose perceiving and thinking, if his own theory is correct, should be exhaustively de-

[2] In *The Philosophical Review*, Volume XXXI, pp. 135-147. This article, published in 1922, was concerned especially with the form of behaviorism then beginning to attain popularity, but the major criticisms still apply to contemporary forms of the doctrine.

scribable in terms of movements of his laryngeal and related muscles, but who (c) in fact thinks, or professes to think, of external objects and stimuli, that is, of entities outside his body, (d) which thinking is obviously neither describable as, nor "accounted for" by, movements of his laryngeal or other muscles inside his body.[3]

In ordinary speech we say, whether we are behaviorists or not, that our thought *refers to* certain objects, and we are normally agreed that this reference is sometimes erroneous. We ordinarily suppose that we refer, in thought, to what turns out to be nonexistent, and then we say we are in error. But this kind of explanation is not possible for the consistent behaviorist.

. . . It cannot even be properly said by a behaviorist that the secondary talking which he calls an "observation" of the primary talking constitutes speech "about" the primary talking. For the category of "about," the conception of "reference to," has no legitimate place in a behavioristic system. It is not a relation definable in physical terms; and all relations not definable in physical terms are (professedly) excluded from the behaviorist's universe. The talking in which he makes both thinking and the observation of it consist would not, in the ordinary sense, have any meaning. To talk does not signify for the behaviorist, so long as he adheres to his principles, to use words to express an awareness of something other than the words; it signifies, once more, nothing but the play of certain complexes of muscles, chiefly laryngeal. If then—to repeat— these muscular (and glandular) changes were all that ever happened in the life-history of a behavioristic psychologist, he would never know that anything of the sort was happening.[4]

Radical naturalism might achieve a fair degree of plausibility were it not the uncomfortable fact that there are observers, that the behaviorist is himself an observer, and that he thinks his own system valid, when, if he is consistent, he must admit that his system makes meaningless the concept of validity.

[3] *Ibid.*, pp. 140, 141.
[4] *Ibid.*, p. 144.

C. THE UNSATISFACTORY ACCOUNT OF HISTORY

We have now seen that both moral judgment and the demand for truth are inconsistent with what is implied in the fundamental hypothesis of naturalism, that of complete mechanical determinism. If naturalism is accepted, nothing is good and nothing is true; therefore naturalism can be neither good nor true. A third difficulty concerns *history*.

History plays a very important part in human experience and is one of the chief marks of spiritual life as against merely physical existence. Only man has a history in the full sense of the word, though some of the higher animals have something approaching it. A stone does not have a history. Past events have occurred which have altered the shape, constitution or location of the stone, but past events, *as past,* do not affect the stone. The only way in which the past affects the stone is by means of *present modifications.* In the experience of man we find something utterly different. Man is affected by past events, not as they have inaugurated a chain of effects leading to the present, but as leaping out of the past into the present.

Modern American philosophers have had reason to be grateful to Professor Lovejoy for his insistence on the reality of time. "To all theories about the nature of reality or of knowledge," Professor Lovejoy has written autobiographically, "I early began to apply one touch-stone before any other—that of congruence with the most indubitable fact of our experience, namely, that experience itself is temporal."[5] Anyone who has ever been Professor Lovejoy's student, whatever his other beliefs, cannot minimize the importance of temporal concepts.

Man's relation to time is, however, as Professor Lovejoy points out, only one of the ways in which *thought* is able to have relations which move into a realm wholly different from those of a merely material order on which the orthodox natu-

[5] Arthur O. Lovejoy, "A Temporalistic Realism," *Contemporary American Philosophy,* Volume II, p. 87.

ralist has set his heart. How truly the mere relation of contiguity is transcended is brought to our attention by the following observation: "A given moment of thought may consist in a representation of a whole world of objects in relations of many kinds—temporal, spatial, logical—in which it is itself, *as represented,* a mere fragment."[6]

Man's peculiar relationship to the temporal process has been strikingly expressed by Korzybski in the term "time-binding." Man is able to be free, in large measure, from the limits of the specious present, because his past is a *living past.* Animals have a past, but not a past which, in most cases, can be an immediate causal factor in behavior. The chief outward evidence of this important difference is the fact that men have *traditions* whereas other creatures must rely either on instinct or on a short span of individual experience. Man, accordingly, is able to profit by the entire past as known. In other words, human events are determined by conscious *knowledge.* Only a creature with our peculiar relationship to time could develop a written language.

The peculiar relationship to the temporal process which man enjoys holds an important place in the argument of A. E. Taylor's famous Gifford Lectures. The crucial part is as follows:

In the merely inanimate world, according at least to the conceptions of "orthodox" mechanics, the past seems to shape the future only in so far as it has not passed, but has persisted during the interval. In the merely animate world, the past which shapes a future seems to do so by the persistence of its contribution in the way of a series of effects through an interval. In the world of intelligent human action, the remembered past seems to be able to mould the future directly and immediately, striking, so to say, out of its own remote pastness, even though there has been no continuous persistence of itself or its effects through the interval.[7]

Now the point is that philosophical naturalism is fully con-

---

[6] *Ibid.,* p. 98.
[7] A. E. Taylor, *The Faith of a Moralist,* London, 1931, Volume I, p. 87.

sistent with the first of these three relations to the temporal sequence; it is less consistent with the second; it is wholly inconsistent with the third. From the point of view of orthodox naturalism, action at a distance, such as men experience when they share in history, is a scandal. It ought not to be, yet it is. It may be scandalous and disturbing that there are men in the world, but we neither avoid nor explain this fact by refusing to look squarely at it.

Naturalism receives most of its plausibility from those manifestations of reality in which time is not an important factor. Thus mechanics approach the naturalistic ideal of knowledge. But once we have determined not to evade the fact of man, we are forced to take time seriously. And time, as experienced by men, involves *physical discontinuity*. The mind can arrive at present decisions by consciously fastening on something which is no longer, inasmuch as it occurred long ago. Similarly the mind can arrive at present decisions by concentration on something which *is not*, in that it has never yet been, because it belongs to the unrealized future. That which is not helps to produce that which is.

In a purely physical, that is to say, a purely naturalistic world this would be impossible. Indeed, it is difficult to see how, in a purely naturalistic world, there would be any novelty at all. But history is the story of the persistent introduction of novelty. Men invent new tools and thereby utilize unsuspected resources. To invent is to alter the course of events by the power of creative thought. "Invention," writes Professor Blanshard, "is purpose assuming authority over the course of ideas."[8]

Professor Blanshard's able and careful study of invention in his recent work on *The Nature of Thought* is sufficient to give pause to any reader who has been inclined to suppose that the introduction of novelty in human history can be accounted for on naturalistic grounds. Invention is a scandal from the natural-

[8] Brand Blanshard, *The Nature of Thought,* New York, 1940, Volume II, p. 129.

istic point of view because it involves the determination of events by causes which are not describable in terms of physical science. It signifies the intrusion into the material order of another order, the order of thought. "Our contention," Professor Blanshard concludes, "is nothing less than this; that in the mind of the successful thinker the spirit of logic itself is at work leavening the unformed mass."[9]

The experience which makes history possible is the kind of experience we know best, the kind in which we share every day. How amazing that men should turn from this to try to find an adequate conception of reality in the kind of experience appropriate to mechanical units, according to which contiguity is an essential condition of effective influence. It seems perverse to hold that we can explain the more familiar by the less familiar. But it is worse than perverse, it is downright unintelligent to deny the actuality of the familiar, solely because it cannot be made to conform to the pattern of the unfamiliar, which has been arbitrarily chosen as the principle of understanding.

D. TRANSITION

We see now the direction in which we are guided by our considerations thus far. We cannot return to the naïve spiritualism which satisfied our ancestors for so many generations. The existence of natural science renders this general conception of the world untenable. The scientific theory of the world has too many successes to its credit to be lightly dismissed. At the same time we cannot rest satisfied with the second stage in our dialectic; we cannot, with intellectual integrity, adopt a system as demonstrably inadequate and self-defeating as philosophical naturalism is. This means that we must press forward to some genuine synthesis. What is this synthesis to be? Will it be closer to spiritualism or closer to naturalism, and, if it combines both, how will we combine them?

[9] *Ibid.*, p. 129.

But what if there were a synthesis already in being, a synthesis made up, not by the application of philosophical glue, but already existent in mature experience? We shall see, in the following chapter, that there is such a system, *theistic realism,* and that it is what William James called a "live option." Many of the faiths which men have held, such as polytheism and pantheism, are not really live options at all, but ethical theism is a live option in that it deserves to be considered among the interpretations of experience which are actually open to our acceptance. The patent inadequacy of naturalism, which is the chief competitor of theism, makes us approach the existent synthesis with eagerness and humility.

Fundamentally there are only two alternatives in belief concerning the nature of the world. These have been admirably stated by Bishop Gore. One of these, the atheistic alternative, means "that we see in the world of which we form a part no signs of anything corresponding to the mind or spirit or purpose which indisputably exists in man—no signs of a universal spirit or reason with which we can hold communion, nothing but blind and unconscious force." The other alternative, the one to which we now turn, is "the recognition about us, within us and above us, of a universal and eternal reason or purpose, with which we can and ought to correspond."[10] No third possibility is really a live option.

[10] Charles Gore, *The Reconstruction of Belief,* pp. 45, 46.

CHAPTER VIII

THEISTIC REALISM

"The God of Christians is not a God who is simply the author of mathematical truths, or of the order of the elements; that is the view of heathens and Epicureans. He is not merely a God who exercises His providence over the life and fortunes of men, to bestow on those who worship Him a long and happy life. That was the portion of the Jews. But the God of Abraham, the God of Isaac, the God of Jacob, the God of Christians, is a God of love and comfort, a God who fills the soul and heart of those whom He possesses, a God who makes them conscious of their inward wretchedness, and His infinite mercy, who unites Himself with their inmost soul, who fills it with humility and joy, with confidence and love, who renders them incapable of any other end than himself."

—BLAISE PASCAL

As we seek an hypothesis which will take us at once beyond naïve spiritualism and naïve naturalism, we are in the fortunate position of having an hypothesis already at hand, already emergent in the course of human history, and already enjoying the intellectual prestige which comes from having won the assent of sensitive minds. We do not need to *construct* a world view which goes beyond the two forms of naïveté, for such a world view is actually held.

A. STABILITY IN RELIGION

One of the most striking differences between science and religion is found in the fact that religious experience seems to be relatively independent of time and change, whereas natural science is not thus independent. Contemporary science has little in common with the science of two thousand years ago, whereas the religious experience of cultivated men two thousand years ago may be seen as practically identical with the religious experience of cultivated men today. Old science, even that of two or three generations ago, almost always seems to us bad science, but old religion may be good religion. Science seems to be engaged in the denunciation of its ancestors, while religion seems to be engaged in the support and confirmation of its ancestors.

In this regard religion is like morality and art, for both of these have an indifference to time which science does not enjoy, inasmuch as aesthetic and moral judgments have achieved an imperviousness to change which most scientific theories have not yet attained. Many of the finest examples of moral excellence or of artistic production appeared long ago, whereas the best scientific production is the newest. This last fact is illustrated by reference to technology, which is the fruit of science, and which shows the tendency in a marked degree. The latest technological development quickly outmodes that which immediately preceded it, but this has not occurred in music, painting or sainthood, even though there have been temporary fashions in all three. Science, by its very nature, is a cumulative procedure, new theories rising on the debris of discarded theories. Each theory is useful as a link in a swiftly moving chain. In religion, on the other hand, the characteristic experience is one in which the newest need not be the best, and in which men speak the same language across great chasms of time and space. Thus an ancient prophet may speak directly to our spiritual need at this moment, though the science of his period seems to us ridiculous.

We can put this in another way by saying that religion has classics as science does not. Augustine's *Confessions* and the *Private Prayers* of Lancelot Andrewes are quite as valuable in the twentieth century as when they were written, and are still widely used. They are classics in the sense that they have catholic appeal and are not limited to one time, location or class. Science has interesting older books, landmarks on the way, but they are now outmoded and have, for the most part, only anti-quarian interest. The characteristic ancient scientific treatise seems quaint, whereas the characteristic ancient religious treatise does not seem quaint. Pascal, we may suppose, was equally in-telligent in his scientific and his religious writings, but whereas the former are *interesting* the latter are quite as valuable now as when they were written almost three centuries ago, and are apparently much more widely read.

Such considerations lead us to suppose that science is sub-ject to progress, with all the attendant advantages and disad-vantages, but religion is not subject to progress. Yet this con-clusion is not wholly true. There has been genuine progress in religion since the dawn of history, *but it is not the same kind of progress* which science presents. Progress comes to pass ear-lier in religion than in science and, once a high level is reached, this progress often appears to end, so far as essentials are con-cerned. Most scientific progress has been recent, whereas the most striking religious progress came long ago, judging by the time scale of modern history. The religious spirit comes to maturity earlier than the scientific. The scientific spirit cannot come to maturity except in a highly complex society with a well-defined division of labor, but the religious spirit can come to maturity in a life close to the simplicity of the desert. In fact, insight into eternal verities may be hindered by a busy modern society and greatly facilitated by relative simplicity of organ-ization.

B. PROGRESS IN RELIGION

The progress in religion which is most striking and most in-structive is that which has come in the Judeo-Christian stream of development. Here we have a record which, fortunately, has been kept with unusual faithfulness, and which tells the story of emerging theism from early nature worship to the mature theism of the Christian faith. It is important to see the entire stream as one spiritual movement. The Hebrew development, standing alone, is an unfinished building, and the Christian faith, standing alone, is a structure without a foundation. Each illuminates the other. One of the most fortunate decisions made by the early Christians was the decision to retain the Hebrew Canon as part of their Holy Scriptures, to accompany the specifically Christian writings. This brought both enrichment and perspective. So eminently satisfactory has this arrangement been that it has not been seriously challenged until today, and now only in neopagan circles. One result of this arrangement is that great numbers of Christians are far better acquainted with the deeds of Hebrew heroes than with the deeds of any of their own remote ancestors.

The main story which reaches its climax in Christian theism may profitably be viewed as a dramatic movement in three parts. The first part is concerned with the rise and development of the religion of Israel, the second part is concerned with the rise and development of Judaism, and the third is concerned with the rise and development of Christianity.

(1) The first movement covers a period of a little more than five hundred years, roughly from 1300 B.C. to about 750 B.C., i.e., from the time of the exodus from Egypt to the appearance of Amos, the first of the classic prophets. A sensitive people, with a background of suffering in servitude, adopted, through the persuasion of a powerful leader, the worship of Yahweh. Up to that time their religion had been fully polytheistic, with a recognition of gods in the storm, in trees, and in fountains of water. There were thousands of local and tribal divinities, each with an appropriate worship.

The powerful leader, whom we call Moses, brought together several wandering tribes and led them to the East Jordan area from which they were able to enter the land west of the Jordan. Success in this enterprise demanded a large share of unity, and this was achieved by the worship of Yahweh. The people came to believe in Yahweh as the God *common* to all the tribes, superseding their tribal divinities. They came to have faith in the power of Yahweh as a Redeemer and Leader, helping them to consolidate their lives and overcome their enemies.

This development, which may have taken place on the peninsula of Sinai, was far from a full monotheism, but it was of great importance for the entire human race since it was a step in this direction. Monotheism, in any significant sense, is the result of a long painful struggle, and it came to the world chiefly through several hundred years of bitter experience on the part of the people of Israel.

Under the leadership of Moses, Israel took a great step beyond the ordinary nature worship of their neighbors, and already had a germ of what is *ethical* in their religion. They had not really chosen Yahweh, but He had chosen *them*, and, if they would follow Him faithfully, giving up the worship of rival gods, He would lead them into a fair inheritance. Thus their battles were fought in a spirit of intense religious faith. Yahweh, at this time, was not supposed to be the *only* divinity and he was not fully ethical in character, but the concept was capable of great development. It was so much superior to the competing nature cults that it held its own and united the people even in the fierce days of settlement in Palestine. They did not always win their battles, but the worshipers of Yahweh considered that failure was the result of their own inattention to their religious duties, rather than to any weakness of their God. If they did not keep God's laws, how could they expect success? The earliest of these laws were largely ritualistic.

We are helped in understanding this progressive record if we realize that much of the present biblical narrative of events in the early period is colored by later convictions. It is only by careful study that we come to realize that the earliest codes of Israel were almost wholly ritualistic. The editors, however, could not think of law apart from the ethical concepts of their own advanced period. Deuteronomy is the key book of the Old Testament, as we know it, since that book exhibits in extreme form what the entire history of Israel exhibits in some degree.

Primitive men of the desert are, on occasion, made to talk like
Jeremiah. Temple's warning on this matter is worth heeding,

The Old Testament contains the record of how a certain nation
came to its faith in One Holy God. For understanding this record
we must first of all remember that it is written, in its present form
at least, by men who accept that faith, but that the story is to a
great extent concerned with people who did not accept it.[1]

As the period of struggle and settlement went forward, it
became increasingly clear that Yahweh was concerned alike with
the powers of nature and the forces of history. He made the
thunder and He likewise helped His servants to defeat their
enemies. Thus we are moving forward in the direction of monotheism. Moreover we find several important people marrying
outside the clan and the new people are adopted into the faith.
The people are unified, not by a common origin, but by a common worship. There was, as yet, no effort to evangelize others,
since the gods of other people might be considered as having
their appropriate places. Furthermore there was, as yet, no real
centralization of worship. All kinds of altars might be suitable
places for the worship of Yahweh.

As Israel became a settled people, with a royal house, there
was an increased tendency to bring in fashionable rival cults
from the outside, producing an eclectic religion. The importance of Elijah lies in the fact that he shows how, in the ninth
century B.C., strong men of faith could resist both the tyranny
of the rulers and the tendency to tolerate alien faiths, especially
those coming through the dynasty of Tyre. Elijah stands out
against the priests of Baal and demands the exclusive worship
of Yahweh by His own people. Inasmuch as Baal worship was
concerned with the fruitfulness of the soil, there were different
Baals in different localities. The insight which came to the
spiritual leaders of Israel was that, though there might be many
Baals, there could only be one Yahweh. It was one and the

[1] William Temple, *Mens Creatrix*, p. 30.

same Yahweh who manifested Himself wherever He was rightly worshiped, whether in the desert or in the settled land. They came to believe that Yahweh was the Lord of the pleasant land as He was the voice in the fierce storm and the leader in battle. Thus we find the people one step farther on the road to a great unity. Yahweh is really the God of Nature, and the old shrines, erected to the nature gods, can be used to glorify Him. This step involved the possibility of corruption and danger, but it was clearly an enlargement of the central idea. Worship was still largely ceremonial, but exclusiveness produced a certain stern purity and brought order out of religious chaos. There is little doubt that the record from Moses to Elijah is a record of progress and not merely of change.

(2) The second movement also covers a period of more than half a millennium, a period which included the rise and development of Hebrew prophecy. It gave to the world the religion which we call Judaism, a religion markedly different, in many ways, from the religion of Israel. From the time of Amos, there were prophets who were able to transmit to posterity the notes of their own discourses.

The eighth century prophets, Amos, Hosea, Isaiah and Micah, considered themselves conservatives, inasmuch as they were calling their neighbors back to the simplicity and brotherliness of earlier days, but they actually marked a forward step of tremendous importance. In the teaching of Amos we learn that Yahweh makes demands that are entirely ethical in character and that he brings judgments upon neighboring tribes as well as on his chosen people. Those who are *not chosen* are under His moral government and those who *are chosen* will be punished for infractions, just as the others. In other words, God does not stoop to favoritism in his moral judgment. This is a stern, but wonderfully enlarging conception of God's nature.

Hosea accepted the doctrine of Amos that God's relationship to His people is a wholly moral one, but Hosea taught that this has its tender as well as its stern aspects. Yahweh will reach out to redeem the fallen and to forgive. And, apparently, the divine forgiveness is not limited by race.

Isaiah and Micah, taking seriously the notion that Yahweh's demands are ethical ones, showed the irrelevance of purely ceremonial worship. They cried out against the folly of ritualism, much of which had ceased to have any deep religious significance, and they said that the divine demand is for pure hearts and sympathy for the oppressed. God asks for honesty in private and public life and for that administration of affairs which relieves the oppressed. Social morality is thus presented, for the first time in the history of the human race, as the highest expression of religious devotion.

It is important to note that this kind of teaching entails complete monotheism. If the people who worship Yahweh are punished for infractions of the moral law, and if other people are judged by the same standard, there must be a common source of all these judgments. The religion is monotheistic *because* it is ethical. If judgment comes because of the capricious will of an injured deity, there may be many gods, but if judgment comes because of infraction of moral laws, then there must be one God for the whole world. Indeed, the power and being of God would in no wise be diminished by the destruction of the very nation which He has chosen.

The remainder of the prophetic movement was devoted to an elaboration of what was implied in the teaching of the eighth century spiritual giants. Perhaps the decisive factor which made the prophetic movement in Israel really unique in human annals was the cumulative effect of many prophets, so that the entire movement had both unity and development. Zoroaster, founder of the Persian religion, almost succeeded in lifting a people from the worship of tribal deities to ethical monotheism, but he stood too much alone, whereas the prophets of Israel supported one another in successive waves. In literary monuments, among which the Book of Deuteronomy stands high, the second and third wave of prophets sought to show how God's will might be done. The growing sense of the oneness of God led to a demand for one central sanctuary. This did not go the whole way to the notion that God, being spiritual, may be worshiped anywhere. To expect this is to expect too much. The step actually taken was a step forward; the abolition of local sanctuaries was a movement in the direction of universalism. Furthermore, there were suggestions, in the words of Jeremiah, already pointing to a fully spiritual conception of the worship of the one true God.[2]

The exile into Babylonia was one of the hardest experiences, yet it was the means of still further progress. Apart from the plight of the refugees it is unlikely that we should have the literary masterpiece composed of sixteen chapters imbedded in the book of Isaiah. One of the least contested points of biblical criticism is the conclusion that Chapters XL to LV of Isaiah are not by the hand of the man who lived at the end of the eighth century B.C. and had a vision in the year that King Uzziah died. The author of the marvelous sixteen chapters lived at least two centuries later than Isaiah, at the time of Cyrus the Great. This anonymous prophet of exile had come to see all history as part of Yahweh's hand; a glorious restoration was not only a future hope, but, in part, a present reality. (Isa., 43:19).

Deprived of the opportunity of worship at Jerusalem, small colonies turned more and more to the solace found in the "book," the record of the history of themselves as a people. These devout and lonely souls began to see that they possessed something of more than national or local significance, something that could be carried on even in defeat and dispersion. It was undoubtedly hard to sing the Lord's song in a strange land,[3] but the truth was that it could be done. The eventual development of the synagogue as a place for the reading and hearing of the "book" was only an extension of what first appeared to the contemporaries of Ezekiel. By loneliness and

[2] Jeremiah, 31:31.
[3] Psalm 137.

suffering, men learned that worship was possible far away from Jerusalem, and when the Temple was finally destroyed by the Romans in 70 A.D. it was never restored, since the synagogue had already taken its place. The prophetic emphasis on moral law had triumphed over the older emphasis on ritual.

In the teaching of Ezekiel the growth of ethical monotheism marked a new step. Ezekiel's insight was that of individualism. Universalism and individualism stand in a relationship of mutual implication. If God treats each human soul fairly and objectively, i.e., if God judges each man by his own deeds and not those of his father, it follows that God sees each man as a *man*, and not as a Jew or a Greek, a white man or a black man. But only if God is the God of all races and nations is this possible. By the end of the great prophetic period we are far, indeed, from the old Mosaic conception of Yahweh as one jealous god among many, and we begin to see that Yahweh is the God of all men everywhere, beside whom there is none at all.

Some of the corollaries of these prophetic ideas were unpalatable to the populace and probably never received full acceptance. The Book of Jonah is a brilliant example of the literary ingenuity which was employed to make the new and revolutionary message understood. Jonah is a caricature of the man who does not understand, a man who so hates the people of Nineveh that he does not want them to hear the message from Yahweh, warning them to repent. He is fearful that they will repent, and he is likewise fearful that, if they do repent, Yahweh will forgive them. Finally, by a combination of semihumorous events, of which the fish ride is only one, poor Jonah arrives in Nineveh and everything turns out just as he feared it might. Jonah is sentimental about a gourd tree which withers, but is untouched by the fate of thousands of persons who are as much objects of Yahweh's care as he is. It is obvious that this clever pamphlet was written by a person who has already come to accept fully the notion of universalistic, ethical monotheism, but the cleverness of his effort is evidence that the reading public had not yet accepted this conclusion and needed a vivid literary cartoon to make them understand.[4]

(3) The third movement in this series is the Christian one. With the rich background of more than a millennium, Jesus could be understood when He spoke of God and the Kingdom of God. Accepting completely the prophetic insight about God's nature, Jesus went on to declare, by the use of matchless parables, the faith that God was more like a solicitous parent than anything else we know. God, we are told, reaches out to welcome the returning penitent, He searches for the one that is lost. God, according to this Christian teaching, holds each individual precious and is ever trying to win the whole world, including all men, unto Himself. Furthermore He sends His Messiah to show people the way, and to herald the coming of the Kingdom, which, though it may appear soon as an historical fact, is already present in less obvious ways.

The worship of God, according to Jesus, is not a matter of time or place, inasmuch as all days can be holy and all places sacred. Since God is to be worshiped in spirit and in truth, the argument whether men should worship at Jerusalem or some other place is pointless. Here we have the climax of a long and interesting development. In the days of Elijah it was an advance to *include* the many local shrines in the worship of Yahweh. In the Deuteronomic reform it was an advance to limit worship to Jerusalem *excluding* local shrines. In the days of Christ it was an advance to reject the notion of place altogether, so far as worship is concerned. The development is best shown by placing together the three propositions:

Many places are sacred.
One Place is sacred.
Sacredness is not a matter of place.

[4] The use of the word "cartoon" in connection with Jonah was, I believe, first made by Henry J. Cadbury in his *National Ideals in the Old Testament.*

If anyone chooses to hold that this movement does not represent progress, it is difficult to know how to convince him. Indeed we have no absolute rule to determine which kinds of change represent progress, and if anyone sincerely supposes that polytheism is better than monotheism, there is little we can do about it. The real question, however, is whether any thoughtful person who honestly considers the history of the development of the Judeo-Christian stream can doubt the reality of the progress involved. To most minds, it would seem the progress is obvious. There is a movement in the direction of unity, of order, of ethical consciousness. There is a growth in the conception of God as personal that is most remarkable. In the early stages Yahweh is partly impersonal, seen better in the voice of the storms than anywhere else, but finally we come to a refined sense of God as personal, not limited as men are limited, but marked by complete love, respect for persons, and complete consciousness of purpose. In the teaching of Jesus about God, all the crudities are gone.

Since the time of Jesus there have been some advances in religion, especially in new conceptions of what is ethically involved in the Christian faith, but these advances are usually admitted to be nothing more than the explication of what was already implicit in the teaching of Jesus. We are still trying to catch up with Him. There may, at some later day, be some new development which will take us beyond anything we now know, but so far it is clear that there is a certain finality in Christ. He brought one stream, and that an important one, to its logical conclusion.

C. THE PLACE OF WORLD RELIGIONS

There have been many religions competing for human attention and devotion, side by side with this Judeo-Christian stream, and these we must not neglect. Since the study of comparative religions is relatively modern, we know far more about them than did our ancestors. One of the most fruitful results of this modern study is the observation that each of the great faiths has become stabilized at some single point, already represented on our line of progress outlined above. Not only do the "dead" religions, such as those of Greece and Rome, mark steps on the ladder of religious progress, but the world's living religions do the same. In a striking manner, comparative religion comes to be the same as the history of religion, except that the history is presented simultaneously rather than successively. Thus Shintoism is really a primitive and undeveloped faith, existing in our day as something of a spiritual anachronism. It matches the religion of Israel before the prophetic reformation in that it is still purely national and has not attained universalism.

Taoism, as practiced, matches the period in the history of Israel when seers and soothsayers were the chief exponents of the religious life. Mohammedanism, though it arose in Arabia six hundred years after the birth of Christianity, is really pre-Christian in character. Its stern monotheism marks it as belonging to the beginning of the prophetic period. Islam is clearly more advanced than was the religion of Israel, but this is about all that we can say in this regard. In many ways the spirit of Mohammedanism may be equated with that at the time of Elijah. Confucianism, seen as a religion and not as an ethic, matches the nature worship which appeared after Israel entered Palestine.

It is more difficult, in a brief survey, to state precisely the way in which Hinduism and Buddhism enter into the scheme of progressive historical sequence, partly because these systems are so complex and involve so many variations within themselves. In passing it may be said, however, that popular Hinduism is largely polytheistic, with great emphasis on ritual sacrifice, and thus falls into the preprophetic category. The major emphasis of Buddhism on the escape from life which is mere flux "strikingly confirms," says Von Hügel, "the whole Jewish and Christian persistent search for permanence in change."[5] The modern development of Buddhism away from the atheism of its origin, points more and more in the direction of an emphasis on personality which finds its climax in Christianity.

Since there is no way of ascertaining truth by getting outside experience, we must see whether there is order in experience, and especially whether religious history is a meaningful sequence. Looking at it as objectively as we can, we are forced to the conclusion that it is neither a cyclical process nor meaningless change, but change in a direction. The emergence of Christianity illuminates all the other faiths, because it shows them as steps on the way, regardless of their dates of appearance. Christianity can satisfy the Confucian or the Jew, whereas Confucianism and Judaism cannot satisfy the Christian. H. G. Wood has put this point well in the following sentences:

> As between Judaism, Christianity and Islam, the crucial issue will turn on whether individual events and the historic process as a whole are more intelligible, more full of meaning from the Christian than from either the Jewish or the Moslem standpoint. To put it in another way, it depends on whether in the course of history Christianity can do fuller justice to Judaism and Islam than Judaism or Islam can do to Christianity.[6]

D. THE RELIGION OF MATURITY

We are now in a position to say something about the main lines of progress in human religion as it has appeared in the last few thousand years. From many sources and in a multitude of dark ways there has come an aspiration or thirst that cannot find its goal except in the knowledge of God who is at once the union of genuine power and perfect love. These two attributes have, indeed, not been fully appreciated in equal degree at all the stages on the way, but neither has been utterly

---

[5] Baron Friedrich von Hügel, *Essays and Addresses on the Philosophy of Religion,* London, 1924, p. 89.
[6] H. G. Wood, *Christianity and the Nature of History,* p. 8.

neglected or can be. It is faith in God so defined which has been slowly coming to birth in so many periods of human history.

The faith which finally emerges in the development of human religion is perfectly understandable to thoughtful people, even when they do not share it. It is a faith which can be described with a minimum of ambiguity or vagueness. This is the faith in the Living God who is objectively real, who is the Object of worship, and who can, in part, be known as finite persons are known. It is important to insist on this clarity and objectivity, because there is a widespread opinion in the modern world that men, when they say they believe in God, are uttering propositions which are either meaningless or platitudinous. Few in our time have done better service in helping to remedy this unfortunate situation than has the late Professor Charles A. Bennett of Yale. According to Professor Bennett the meaning of the proposition "God exists" is: "In addition to all finite selves there is a being called God, numerically distinct from them, an independent centre of consciousness, with his own unique life and purposes, with a differential activity of his own."[7]

There is much more to be said on the subject, as Bennett well knew, but this minimum definition is strictly in accordance with the teaching of Jesus as recorded in the New Testament and is also in harmony with the major Christian teaching of subsequent centuries. God, as Christianity has taught, and as the common man supposes, is not some abstract quality. He is not to be equated with Power or Love or Beauty or Goodness or Truth or Human Aspiration or even the Absolute. In the words of Pascal's most revealing document, we are concerned about the existence of the God of Abraham, Isaac, and Jacob, not the God of the philosophers. An important insight of many philosophers is the recognition that it is the faith of the nonphilos-

[7] C. A. Bennett, *The Dilemma of Religious Knowledge,* Yale University Press, 1931. p. 50.

ophers which is supremely worthy of philosophical consideration.

In making this advanced idea of God clear we must be at great pains to distinguish it sharply from any of the ideas of God which arose in Greek philosophy. Reading the Greek philosophers now, in the light of Christian history, and conscious of the Christian adaptation of Greek conceptions, we are inclined to attribute higher notions of divinity to the most influential of the Greek thinkers than their actual teaching warrants. For example, it is almost impossible for us to read Plato's words about the Good, without equating this with God or supposing that the supreme goodness exists in the mind of God, but Plato did not take this step. It is to the credit of Professor Etienne Gilson that he has insisted on this point until he has made his criticism current philosophical knowledge.[8] It is difficult to point to a single, unifying, and fully critical idea of God in the Platonic corpus, and certainly we cannot point to anything comparable to the advanced notion of God as the all-loving and all-powerful Creator and Sustainer of the universe.

Greek thought, reacting against the primitive mythical conceptions of the gods of Olympus with their human frailties, adopted a conception which went so far in the opposite direction that divine beings ceased to be contemplated as living realities at all. The satire of Xenophanes was no doubt effective in this radical shift in belief. This is a thoroughly understandable reaction, but essentially an unfortunate one. At best it fails to maintain a sharp distinction between God and the world, and the popular mysticism, to which it gives rise, is insufficiently ethical in content. Dr. Albert Schweitzer's conclusion on this point is instructive. "In the Graeco-Oriental religion," he says, "there is no living conception of God. To it God is nothing, but pure spirituality. The God of Jesus is an active God, who works in man."[9]

[8] See his *God and Philosophy*, Yale University Press, 1941, Chapter I.
[9] Albert Schweitzer, *Christianity and the Religions of the World*, p. 28.

The central Aristotelian conception of God, though not inconsistent with the one which emerged in Palestine, is nevertheless far from identical with it. For Aristotle God was One who gave meaning to the universe, but not One who could be touched by our infirmities or One with whom we could have fellowship in prayer. In fact, Aristotle's God was an "it," not One for whom a fully personal pronoun could reasonably be used. The fully developed Christian view, on the other hand, is that of One for whom we can honestly use, not only the third personal pronoun, but the *second*. The characteristic Christian pronoun, in reference to God, is "thou." "I thank *thee*, O Father, Lord of Heaven and Earth." "O Lord, *thou* hast made us for *Thyself*."

The upshot of this development, then, is that we have at last arrived clearly and unambiguously at the notion of God as *personal*. The highest attributes we know are those which we call personal, including consciousness, self-consciousness, and the appreciation of value. Just as a living being is of a higher order than a nonliving, because its experience is more inclusive and involves new modes of behavior, so there is a real sense in which a personal being is vastly superior to an impersonal one, regardless of size or power. By common consent, it is Pascal who has made this clearest to people of the Western world. The classic fragment is as follows:

Man is but a reed, the most feeble thing in nature; but he is a thinking reed. The entire universe need not arm itself to crush him. A vapour, a drop of water suffices to kill him. But, if the universe were to crush him, man would be more noble than that which killed him, because he knows that he dies and the advantage which the universe has over him; the universe knows nothing of this.

The idea of God as fully personal means that God is a center of consciousness and of self-consciousness and therefore utterly different from mere brute power or the reign of law, though God is undoubtedly the source both of power and of natural law. God, in the most advanced thought, especially of Christians, is never equated with some abstract quality. The phrase "God is love," though it appears in the New Testament, cannot be considered a definition or an exhaustive statement, and must be understood in connection with other statements such as "God so loved the world." Love without a lover is a pure abstraction. "The gospel is good news of God," explains H. G. Wood, "good news not so much concerning God's eternal nature in the abstract, but concerning God's action in time through which His eternal nature is expressed and understood."[10] For this reason history plays an important part in the logic of our belief.

If God is defined as less than personal, we are forced to contemplate the wholly irrational situation in which God is inferior to some finite creatures. If a man can have knowledge of God, but God does not have knowledge of the man, there is an important sense in which the man is superior to God. God may be far *more* than personal, but if He is *less* than personal, faith in His existence is hardly worth all the trouble of laborious examination.

Frequently the definition of God in terms of the highest we know, instead of some lower category, is dismissed, not by argument, but by the use of an intimidating adjective, "anthropomorphic." But there is no good reason to be frightened by such a term. Is there anything really absurd about the guess that God is *at least* the highest we know or can imagine? What we need to do is to define, refine, and enrich our anthropomorphic conception. The late Paul Elmer More, in the most mature phase of his thought, insisted on this point:

Growth in religion is thus in the direction of a deeper and broader anthropomorphism; *but not away from anthropomorphism.* And this is a corollary of faith that must not be forgotten. So long as God remains a purposeful Being—and to faith He can be only that—He must be imagined as working out a design, just as man is conscious of doing, through some sort of obstacle or hindrance and by the

[10] H. G. Wood, *Christianity and the Nature of History*, p. 29.

lingering processes of time. There can in part be no conception of purpose without such limitation, though with deepening self-consciousness the inference of limitation may change in character . . . and so God's freedom will correspond to man's liberty of choice, developed to that self-determination to choose only good which man sees as the far off goal of his own endeavour.[11]

The anthropomorphism, which is frequently mentioned for purposes of ridicule, pictures God as having a body in human form. This is wholly a creature of straw, since belief in God in this sense has not been seriously entertained for centuries and was branded long ago by Christians as a heresy. Moreover critical theists are greatly misunderstood if they are supposed, in their emphasis on God as personal, to deny that God is *different* from men. We are reminded by an able Christian philosopher, Professor Webb, that "a true Theism is never 'anthropomorphic' in the sense of drawing no essential distinction between man and God, of merely making God in the image of man, as it is often supposed to do."[12] The paradox is that God is seen as both *akin* and *alien*. The worshiper cries, "O Father," but he hears God say, "My thoughts are not your thoughts, nor my ways your ways."

One of the most striking features of modern religious thought is the way in which the reproach of anthropomorphism is boldly accepted without apology. The Dean of St. Paul's Cathedral goes so far as to show that anthropomorphism, far from being a primitive absurdity, is the principle on which progress depends. "Anthropomorphism is the road along which the believing mind has traveled from superstition to noble creeds."[13] Man alone, of all known finite objects, has the potentiality of infinite development. Man is a creature who can make progress, while other creatures are strictly limited and carry on identical patterns of behavior over many centuries. The fact that God

[11] Paul Elmer More, *The Sceptical Approach to Religion*, p. 17.
[12] C. C. J. Webb, *Religion and Theism*, New York, 1934, p. 137.
[13] W. R. Matthews, *God in Christian Thought and Experience*, London, 1930, p. 31.

came to be understood after the analogy of the human spirit meant that men's ideas of God's nature had unending capacity for growth within this analogical framework.

Increasingly the term we have adopted in connection with higher and critical anthropomorphism is "The Living God," a term already mentioned in the quotation from Dr. Schweitzer as indicating the chief contrast between Christianity and the Graeco-Oriental religions. This term leaves open the question whether God is *more* than personal, and frankly recognizes the probability that God is infinitely more than we can think. We can agree with Lord Balfour in his guarded statement, "The attribution of personality to God, though much truer, I think, than the denial of it, is manifestly inadequate to the full reality we are struggling to express."[14] We know Him, but only "in part." The term "Living God" suggests one who really makes a difference, the existence of whom is neither a primitive absurdity nor a sophisticated truism, but an exciting possibility. Furthermore God's will is the primary factor in the actual history of the present world. This notion has been elaborated by Archbishop Söderblom and many others, but one of the best compact accounts is that of G. A. Johnston Ross in his West Lectures at Stanford University.[15]

I believe it will come to be seen that the fullest view of human nature and life is that which predicates conscious vitality in the powers behind the things we see and which perceives that Man is morally related to these powers and under obligation to them; and, further, that these powers outside of Man are ultimately one Power and that that Power is identical with the Fact or Person which (or who) causes Man to suffer and be inhibited in the region of what we call conscience. The Christian view, that is, of all that we see without and feel within as bathed in an atmosphere of living Deity will, I believe, in the end prevail when the tyranny of words (even of sacred words) has come to an end.

[14] A. J. Balfour, *Theism and Humanism*, p. 35.
[15] G. A. Johnston Ross, *Behavior and Destiny*, Stanford University Press, 1931, pp. 10, 11.

Here then is the first element in the background of the Christian's view of life, physical and moral: it is pervaded by the living God.

The hypothesis which theism thus presents for the consideration of thoughtful minds is a daring one, but it is not preposterous or inherently impossible. The hypothesis is to be distinguished, as sharply as may be, not only from atheism, but also from pantheism, on the one hand, and from subjectivism on the other. It is the conviction that God exists both as transcendent reality and as immanent purpose. It is the belief that God is the Creator of the world, but by no means confined to the world. This conviction is wholly realistic in that God is seen as existing independent of our knowledge of Him. *The Christian idea of God is that God is, apart from our idea of Him.* His will is expressed in the slow and painful evolution of the universe; He is witnessed to by conscience; direct experience of acquaintance with Him is reported either explicitly or implicitly by millions. *The hypothesis is that the kind of order we know best, the order of purposive mind, is the ultimate explanation of the order of the universe.*

When we use the word hypothesis in connection with faith in the Living God, we are aware that such faith is not merely an hypothesis. It is not entertained in detachment, and, in practice, it is more akin to courage than it is to belief. It is not normally envisaged as a mere supposition to be tested by scientific method. Nevertheless, the philosopher of religion, knowing this full well, is at liberty to examine theistic faith *as he would examine a scientific hypothesis*, for this is a method which serves his purpose of rational inquiry. We cannot expect such a method to do justice to the subject, and no method can, but it may shed welcome light upon it.

Here then is our method: We present an hypothesis and we look into various aspects of experience to see whether the hypothesis is supported by the facts. We must consider both those facts which support our thesis and those, if there are any, which make the thesis difficult to maintain. The fact that our thesis appears to be the end product of a long spiritual development in many races and peoples does not prove that our thesis is correct, though it undoubtedly makes any honest thinker approach the subject with unusual respect and actually tips the logical scales somewhat in favor of the hypothesis. It is not enough that our hypothesis appears at the end of a line of manifest progress; we are not satisfied until it is verified by a method harmonious with the method of science. Scientific verification does not, as we have indicated earlier in this book, give absolute proof, but it gives something with which most of us are satisfied.

The problem we now face, to which the succeeding chapters are addressed, is not merely, "Does God exist?" More accurately it is, "How is the universe to be understood?" We find that there is in the world one bold theory which stands out from its rivals as especially worthy of attention, the theory of the Living God. Is the world more reasonably understood on this basis than on any other? Will this assumption best order all known facts into a reasonable whole?

There are many features of the known world which can be understood on the theistic hypothesis, but which are not understandable on any other known hypothesis. Our procedure is to consider them one by one. Singly, they are by no means conclusive, just as a single corroboration is no verification, but together their cumulative effect is very great. And it is in such cumulative effect that the whole strength of verification lies. We have examined the reasons for belief in *anything*; we have presented one particular belief, perhaps the most important in the world; we are now to ask whether the evidence for this belief is good evidence.

CHAPTER IX

THE EVIDENCE OF NATURE

"The absence of haphazard and conduciveness of everything to an end are to be found in Nature's works in the highest degree, and the resultant end of her generations and combinations is a form of the beautiful." —ARISTOTLE

We now have before us a great and daring hypothesis, not a hypothesis developed as a brilliant guess by some lone thinker, but one which has grown by the cumulative insight and experience of millions of men, not of one time merely, but representing several thousand years. This hypothesis is, of course, far more than an hypothesis, since it is also a living faith for which men will die, but the task of philosophy is to consider the tremendous claim with scientific detachment. Can it be supported when examined in this fashion? The answer to our question comes as we investigate, one by one, the various areas and levels of the experienced world, to see whether we actually find what we should expect to find if the daring hypothesis is really true. The first area or level to be so investigated is that of the external world of nature.

If it is really true that, in addition to all finite spirits, there is an infinite Spirit, the divine Mind, who is not only the Companion of our spirits, but the Creator and Sustainer of the world order, it is reasonable to expect to find evidences of the divine Mind in the process which goes on relatively independent of the will of men. Specifically, we should expect to find various aspects of the natural order which are not understandable except by reference to the hypothesis in question. If God really is we should expect the heavens to declare His glory and the firmament to show His handiwork.

A. The Existence of Science

The discipline which we call natural science is the best means at our disposal of knowing the secrets of the external world. By means of science we learn more and more about a vast system ranging all the way from distant stars to microscopic phenomena, and all the way from inorganic substance to highly sentient and conscious beings. The process by which we have accomplished so much in the enlargement of the area of scientific knowledge has been slow, laborious, and halting. Beginning with an unreflective experience of adjustment between organism and environment, we have finally arrived at the point where we distinguish sharply between subject and object, seeking to consider the world as it is apart from subjective wishes. We are thus driven to the conclusion that the world exists, independent of our knowing it. Most of the natural order would go on just as it does if there were no scientifically minded creatures on the earth. Perhaps the best evidence of the independence of the natural order is that *it actually did go on a long time before the advent of man.*

Man, when he came to be genuine man, entered into a going world, waiting to be known. The human mind exists in the world, not the world in the human mind. But mind, though a late comer in the temporal sequence, has been remarkably successful in unlocking the secrets of the world which is older than itself. The world has been able to spawn something which can apprehend that which spawned it.

The most amazing fact about scientific knowledge is the evidence it provides that there is an actual correlation between the mind and the natural order which it apprehends. This correlation is so great and so fundamental that we seldom reflect upon it. When we do begin to reflect upon it we begin to realize that the most stupendous conclusion to which science leads is the conclusion that ours is the kind of world in which science is possible. There are many ways of adjusting to environment, but the more rational the adjustment is, the more adequate it becomes, and the test of adequacy is success in manipulation. This tells us something highly significant about our world. It is the kind of world which yields its secrets, in physical and chemical and biological laboratories, to men who conduct precise mathematical calculations. Archbishop Temple has made this point so well that we can do no better than reproduce a few sentences from his Gifford Lectures.

But this fact of knowledge is more remarkable than all the varieties of known objects put together. For the mind which knows is in a perfectly real sense equal to what it knows, and in another real sense transcends it, unless what it knows is another mind which also knows. The mind of the astronomer is equal to so much of the stellar system as he grasps, and transcends it in so far as he knows it while it does not know him. That there should "emerge" in the cosmic process a capacity to apprehend, even in a measure to comprehend, that process is the most remarkable characteristic of the process itself. For though minds emerge as episodes within the process, it is, as will appear, essential to their nature as minds that they are not mere episodes. Thus the cosmic process gives evidence that it is not only process, and history supplies the proof that reality is more than historical.[1]

When a human mind comes to know an object with any accuracy, there is a one-to-one correspondence between the thought and the object. They match! This is what is meant by saying a mind is equal to what it knows. When an astronomer knows the moon, each feature of the moon's surface is matched by an item of the astronomer's thought. The wonder of such matching becomes most apparent when we engage in actual prediction of physical events, a prediction constantly illustrated in astronomy. Valid mental processes go on for a considerable time, unchecked by reference to events, but when the mental processes *are* checked, they are found to have followed events

[1] William Temple, *Nature, Man and God,* p. 129.

perfectly. Nature "obeys" the rules of logic; predictions, made on the basis of logical calculations, come true.

Whatever our explanation of this correspondence, and it may be said in passing that the existence of God, who is at once the Creator of the natural order and the Creator of man's mind, is a fully adequate explanation, there is no avoiding the fact that actual kinship between mind and nature exists. This kinship is the chief basis of whatever success science achieves. It is what we mean when we affirm the existence of an intelligible world. The world, of course, is not now fully intelligible, and it may, for all we know, involve fundamentally irrational elements, but the history of science has been the elimination of many supposed irrationalities, which have finally been understood.

The meaning of these observations becomes more apparent when we consider the significance of *explanation*. Sometimes we say we have explained physical events by reference to prior events of the same order, but reflection shows that this merely pushes the mystery back one step, and does not explain at all. To say that it rains today because there was a certain atmospheric disturbance yesterday is to say very little, indeed. All that we do in this case is to enlarge slightly the temporal span of our description of the physical event. The process of explaining must come somewhere to an end, and it comes to an end only when we reach "principles deducible from nothing prior to themselves."[2] In explanation we seek a connection between what is to be explained and what we already understand, at least in some measure. "The business of philosophy," as a brilliant contemporary thinker has reminded us, "is not so much to explain things, as to find the things that explain themselves."

A situation is never understood until we have some intimation of why it has occurred and we never have an intimation of "why" until we come into contact with purpose. Purpose, in turn, is meaningless apart from a mind which entertains the

[2] H. W. B. Joseph, *An Introduction to Logic*, p. 503.

purpose. "When we find," says Archbishop Temple, "that the position of a given set of material objects is due to their having been arranged with a view to facilitating the accomplishment of some intelligible purpose, our minds are satisfied. That a plank should lie across a stream may call for much explanation if no human beings have ever placed it there; but if men laid it across to form a bridge, so that they could cross over dry-shod, no further explanation is needed."[3]

Not only is purpose a self-explanatory principle; there is, so far as we are aware, no other. All other types of explanation leave the fundamental questions unanswered. We go on asking "Why?" *in exactly the same way as before*. When we are told that gas pressure is explained by movement of molecules, we ask why the molecules move, and we are asking precisely the same kind of question again. When we trace an occurrence to the purpose of an intelligent being, however, the situation is completely altered. We may, indeed, ask why such a purpose is entertained, but, when we do so, we are asking a question of a different order. We have come to the end of one road and we are starting on another. The causes which *produce* a purpose are entirely different from the set of secondary causes which *result* from a purpose.

If a nail is being driven we discover a set of secondary causes reaching all the way from the purpose of the carpenter to the completed process. The nail goes in *because* the hammer hits it. The hammer head moves *because* it is moved by the muscles of a man's arm. The arm muscles move *because* they are directed by nerve impulses. But the whole enterprise takes place *because* a man has a reason for driving a nail in a board. Perhaps he wants to build a house for his friend. Our ordinary language obscures the true situation in that we use the same word "be-cause" in each case, but reflection shows that the word in its fourth use means something very different from what it means in the first three uses. The first three do not really explain, but

[3] William Temple, *Nature, Man and God*, pp. 131, 132.

the fourth *does* explain. This remains true even when we ask why the man wants to build the house. We have solved our first problem and have turned to another.

When we try to explain a purpose we find that our only recourse is to refer to other and more inclusive purposes. Thus Purpose is really an ultimate principle of explanation, and the only adequate explanation of the world would be the Purpose which includes the whole process. If the world is understandable, such a Purpose must exist. But the belief in the existence of such a Purpose is theism. Because science shows the world to be intelligible, at least to a considerable degree, science becomes a witness to intelligent Purpose in nature and consequently it bears testimony to the credibility of theism.

Few modern philosophers have grasped this logica' conclusion of science better than did the late Baron Von Hügel. His words may be used as a summary of, and therefore a fitting conclusion to, this section of our analysis:

Already Mathematics and Mechanics absolutely depend, for the success of their applications to actual Nature, upon a spontaneous correspondence between the human reason and the Rationality of Nature. The immensity of this success is an unanswerable proof that this rationality is not imposed, but found there by man. But Thought without a Thinker is an absurd proposition. Thus faith in Science is faith in God.[4]

B. THE FACT OF EVOLUTION

Though there are many minor arguments about the precise mode of evolution that has occurred and is occurring in the natural order, there is little argument in the modern world about the general principle to the effect that the forms which we see at present have come by innumerable steps, longer or shorter, from other and different forms which have preceded them. The principle of evolution, thus broadly understood, is

[4] Baron Friedrich Von Hügel, *Essays and Addresses on the Philosophy of Religion,* p. 71.

to be distinguished, both logically and historically, from Darwinism, the special evolutionary theory which seeks to make the notion of natural selection a sufficient means of explanation. The Darwinian is necessarily an evolutionist, but one can be an evolutionist without being a Darwinian.

The conclusion to which most biological scholars have been driven is that all living creatures are the descendants of earlier and, in many cases, less developed living creatures. Species, we now believe, have not been immutable from the beginning, but have arisen from other species. It is likely that the earliest form of life, and possibly the ancestor of all living things, was a unicellular organism, popularly known as "primordial ooze." The evidence we have is by no means adequate to demonstration, and there is truth in the contention of skeptics that evolution is a highly speculative theory, but the evidence is sufficient to satisfy most minds which have considered it fairly.

It is well known that the great intellectual struggle over evolutionary theory which took place three quarters of a century ago was occasioned largely by the inclusion of man in the evolutionary scheme. For a number of reasons it was widely supposed that this inclusion, if sustained, made religious faith difficult or even impossible. Curiously enough, it is this very inclusion which subsequent reflection has fastened upon as one of the chief features of the natural order among those which substantiate and corroborate the theistic hypothesis.

The evidence that man is akin to other living creatures by virtue of descent is abundant. Alfred Russel Wallace's summary of this evidence, though made fifty years ago, would hardly be changed by contemporary scholars.

The facts now very briefly summarized amount almost to a demonstration that man, in his bodily structure, has been derived from the lower animals, of which he is the culminating development. In his possession of rudimentary structures which are functional in some of the mammalia; in the numerous variations of his muscles and other organs agreeing with characters which are constant in some apes; in his embryonic development, absolutely identical in character with that of mammalia in general, and closely resembling in its details that of the higher quadrumana; in the diseases which he has in common with other mammalia; and in the wonderful approximation of his skeleton to those of one or other of the anthropoid apes, we have an amount of evidence in this direction which it seems impossible to explain away. And this evidence will appear more forcible if we consider for a moment what the rejection of it implies. For the only alternative supposition is, that man has been specially created—that is to say, has been produced in some quite different way from other animals and altogether independently of them. But in that case the rudimentary structures, the animal-like variations, the identical course of development, and all the other animal characteristics he possesses are deceptive, and inevitably lead us, as thinking beings making use of the reason which is our noblest and most distinctive feature, into gross error.[5]

Wallace, it may be remembered, held back from the conclusion that man's higher life also came out of nature, but he seems to have been impelled by the fear that this would involve some disparagement of this higher life. But the higher life of man, found in his mental and spiritual powers, is dependent on the long series of events which Wallace helped so greatly to describe. Unique as man's mind undoubtedly is, man shares much of his mental experience with the humbler creatures. Mind is man's glory, but there are thousands of stages of mental development to be observed in the natural order. Thought and language, now so highly developed, have already been developing for a very long time in order to reach the stage illustrated in the most primitive tribes we now know. Many animals have a kind of language, even though it is qualitatively different from human language. "Thinking is grounded in the process of adjustment between organism and environment and is indeed an extension of that process."[6]

[5] Alfred Russel Wallace, "Darwinism as Applied to Man" in *Representative Essays in Modern Thought,* pp. 247, 248.

[6] Temple, *op. cit.,* p. 128.

The highest point in creation, so far as we know, is the capacity to comprehend the world, but this capacity has arisen by degrees in the natural order. At one end of the evolutionary series is unconscious life and at the other is self-conscious life, but *it is all one series*. It is reasonable to suppose, as Aristotle taught, that the conclusion of a process gives a more adequate insight into its character than does the beginning. "Primordial ooze" and scientific accuracy belong to a single comprehensive system of historical and genealogical relations, but the science is more revealing than is the ooze.

The fact that a process is rational, does not mean that the ground of that rationality is necessarily revealed in the beginning. In fact the ground of the rationality need not appear until the end of the series of events and then it illuminates the entire process. This is well illustrated in dramatic poetry and in the lives of good men. Seen in retrospect such lives are thoroughly rationalized wholes, because of what, all along, they were *becoming*.

If the general evolutionary theory is true and if man's life be included in the theory, we cannot escape the conclusion, once more, that mind and nature are akin. We saw earlier that mind and nature are akin because mind truly comprehends nature. We now have an independent line of evidence in that mind arises out of nature. It is genealogically as well as cognitively akin. The convergence of two lines of evidence on one conclusion is a matter of great importance. The relation "akin to" is a symmetrical relation. If mind is akin to nature, nature likewise is akin to mind.

We are thus led to the conclusion, not that a naturalistic metaphysic is adequate, but that the explanation of nature is to be found in mind. Inasmuch as Archbishop Temple has had the honor of emphasizing this point more than most contemporary thinkers, it is appropriate to quote his conclusion, a conclusion which he rightly prints in italics. *"The more completely we include Mind within Nature, the more inexplicable must Nature become except by reference to Mind.*"[7] A boldly accepted naturalism leads directly to supernaturalism. How can nature include mind as an *integral* part unless it is grounded in mind? If mind were seen as something alien or accidental, the case would be different, but the farther we go in modern science the clearer it becomes that mental experience is no strange off-shoot. Rather it is something which is deeply rooted in the entire structure.

Science knows nothing of the wholly fortuitous. Though there are some events, especially in sub-atomic physics, to which we cannot assign causes, the general assumption is that there are causes for these events and they would be intelligible if known. This assumption has been well justified by former experience in which the apparently fortuitous or haphazard was finally seen as conforming to an intelligible rule. If, as seems likely, there are no uncaused events, then mind which comes at the apex of the world process, so far as we know it, is really an integral part of the system and a revelation of the nature of nature.

This general conclusion is greatly strengthened by modern studies which stress, in a new and striking way, the fact that the world as we know it is wonderfully adapted to the production of life and, thereby, of the consciousness which depends on life. Professor L. J. Henderson of Harvard University, approaching the subject in a mood quite unlike that of orthodox teleology, and with no theological presuppositions, has shown that a truly amazing combination of circumstances was required to make possible life on the only planet we really know. We have an environment peculiarly fitted for the emergence of life, mind, and spirit. "The fitness of the environment results," we read, "from characteristics which constitute a series of maxima —unique or nearly unique properties of water, carbonic acid, the compounds of carbon, hydrogen, and oxygen, and the

[7] Temple, *op. cit.*, p. 133.

ocean—so numerous, so varied, so nearly complete among all things which are concerned in the problem that together they form certainly the greatest possible fitness."[8]

It is important to stress what Professor Henderson says about maxima. For life and consciousness to appear, it is necessary that there should be a combination of winning throws, each of which is as unlikely as a run of several hundred "heads" in tossing an honest penny. The combination is almost fantastic.

There is, in truth, not one chance in countless millions of millions of millions that the many unique properties of carbon, hydrogen, and oxygen, and especially of their stable compounds water and carbonic acid, which chiefly make up the atmosphere of a new planet, should simultaneously occur in the three elements otherwise than through the operation of a natural law which somehow connects them together. There is no greater probability that these unique properties should be without due cause uniquely favorable to the organic mechanism. These are no mere accidents; an explanation is to seek. It must be admitted, however, that no explanation is at hand.[9]

The most fruitful conclusion of such studies lies in the revelation that "cosmic and biological evolution are one." There seems to be a single orderly development with mind and matter belonging to the same inclusive system. In short, studies regarding the fitness of the environment emphasize in a new way the great lesson of evolution to which we have already pointed. "For undeniably," concludes Professor Henderson, "two things which are related together in a complex manner by reciprocal fitness can make up in a very real sense a unit—something quite different from the two alone or the sum of the two or the relationship between the two. In human affairs such a unit arises only from effective operation of purpose."[10] Thus the evidence

[8] L. J. Henderson, *The Fitness of the Environment,* New York, 1913, p. 272.
[9] *Ibid.,* p. 276.
[10] *Ibid.,* p. 279.

grows that mind is not accidental in nature, and that nature, consequently is not alien to mind.

C. THE SECOND LAW OF THERMODYNAMICS

Of all the conclusions reached by the last two centuries of careful scientific work, one of the most revealing, as well as disturbing, is that which points to the degradation of energy. The notion of the progressive degradation of energy, which is based on what is called the "Carnot principle" and finds its formal statement in the Second Law of Thermodynamics, has been known for a century, but we have been surprisingly slow to see its metaphysical implications.

The Second Law of Thermodynamics must be understood in connection with the First Law, that of the conservation of energy. This principle, to be distinguished from the principle of the conservation of matter, was reached independently by several scholars. Mayer, in Germany, announced his conclusions in 1842 and Joule, in England, announced his in 1843. The law holds that the amount of energy in the world is constant, though it changes in form. The fact that the amount of energy is constant does not mean that energy is always available. In so far as we can see the time will come when energy is not available for work. Because there is constant diffusion, and because there is no *addition* to the total energy, we must contemplate a final condition of absolute stagnation. And it is precisely this to which the Second Law points.

In all physical systems we note a leveling process. A stone thrown in a pool raises waves, but these slowly dissipate until they are no longer observable. The hot stove radiates its heat into the closed room until a uniform temperature is reached. Just as nature may be said figuratively to abhor a vacuum, so nature abhors differentiation and concentration of energy. Thus the stars radiate their energy and this energy, so far as we know, never makes a return trip. It is a one-way process. This increase of leveling is called the "increase of entropy." There are many excellent definitions of this, but the following is one of the clearest: "As the useless energy increases, the useful decreases by the same amount. This ratio of useless to useful energy is called *entropy*. The law of entropy states that the ratio is constantly increasing. This means that the amount of energy available for the energizing process of the world is ever growing less."[11]

The reason why we can get work out of a heat engine is that there is a temperature differential, and the reason we can get work out of a waterfall is that there is a difference in level. The waterfall is useful because there is a low place into which the water can descend. If the leveling process were ever completed, all work would be at an end. "We cannot convert the heat of a cold body into work," says Barnes, "for then, without consumption of fuel, we should get unlimited supplies of motive power. Hence we may conclude that the efficiency of a perfectly reversible engine is the maximum possible, and further that it depends solely on the temperatures between which the engine works. It is always possible to get work out of the heat of a body which is hotter than surrounding bodies. But, just as you cannot get blood out of a stone, so you cannot get work out of a body which is colder than surrounding bodies. On this simple fact the second law of thermodynamics is based."[12]

Though the law of entropy is partially a matter of speculation, inasmuch as the conclusion is large in comparison with the field of observation, the conclusion reached is far from fanciful. In fact, no less a physicist than Sir Arthur Eddington calls this law the most certain and the best grounded of all the laws of physics.

"Carnot's principle," wrote Emile Meyerson, "is a fact, and by far the most important fact, of all science."[13]

It is always possible for some new force, now unknown, to

[11] J. A. McWilliams, *Cosmology*, New York, 1933, p. 42.
[12] E. W. Barnes, *Scientific Theory and Religion*, p. 233.
[13] Emile Meyerson, *Identity and Reality*, p. 278.

enter, but, on the basis of present observations, there seems to be no rational escape from the prospect of an ultimate dissipation of all energy. This means not only the "death" of our particular solar system, but of any physical system.

This prospect has appealed strongly to some modern minds and has been used for different purposes. The late Henry Adams accepted the concept as valid, not only for physical systems, but also social and political ones as well. Accordingly he wrote *The Degradation of Democratic Dogma*. To Bertrand Russell and others the concept has seemed to provide adequate ground for despair in the grand manner, a fit subject for rhetorical flourish.

A more careful and critical examination of the metaphysical implications of the Second Law came early from the philosopher, Josiah Royce. Royce was quick to see that the principle we are considering undermines what may be called a religion of progress. Many have sought a substitute for theism in the notion that this world, in spite of occasional relapses, is coming to be more and more a place which harmonizes with man's moral growth. Here is an aspect of the natural world which may be termed a power which makes for righteousness, and this power, it is supposed, is sufficient to meet man's religious needs. But, said Royce, the Carnot principle shows us that progress, as we know it, is a fact of transient significance. "Progress," wrote Royce, "is an incident of a certain thermal process, a kind of episode in the history of the dissipation of the energy of our particular mass of matter, and thus, insofar as we yet know, a present occurrence just in our neighborhood, a local item in the news of the universe."[14]

Professor Royce's contention that the Second Law of Thermodynamics undermines a religion of progress was not based solely on considerations of time. It is true, of course, that something can be splendid or even perfect without lasting forever. The difficulty, in Royce's mind, was the deeper one of cosmic indifference. "It is not because progress is to endure on this planet

[14] Josiah Royce, *The Religious Aspect of Philosophy*, p. 244.

for a short or for a long time, but *because the world in which this progress is so to end seems, thus regarded, wholly indifferent to progress*—this is the gloomy aspect."[15]

But while the Second Law of Thermodynamics thus limits the rational appeal of an alternative to our grand hypothesis, it actually supports the theistic claim in a remarkable way. In the first place it now seems clear that the physical world, which we have come to know, is something which not only will have an end, but also something which had a beginning. "If the universe is running down like a clock," says Dr. Inge, "the clock must have been wound up at a date which we could name if we knew it. The world, if it is to have an end in time, must have had a beginning in time."[16] This follows strictly from the fact that the law of entropy is irreversible. A clock which always runs down and is never rewound cannot have been running forever.

At first sight it looks as though there is a possible escape from this conclusion in the concept of the physical world as infinite in extent or in amount of energy. But this, in fact, is no solution of the problem, since the notion of an infinite quantity is really meaningless. The term "infinite sum" has no meaning. However much there is of energy or of matter there is just that much and no more. Energy cannot be infinite in amount because it is concerned with actuality. Time, however, can be infinite in the sense of possibility of events.

The chief metaphysical significance of the law of entropy consists, not of the evidence of a beginning in time, important as that is, but rather in *the evidence that the natural world is not self-explanatory*. According to natural law, energy loses its efficacy. But without the operation of a totally different principle, there would be no energy to lose its efficacy. *Nature points beyond nature for an explanation of nature.* The Second Law of Thermodynamics thus points directly to theism as an explana-

---

[15] *Ibid.*, p. 245. The italics are Royce's.
[16] W. R. Inge, *God and the Astronomers*, p. 10.

tion of the world and the reasoning based upon it provides a modern counterpart to the cosmological argument.[17]

Though we have, in this section, stressed the importance of time, it should be made clear that the reference to time is not strictly necessary to the validity of the argument in general. All of the changes which we know in the world of nature are dependent changes. We refer changes in plant growth to changes in soil, we refer the changes in soil to still other changes, and so on. No single step in the process would even occur apart from the other steps upon which it depends. Therefore the entire chain of causes presupposes the existence of a power which is truly originative, able to account not only for others, but also for itself. "The dependence meant in the argument," says Professor A. E. Taylor, "has nothing to do with succession in time. What is really meant is that our knowledge of any event in Nature is not complete until we know the reason for the event. So long as you only know that A is so because B is so, but cannot tell why B is so, your knowledge is incomplete. It only becomes complete when you are in a position to say that ultimately A is so because Z is so, Z being something which is its own *raison d'etre*, and therefore such that it would be senseless to ask *why* Z is so."[18]

The chief strength of atheistic naturalism has lain in the notion that the material world needs no explanation, *external to itself*, that it is, indeed, a perpetual motion machine, which had no beginning and will have no end. But when we take the Second Law of Thermodynamics seriously we can no longer

[17] The cosmological argument for the existence of God is the argument from the necessity of cause. The argument received its classic formulation in Book X of Plato's *Laws* and was greatly refined by St. Thomas Aquinas. Though criticized by Kant, it has received the assent of many modern thinkers, especially Catholic philosophers. For a good modern statement see George Hayward Joyce, *Principles of Natural Theology,* Longmans, Green and Co., 1934, Chapter III. The heart of the argument is the necessity of a First Cause, which arises from the impossibility that a series of secondary causes should be infinite.

[18] A. E. Taylor, "The Vindication of Religion," *Essays Catholic and Critical,* edited by E. G. Selwyn, London, 1938, p. 50.

hold to this doctrine. The universe as we know it, by the aid of modern science, could not have originated without the action of a creative Source of energy outside itself, and it cannot be maintained without it.[19] But a creative Source of energy outside the natural order is God.

The more we delve into the secrets of nature, the more it becomes clear that nature cannot account for itself in any of its parts or in its entirety. It is no valid answer to say with Hume's skeptical critic in the *Dialogues Concerning Natural Religion* that the necessary being which accounts for all the contingent parts may be nothing else than the *world as a whole*. It is precisely the "whole" which most demands explanation, and there is no line of evidence which makes this more clear than that which leads to the general acceptance, among scholars, of the Carnot principle.

[19] For an able discussion of this, see Joseph A. Leighton, *The Field of Philosophy,* New York, 1923, pp. 207 f.

CHAPTER X

THE EVIDENCE OF MORAL EXPERIENCE

"The breach between ethical man and pre-human nature constitutes without exception the most important fact which the universe has to show."
—ANDREW SETH

Ours is a world which has men in it. This fact would seem to be so obvious that it could not fail to be observed, since it is usually men who do the observing, but it has, indeed, frequently been overlooked in high places. It is, of course, much easier to exclude the observer from the totality of what is observed, but this can be done only at the price of falsification. Generalization about the nature of reality is greatly simplified if men are left out of consideration, for men are highly embarrassing phenomena. The most glaring example of such a radical omission is found in the several varieties of philosophical mechanism. There is a famous story to the effect that Laplace, who sought valiantly to be a consistent mechanist, told Napoleon that in his (Laplace's) system there was no need for the hypothesis of God. He might well have added, as a distinguished Gifford lecturer has suggested, that there was likewise no place in his system for the creative activity of man.[1] The old-fashioned mechanistic scientist of the nineteenth century, who even yet is not wholly extinct, created "a paradise of intelligibility" by the simple expedient of excluding himself. It is relatively easy to reduce the world to order according to the laws known to physics if one elects to overlook the persons who change the course of events by the discovery and use of the laws of physics. But the truly modern man is so infected with the virus of

[1] E. W. Barnes, *Scientific Theory and Religion*, p. 583.

realism that this simple method is not open to him. For better or for worse, we must seek to reckon with the fact that the world has men in it. We see the joke when Whitehead writes, "Scientists animated by the purpose of proving that they are purposeless constitute an interesting subject for study."[2]

A. THE PHENOMENA OF CONSCIENCE

In Chapter IX emphasis was placed on the degree to which man's mind is rooted in external nature and fundamentally akin to it. In order to keep a proper balance it is necessary to point out that there are striking ways in which man's mind is unique. It was the distinction of Thomas Huxley, in his famous Romanes Lecture, to produce what has become the classic statement of the uniqueness of man's moral life. Huxley shocked both conventional Christians and conventional naturalists by his insistence that there is a vast chasm between man's moral life and all the rest of reality. He shocked the conventional Christians because he affirmed the moral life without reference to God, and he shocked the conventional naturalists because he cast scorn on the notion that the evolutionary process provides guidance concerning what man ought to do. Differing sharply from Herbert Spencer, who taught that man's task is to fall in with the evident trend of nature, Huxley held that it is man's high vocation to *go against nature*. "Social progress means a checking of the cosmic process at every step and the substitution for it of another, which may be called the ethical process; the end of which is not the survival of those who may happen to be the fittest, in the respect of the whole of the conditions which obtain, but of those who are ethically the best."[3]

Though it now seems evident that Huxley overstated his thesis,[4] making the contrast greater than it is in fact, the funda-

[2] Alfred North Whitehead, *The Function of Reason*, p. 12.
[3] *Evolution and Ethics*, p. 81.
[4] One of the best criticisms of Huxley's position is that of Andrew Seth. It is the first essay in his volume, *Man's Place in the Cosmos*, New York, 1897. The quotation at the head of this chapter is from Seth's essay. A fuller treatment of Huxley's contribution will be found in Chapter XIV.

mental conviction which he expressed must always be included in any thoroughgoing attempt to understand the nature of the world. Man's mind is, indeed, rooted in nature, but man has the honor of being the lone exhibitor of some of the aspects of reality potential in the universe. It is important to call attention to these aspects because they tell us something about the world which we might otherwise miss. Because they tell us something about the world, they may have important bearings on the grand hypothesis which we are seeking to test by reference to experience.

It is beyond dispute that the human animal is concerned very largely *with what he ought to do*. In this enterprise he is, no doubt, frequently confused and baffled, but he goes on asking the question. Man falls to depths such as no mere beast can experience, but he is frequently conscious of his fall and self-condemnatory accordingly. Man is a self-conscious being who not only acts, but *judges* his own acts, as well as the acts of others. He not only uses intelligence to gain his ends, but he asks whether certain ends ought to be gained. He not only seeks praise, but, at least in fleeting moments, seeks to be worthy of praise. Frequently he does what is customary, but generation after generation he asks whether what is customary is really right.

The point to make clear here is that, in dealing with the phenomena of conscience we are dealing not with something transitory or local, but with something permanent and universal. No matter how evil men are, all seem to have what have been termed "splendid incapacities"; there are acts which they cannot do and keep any self-respect. In any case it is true that, *unless* there are some things which a man will not do, whatever the personal cost, we can have no respect for him and it is doubtful if he is a moral being at all. This point is forcefully presented in the later work of Paul Elmer More, especially in the following paragraph:

A man's moral sense may be very low and shifty, but no man, whether in a state of savagery or of advanced civilization, escapes remorse if he commits an act flagrantly at variance with his code of right and wrong; and no man, though his resolution may be extremely feeble, lacks at least a velleity, or slightest stirring of the will, to act in the future so as to avoid remorse. I do not believe you will discover anywhere, or at any time, a human being who does not feel ill at ease if he is conscious of having betrayed a friend, and who does not, under the sting of shame, form some sort of resolve for the future. In other words, so far as we can judge from what men say of themselves, the teleology of conscience is universal.[5]

An experience so important to human life must be taken seriously, yet we have seen that the attempt to account for the convictions of conscience on the naturalistic hypothesis is bound to fail. Naturalism, seeking as it does to explain developments by reference to survival value, cannot give a reasonable explanation either of the rise and development of moral experience or of its authority. Naturalism erases the distinction between what is prudent and what is really right, just at it erases the distinction between what is genuinely true and what is necessitated by conditioning, thus making its own position untenable. If the only kind of value is survival value, then there is no value at all, "for it is clearly nonsense to speak of the race as having value in the sense that it tends to preserve the race."[6]

To show that naturalism is unable to account reasonably for moral experience, important as that is, is not sufficient. Nor does this, of itself, give positive verification of our hypothesis, though it prepares the way for the humble acceptance of positive evidence if any is forthcoming. We are well on our way when we begin to ask seriously the question: *What must be the nature of the universe which gives birth to a being tormented by a sense of obligation?*

---

[5] Paul Elmer More, *The Sceptical Approach to Religion*, p. 5.
[6] W. R. Matthews, *Studies in Christian Philosophy*, London, 1921, p. 123.

B. THE OBJECTIVE FACTOR IN MORAL EXPERIENCE

Every person who engages in moral judgment, and this includes, so far as we know, all members of the human race, implies by his judgment the existence of an objective moral order. The relationship called judging involves at least three terms, the person who judges, the action that is judged, and the standard of judgment by which the judged action is measured. This last, if moral experience is to make sense at all, must be something independent of both of the other terms.

There is hardly any field in which sensitive men have been so concerned with the distinction between appearance and reality as that of moral experience. This has led, in all generations, to the rejection of the *mores* in favor of what really ought to be. It has often been customary to accept bribes, but the moral pioneer arises as "he that despiseth the gain of oppressions, that shaketh his hands from holding of bribes."[7] Good men in all ages have interpreted their moral decisions, not in terms of something they have *made*, but in terms of something to which they have become sensitive.

According to almost all the testimony of moral experience, ethical propositions are genuine propositions, i.e., statements capable of being true or false. To this we all bear witness when we criticize others for doing wrong or making wrong decisions. If there is a possibility of moral error, then there is a possibility of moral truth, even though we may not be sure when we attain it. If there is a possibility of moral truth, then ethical propositions refer to a realm which is as independent of the individual observer as are natural laws.

The objective reference which is inherent in all ethical judgment is fully consistent with a species of relativity, in that the precise relationship to the objective order is different in each particular situation. The duty of the married man is not the same, in certain emergencies, as is the duty of the single person.

[7] *Isaiah*, 33:15.

This kind of relativity is not only consistent with the notion of objectivity, but is necessitated by it. Two men starting from opposite shores to swim to an island in a stream must swim in different directions to get to the common goal, not because there is no objective order, *but because there is*.[8] Though the fundamental truths about what is really right no doubt remain the same, as do the fundamental truths about physics and chemistry, when situations change, new and different acts are demanded if fundamental moral consistency is to be maintained.

How can the conviction of objective reference in moral experience be accounted for? What is it that is objective to which all ethical judgments refer? They clearly refer to a moral order which is part of our environment, as genuine a part of our environment as the physical order of which we are so conscious. Unless this is the case we are referring to nothing at all, since it is already clear that we are not referring to something in the natural order. When a man says an action is wrong he clearly does not mean that it will hinder survival, that it is imprudent, that it is mechanically impossible. He is seeking to refer to something utterly different from all these, or at least such is the constant testimony of men whom we most delight to honor and trust. But if there really is a moral order which is part of our environment and to which we must adapt ourselves, this is a clear evidence of the theistic hypothesis. "Only to a being who has in his structure the adaptation to the eternal can you significantly say 'You ought.' "[9]

When we recognize an objective factor in ethical judgment we cannot be considering something tangible or observable by the physical senses. All that we can reasonably mean is an ideal, but not one of our own making. It must, therefore, to use Dean Matthews' sharp expression be "in the form of a completely

[8] This aspect of ethical theory is worked out carefully by Professor Henry Lanz in his prize essay which was successful in the international competition inaugurated by the Swedish Publishing House in 1936. It is now published by the Stanford University Press under the title, *In Quest of Morals*, 1941.

[9] A. E. Taylor, "The Vindication of Religion," *op. cit.*, p. 63.

conceived, but imperfectly achieved purpose."[10] Such a purpose involves a transcendent teleology, and this is another way of referring to the reality of God, who is the Purposive Intelligence revealed in the actual world, but not identical with it.

If God really is, in the sense defined earlier, if, in addition to physical constituents there is One who purposes the good, then the experience of self-conscious creatures who are concerned with knowing what is right, becomes abundantly reasonable. The fact that men differ concerning what is right is no impediment to this interpretation for men naturally are affected by their human environment and break with it only after effort and strain. It is not surprising that men, especially ignorant and savage men, should have all kinds of absurd ideas about the supernatural or moral order, since they have all kinds of absurd ideas about the natural order, and no person supposes that this means that the natural order is nonexistent.

It is not difficult to show, as we have seen, that actual objective moral reference really implies the theistic hypothesis and can only be justified on this hypothesis. There are many, however, who maintain that mankind as a whole is deluded in supposing they are experiencing something objective when they make moral decisions. Perhaps, it will be said, they merely objectify their own personal whims or the passing *mores* of their particular tribe.

There has been a marked tendency in recent times to believe that sociological research has practically demonstrated complete relativism and subjectivism in morals. There have been several careful studies of the natural history of morals, notably those of the late Professor Westermarck and his collaborators, which are widely supposed to show that there is no agreement in moral judgments. Some tribes, we are told, are conscientiously favorable to cannibalism, and other tribes are conscientiously opposed to cannibalism. In the same manner, wide differences of ethical judgment in regard to sexual practices are reported.

[10] W. R. Matthews, *Studies in Christian Philosophy*, p. 140.

Considerations of this kind have led many to the complete subjectivism popularly and superficially expressed by the hackneyed
quotation, "There's nothing either good or bad, but thinking
makes it so."

When we consider the matter carefully we find that the case
for ethical realism, according to which ethical propositions are
genuine propositions, capable of being true or false, is strictly
parallel to the case for physical realism. There are the same
reasons for believing in a moral order to which our ethical
judgments may or may not conform, as there are for believing in
a physical order to which our scientific judgments may or may
not conform.

It is pointless to insist that ethical judgments are subjective,
in that they take place in the mind. All mental events occur in
minds, whatever order they may represent. All states of mind
are states of some self or ego, but they *may* refer to what is
beyond the self, and there is no reason *a priori* why they might
not truly refer to a moral order as to a physical order.

What we must do is to examine the data without prejudice.
All that we know, we know by experience of some kind, and
there is always a chance that we are deluded, but we have a
right to be satisfied when we have honestly examined experience and found it to point to something beyond ourselves.

In passing, it may be pointed out that there is a really convincing dialectical argument against ethical subjectivism. If no
ethical judgment involves anything more than subjective reference, if each man who says "This is right" is merely talking
about a feeling which he happens to have, we cannot escape the
startling conclusion that no two people ever differ on an ethical
question. If we are referring to something confined to ourselves,
as the thoroughgoing relativist holds, we are referring to *our*
whims and the other fellow is referring to *his* whims. It is as
though Paul, when he says "This murder was unjustified"
should say, "I don't like spinach," and Peter, when he says,
"This murder was justified," should say, "I do like spinach."

Unless there is objective reference, one is not even denying what the other says, for they are not talking about the same thing.

Now it is well known that men *do* differ on ethical questions, that they differ on these more than on anything else, and that they constantly refuse to let each man be an ethical solipsist. To Paul's "I don't like spinach," Peter may reply, "But *you ought* to like spinach," and he doesn't mean, "I like it." A theory which goes against so much experience must be suspect, and the theory of subjectivism does go against it. Apart from the ascription of objective reference ethical questions could not even be discussed, but they have received their most careful discussion from the men, such as Plato and Kant, whom we have had most reason to honor.[11]

The best evidence for ethical objectivity, however, is not this dialectical argument, but the fact that there is really a significant agreement in moral convictions, an agreement too great to be accounted for by coincidence. The convergence of ethical testimony is parallel to the convergence of opinion regarding physical factors. Just as people on the savage level exhibit the widest difference of judgment in regard to astronomical or geographical objects, so people on the same savage level exhibit considerable difference of opinion on moral questions, but with the growth of sensitiveness and the development of the human mind, the difference of judgment concerning both the moral and material order is greatly diminished. That there is never full agreement is easily accounted for by the fact that there are many reasons for *moral blindness.*

In fairness to Professor Westermarck it should be said that his researches do not show utter confusion in moral ideas among backward people as they are popularly supposed to do. What he shows is substantial agreement in spite of some striking differences, and *the possibility of authentic development* in these matters. The substantial agreement found by Westermarck re-

[11] For a fuller statement of this interesting argument, see G. E. Moore, *Ethics.*

fers to *hospitality, care of children, fidelity, a certain respect for life and liberty.* These are among the major virtues that have been practiced, though imperfectly, by countless peoples. On the other side we must set different rules concerning what constitute incest and adultery, the exposure of defective children or supposedly superfluous female children, etc. These are, in most instances, relatively minor, important though they may be. The most significant factor is what seems to be authentic development roughly parallel to scientific development from magic to modern science.

C. THE AUGUSTNESS OF OUGHT

The august quality of moral obligation, though it is closely allied to the recognition of an objective factor in moral experience, is really different and takes us farther on our road. It has long been noted that the demands of conscience have an imperative note not found elsewhere in all experience. This is shown by the witness of men and women of widely different temperaments and vocations from saints and martyrs to statesmen and scientists. Many scientists could win fame and other rewards for apparent new discoveries, if only they would alter their figures, but in countless cases this temptation is scornfully rejected, even when there is no reasonable probability of detection and exposure. Such action is by no means limited to those who have a positive theistic belief, but finds some of its clearest expressions in the lives of supposed atheists.

Few men have been more uncompromising than W. K. Clifford, who wrote his brilliant and convincing essay on "The Ethics of Belief," with special reference to the religious belief which he did not have. Similarly the unbelieving Huxley wrote to his friend Kingsley of his refusal to believe in the comforting doctrine of immortality while he was grieving for his dead son. He could not play fast and loose with truth.

What all bear testimony to is the fact that a man who genuinely says, "I ought," means, "I ought, though the heavens fall." The command is not conditional, but categorical. Of course conditions make a difference, but *once the conditions are recognized*, there is a genuine imperative. "Whoever says 'ought' at all, must mean that at least *when* the requisite conditions are fulfilled the obligation is absolute."[12] This augustness of "ought" is by no means felt in all situations, but it seems a misuse of language to call a situation a moral one if this note is wholly absent. Kant, whose judgment cannot be lightly dismissed, thought reverence for the moral law was the one and only specific moral feeling.

We may now ask what this implies. What conception of reality is required if we are to make sense of this all but universal experience? The striking fact is that the augustness felt is similar to that felt in connection with persons and is not reasonable in other connections. We do not feel shame or pollution when we harm *things* or even when we transgress impersonal *laws*, but we do feel these when we violate the rights of *persons*. Why should men like Clifford and Huxley be so finicky about the "truth" if there is nothing in the world but matter and our feeble lives? Their carefulness becomes fully rational *only if there is One to whom their dishonesty becomes disloyalty*. The practice of the honest atheist frequently denies the conscious import of his words, because he is acting in a way which makes no sense *unless his conscious conclusions are untrue*. Temple has made a similar observation by pointing out that "this quality of reverence for Truth is specially evident among those who have felt bound, out of loyalty to Truth itself as they have been able to receive it, to abandon the belief which alone could justify it."[13] In this regard the atheist often bears a more eloquent witness to the being of God than does the believer, since the latter may let himself be influenced by his desires.

The theistic implication of the augustness of moral obliga-

---

[12] A. E. Taylor, "The Vindication of Religion," *op. cit.*, p. 62.
[13] William Temple, *Nature, Man and God*, p. 251.

tion takes us beyond what is implied by objective reference, because the augustness is more fully suggestive of some tremendous reality. No theory regarding custom can adequately account for something so insistent in the lives of the best trained and most independent minded of men. This becomes particularly clear in the case of martyrdom. "No man," as Cardinal Newman well said, "will die for his own calculations: he dies for realities." When men go against some received opinion standing alone like Luther at Worms, their action is difficult to explain except on the assumption that they have a genuine perception, however dim and faulty, of a supernatural order which is part of their total environment. *The augustness of "ought" is what we should expect to find if theism is true and it therefore constitutes part of the verification which scientific method demands.*

It may be countered that moral experience does indeed imply theism, but that the whole logical enterprise is vitiated by the delusive character of moral experience. Perhaps moral experience is a cheat and a liar, utterly undependable. There is, of course, no coercive answer to be made to one who chooses to think this about his own experience and that of most of his fellow men, but this kind of doubt is so far-reaching that it is hard to see how *anything* could be considered reliable on such a basis. Actually there would seem more reason to trust the human spirit in its exalted moods than in its more humdrum pursuits. At least we are conscious of living more adequately in times of courageous moral decision than at other times. No doubt most careful thinkers will have sympathy with the late Paul Elmer More when he asserted that he found the hypothesis of mass delusion really incredible. "You ask me to believe," he wrote, "that nature has planted in me, and not in me alone, but in all men, desires which I must eradicate as pure deceptions, that I am the victim of a cosmic jest only the more cruel if unintended, that the ultimate fact of existence is a malignant mockery."[14] When the matter is so stated it is no wonder that Professor More went on to say that "the so-called dis-belief of the infidel is an inference which, if honestly examined, demands an act of almost impossible credulity."

D. THE PARADOX OF FREEDOM

Freedom is an aspect of human experience which is associated most intimately with moral endeavor, but is by no means limited to this area. For this reason it seems proper to consider freedom in the chapter dealing with moral experience, but in a separate section of the chapter. The close connection between freedom and morality lies in the notion of responsibility. Unless there is some real sense in which man is free, he cannot be held responsible for his acts, and, if he is not responsible, it is meaningless to speak of his actions as having ethical significance. The boulder on the mountainside, which is caught up in a snow slide, and accordingly crushes the life out of a man in the valley below, is not guilty of a crime and has not engaged in a moral enterprise at all. The boulder has no choice, makes no decision, and accordingly has no moral responsibility. If men are so constituted that their acts are determined as is the movement of the stone, all discussion of moral obligation, duty, and the claims of conscience is empty talk. This remains true in spite of the fact that a man is conscious whereas a stone is not. Consciousness makes no *moral* difference if all action is predetermined by the same kind of factors which are determinative of the behavior of physical constituents.

If man is not free, even in a small measure, both praise and blame become utterly meaningless. We do not praise a man for doing what he could not avoid doing, and neither do we blame him in the same situation. If a man were convicted of murder, and if it could be demonstrated that some kind of inherited glandular disturbance made the murderous action inevitable, it would be silly to blame the man, even though we might con-

[14] Paul Elmer More, *The Sceptical Approach to Religion,* p. 24.

fine him in order to avoid a repetition of his act. In fact, we should hardly speak of the murder as a human act at all. "Man's will is called *animal*," says Kant, "if necessitated pathologically."[15]

Though the complete denial of freedom makes moral experience meaningless, the complete affirmation of freedom, in the sense of indeterminism, has the same result. This striking paradox arises from the fact that complete indeterminism would be inconsistent with the continuity of character. A wholly unpredictable man would by no means be a good man. He would, indeed, be no more an ethical being than is a tossed coin. He would face a decision and, if wholly undetermined, there would be no way of having any idea what his decision might be. Choice, so understood, would be indistinguishable from chance. Furthermore, praise and blame would again have no bearing. The blamed man would be able to say, "I chose that action yesterday, but I do not choose it today." Praise and blame are as meaningless apart from continuity of character as they are meaningless apart from some kind of freedom.

We thus find ourselves in a serious dilemma. It seems that, in order to have real responsibility, we must reject determinism and that we must likewise reject indeterminism. The good man is one who is conscious of making a free choice so that he is not an automaton; but the good man is, at the same time, one whose actions are largely predictable because there are enduring elements in his character. The chance that a man of lifelong integrity will steal his friend's purse is almost negligible. But if there were something about his *physical* make-up which made theft impossible, we should not ascribe any *ethical* significance to his apparent honesty.

How shall we escape from the horns of our dilemma, finding some way in which the claims of the moral life can be reasonably maintained? Unless we do, we must be prepared to hold

---

[15] *Critique of Pure Reason*, Transcendental Dialectic, Book II, Chapter II, Section IX, ¶ III.

that a great portion of human experience, and precisely that portion which has seemed the noblest, is sheer delusion. This, which is merely a counsel of despair, most thoughtful people are not willing to accept.

The problem is really enlightened by the consideration of an added paradox. This new paradox lies in the fact that what seems like freedom from the inside looks like determinism from the outside. It is admitted by all people, either directly or implicitly, that they experience freedom of choice in their own personal lives, whereas it seems possible to explain all other events, including those in the lives of other people, on a basis of strict causal determinism. John is conscious of difficult decisions in his own life, certain that he could go in several different directions if he so chose, but he looks at the action of James and thinks he sees that James was helpless in the presence of external forces and prior conditioning. Herein lies whatever plausibility orthodox behaviorism has, in spite of its fundamental inconsistency, as pointed out earlier. The behaviorist avoids the paradox by the simple expedient of observing all events, mental or physical, from the outside. He looks at other men rather than himself. He looks at men precisely as he looks at rats or at stones. He even goes so far as to state, in a doctrinaire manner, that this is the only way in which observation is possible, so that when a man observes his own mind he observes nothing at all.

Now it must be agreed that a good case can be made for the complete causal determination of all acts. The notion that there are no uncaused events, though it is an article of faith in our scientific society, is one which seems unavoidable. The alternative is sheer chance, a concept to which it seems more and more difficult to assign any clear meaning. What we ordinarily call chance is nothing but ignorance of determining conditions, as is obviously the case when we toss a coin or throw a die. There is *some reason* why the die turns up the face it does turn up. In like manner it is difficult to avoid the conclusion that there is

some reason why a man chooses as he does. Every man is naturally affected by his past training, by the standard of his group,
and by the condition of his body. The fact that moral decision
can be weakened by the use of drugs is a most sobering consideration. Perhaps there are other factors, quite as determinative as drugs, of which we as yet are ignorant.

If a man's action is lawless it is amoral, and we cannot
profitably carry the investigation further. Even when we look
back on our own lives we can look at our former decisions in
some detachment and see why we acted as we did. But at the
moment of choice we are fully conscious that we do actually
choose and that we are responsible as the automaton is not.
Even those who write in defense of determinism, interpreting
the actions of other men as they interpret the actions of dogs
who are conditioned to produce saliva at the ringing of a bell,
look upon their own actions as the result of intelligent choice.
Even the most orthodox behaviorist apparently is unwilling to
believe that his book on the subject is the result of his conditioning, just as that of his opponent or critic is the result of
other conditioning. This would eliminate the possibility of one
being more true than the other. Other men may be the mere
victims of circumstance, but not himself! In the expression of
this paradox it is difficult to go beyond the classic words of
Dr. Samuel Johnson when he said in another connection, "All
argument is against it; but all belief is for it."

We begin to see light on our problem when we realize that
moral experience may be caused, in that it is not fortuitous and
lawless, but caused by a different set of factors than those which
determine the action of the boulder in the snow slide. The
hypothesis which saves both freedom and causality is the hypothesis that the human being is a creature who comes into
contact with causes of a different order from those which obtain
in physical sequence. The paradox of freedom ceases to be a
paradox if man's environment includes spiritual as well as

physical reality, and, furthermore, if this spiritual reality can be apprehended. When it is apprehended, the introduction of a new causal order occurs. We then have, not the indeterminism we are bound to reject, but a determination by *something* other than efficient causation. A man's action, then, is not lawless, but it could not be predicted unless we could know all his unrealized ideals, which indeed he cannot even know himself. The only theory which we know which avoids absolute contradictions in regard to freedom is the theory that man is affected in his action, not only by conditioning and by physical factors, but also by the true and the good as apprehended. *"Freedom,"* the Archbishop of Canterbury has said, *"is not absence of determination; it is spiritual determination as distinct from mechanical or even organic, determination. It is determination by what seems good as contrasted with determination by irresistible compulsion."*[16]

The chief reason why so many discussions of freedom have been so confused and unprofitable is that the billiard table conception of causation dominates the thought of the examiner, and on this basis there seems to be no solution at all. The truth, as we all know, is that man's acts are determined differently from the movements of billiard balls, and the difference seems to all of us to be one of kind rather than degree. If God really is, if there is a spiritual order as well as a material order, and if man is a creature capable of responding to both orders at once, the mystery of freedom is largely dispelled. How this is to be understood can hardly be better expressed than in another passage from Dr. Temple's great work:

But there is another environment besides that of nature and human beings; it is that Mind in which the Cosmic Spirit is grounded, that Spirit of the Whole, which is most adequately conceived on the analogy of Personality such as our own, but freed from our limitations and fulfilling all that in us is potential only. If it be possible to

16 William Temple, *Nature, Man and God,* p. 229.

establish fellowship between the human soul and that Spirit, such fellowship would be the source of the true freedom of man.[17]

Again we realize that we have found genuine evidence of our grand hypothesis. If there are aspects of human experience which that hypothesis will illuminate and explain, whereas we can find no competing hypothesis that will do so, we are well on our road, the road of scientific verification. We find that the chief features of moral experience and of the experience of freedom are made reasonable in the same way. We begin with facts, such as the fact that freedom is universally experienced, and then we ask what kind of a world it must be for such facts to occur. We find that we are forced to the conclusion that the environment of man is larger than that which appears to the senses. The experience of freedom implies that there is an area of reality in which truth and goodness are to be genuinely apprehended. But that there is such an area is precisely what theism contends.

It will be noted that the present segment of our study does not stand alone. We found in Chapter IX abundant evidence that nature is akin to mind and therefore most rationally understood if it is the product of divine mind. We now find that moral experience is an absurdity and a delusion unless there is a divine Mind to whom our moral obligation refers and to whom we are disloyal when we fail. Nature and moral nature are thus two witnesses who, without collusion, confirm one another's testimony. The relationship between these two is carefully stated by Professor Taylor as follows: "In Nature we at best see God under a disguise so heavy that it allows us to discern little more than that someone is there; within our own moral life we see Him with the mask, so to say, half fallen off."[18]

Kant, as is well known, rejected almost entirely both the evidence of nature and the evidence of religious experience,

[17] *Ibid.*, p. 243.
[18] A. E. Taylor, "The Vindication of Religion," *op. cit.*

making the moral argument for theism the only one. We can now see that this was a mistake and an unnecessary impoverishment. But Kant was fundamentally right in his positive doctrine; the moral argument for theism is not the only valid argument, and it is greatly helped when it is corroborated by others, but it is an argument which could bear the weight of the logical structure alone if that were necessary.

CHAPTER XI

THE THEOLOGICAL SIGNIFICANCE OF AESTHETIC EXPERIENCE

"A man's moments of serenity are few, but a few will sustain him a lifetime."
—ADMIRAL BYRD

In our humble efforts to understand something of reality we dare not neglect any of the approaches to reality which have seemed trustworthy to men whom we have reason to honor. In the verification of the theistic hypothesis we have found that both scientific and ethical experience are more intelligible and less marked by absurdities if the reality of God is assumed than on any other basis of which we can think. Since the experience of beauty has been so widespread and has seemed to great parts of the human race so important, we ought to include the aesthetic experience in our process of verification. What is this experience, what does it imply, and in what framework does it form a rational and coherent whole?

A. THE OBJECTIVITY OF BEAUTY

The relation between science, ethics, and aesthetics is interesting and curious. All seek to deal with different aspects of reality, yet some of their objects of contemplation are the same. Thus aesthetics overlaps both the field of science and the field of ethics and may be said to be the middle term in the series. It overlaps the field of science because both aesthetics and science are concerned with the external world. It is the *same flowers* which, according to scientific experience, are classified, and, according to aesthetic experience, are held to be beautiful. But aesthetics overlaps, at the same time, the field of ethics in that both are concerned with value. It is not, however, the *same* value, for beauty and goodness are far from identical.

Though aesthetics deals with the external world, including the beauty of both art and nature, and though the ordinary observer supposes the beauty to reside in these objects, there has been, especially in late years, a strong tendency to suppose that aesthetic experience tells us nothing about the nature of the world at all, but only about the shifting subjective feelings of certain people. The subjectivistic interpretation of aesthetics is strictly parallel to the subjectivistic interpretation of ethics and based on similar arguments, which we have already noted. The subjectivistic interpretation may be simply stated, in Professor Montague's words, as the conviction that "the adjective *beautiful* is nothing but a somewhat solemn and decorative synonym for the adjective *pleasant*."[1]

The notion that the sense of beauty is wholly subjective, telling us nothing about ultimate reality or the nature of the universe, receives at least superficial support in the fact that standards of beauty seem to change according to fashion. It is common knowledge that this is true of clothing. What seemed to be suitable apparel only a few years ago now seems comical or even disgusting. That such change is by no means limited to clothing is apparent when we think of the rise, in each generation, of some new school of art or poetry. Once Tennyson was almost universally admired, but more recently it has been the mode to belittle him. No doubt the more enduring verdict will rest somewhere between these extremes, but in the meantime there is no stability of judgment.

The fact that fashion plays a part, and indeed a great part, in aesthetic enjoyment is generally admitted and needs little documentation.[2] Those who hold that there is an objective

---

[1] W. P. Montague, *The Ways of Things,* New York, 1940, p. 126.

[2] Careful psychological studies of the effect of fashion on conceptions of beauty have been made. My colleague, Professor Paul R. Farnsworth, will publish a study on this in the near future, "Stereotypes in the Field of Musical Eminence."

factor in the sense of beauty have been as quick to admit the fact of change as have been their subjectivist opponents. Indeed, one of the best available statements of the effect of aesthetic instability is to be found in Lord Balfour's chapter, "Naturalism and Aesthetic," in *The Foundations of Belief*. But Lord Balfour, like so many other philosophers who have analyzed the experience of beauty, found that there was a significant remainder which mere fashion could not explain.

It is evident that the same argument, used in the immediately preceding chapter, concerning objective reference in ethics, applies here as well. If all experience of beauty is merely subjective, we find ourselves in a position in which some people like rice pudding and other people do not like rice pudding, which is then the conclusion of the matter. In short it would mean that no two people have ever differed or ever can differ on a question of beauty. When one person says the Philadelphia City Hall is more beautiful than the Parthenon and another person denies this, they are not, on the subjectivist theory, arguing at all. One man is telling about his *insides* and the other man is telling about *his* insides. If someone wishes to contend that the works of a contemporary leader of a "swing band" are aesthetically superior to the works of Beethoven, there is, subjectively speaking, no suitable rejoinder.

This situation, however, is too absurd to be accepted by thoughtful critics as the last word on the question. The fact is that people *do argue* about aesthetic judgments and the subjectivists argue as much as anybody else. A theory which is so markedly at variance with practice, including the practice of the most critical and sensitive natures, is rightly under strong suspicion. It is instructive to note that those who take beauty most seriously tend to hold that those who fail to see what they see, really *ought* to see it, and, with sufficient clarification of sight, *would* see it. The maxim *de gustibus non disputandum est* is apparently believed by nobody, and has lived only because it is a kind of joke. Far from taste being beyond dispute it is the subject of endless dispute. Conversation would be dull indeed if the maxim were taken seriously, which fortunately it never is.

Kant goes farther than the mere rejection of the familiar maxim and points out the imperative note which is essential to aesthetic judgment, a note similar to that which we found in moral judgment. To assert that a thing is beautiful is to blame those who do not agree. If I am right, they are wrong. How seriously Kant's dictum should be taken is suggested by the estimate of a contemporary philosopher, the distinguished realist Professor Montague, who says, "It seems to me that Immanuel Kant, in his theory of esthetics set forth in *The Critique of Judgment*, dealt more justly and more penetratingly with the two aspects of beauty than any other philosopher."[3] The relevant passage from Kant's pen follows the assertion that it would be laughable of a man to justify himself by saying, "This object is beautiful *for me*."

Many things may have for him charm and pleasantness; no one troubles himself at that; but if he gives out anything as beautiful, he supposes in others the same satisfaction—he judges not merely for himself, but for every one, and speaks of beauty as if it were a property of things. Hence he says "The *thing* is beautiful"; and he does not count on the agreement of others with this his judgement of satisfaction, because he has found this agreement several times before, but he *demands* it of them. He blames them if they judge otherwise and he denies them taste, which he nevertheless requires from them. Here we cannot say that each man has his own particular taste. For this would be as much as to say that there is no taste whatever; i.e., no aesthetical judgement, which can make a rightful claim upon every one's assent.[4]

When people dispute about questions of taste, it is clear that they are not concerned with the statistical calculation of pleasure. At the present time it is probably true that the number of Americans who find pleasure in the poetry of Edgar Guest is

[3] W. P. Montague, *The Ways of Things,* p. 132.

[4] Immanuel Kant, *Critique of Judgement,* translated by J. H. Bernard, second edition, revised, 1914, I, I, 7.

greater than the number who find pleasure in the poetry of Archibald MacLeish, but this is not generally regarded as settling the question. In other words, we habitually distinguish between what men actually think beautiful and what they *would* find beautiful if their area of awareness were deepened and broadened. This implies that the change of fashion is a change in the observer, but not a change in that which is observed, namely the beauty itself.

Such an implication of our universal experience is greatly strengthened by the consideration that people actually do change in their tastes, with developing maturity, in ways which we can hardly interpret as other than progressive ways. It is a common experience for young people, as well as some older ones, to get their greatest joy in music from obvious tunes like "Home on the Range," but, with expanding interests, they discover a keener joy in musical productions which are far more complex and less obvious. The same kind of development occurs in the other arts and in the appreciation of nature. If subjectivism is an adequate account of the sense of beauty this is mere *change*; it cannot be interpreted as *progress* unless there is objective reference in aesthetic judgment. If there is any way in which the critic's appreciation of beauty is superior to that of the savage, subjectivism is thereby refuted and rejected.

A further relevant consideration is the fact that aesthetic judgment actually gives far more evidence of permanence than superficially appears. In spite of the constant arguments about contemporary works, there are many judgments which are not seriously disputed or doubted by any persons who have given the matter serious attention. Though the contemporary poet is on trial, Shakespeare is not on trial. We debate contemporary art, but we do not seriously debate classic art. That is why there are any classics at all. If we take into consideration a long time span there is far more agreement in aesthetics than there is in science.

The observation that great works of art are more nearly dateless than great scientific conclusions, seems startling at first, but the explanation is easily available. The explanation is that scientific conclusions are necessarily interconnected, each depending upon a host of former generalizations. If one of these generalizations is proved inadequate, as knowledge grows, the other generalizations dependent on it are thereby affected. All kinds of laws required radical restatement after the Copernican hypothesis was accepted. Art, on the other hand, is always individual and particular. It is not a generalization and therefore is not dependent on the general context or world view. A change in astronomical theories does not affect Michelangelo's statues in the least. The nature of all art, and not merely painting, is symbolized by the frame which frees art from its setting making it relatively independent of contextual change.

There is no serious dispute about the merit of Phidias or Rembrandt or Dante. These men are now practically free from the irrational changes of artistic fashion; their works move us as they moved the first to enjoy them. Sometimes the really great work of art may need interpretation or translation, but it is never merely quaint. If it be said that this permanence of aesthetic judgment is to be explained by the prestige value of a long past, according to which men praise the work of the masters, because they are ashamed not to do so, an adequate reply is that the famous works are often *rediscovered* with manifest excitement by successive generations, for whom lip service is changed into enduring gratitude. Such a rediscovery is the whole point of Keats' sonnet, *On First Looking into Chapman's Homer*. Not only is the testimony of John Keats impressive, but this is augmented immeasurably by the experience of the thousands who have loved the sonnet because it has expressed what they also have known, but have not been able to say so well. What Keats discovered about Homer, through the instrumentality of Chapman's translation, others have discovered about Bach or Velásquez or the unknown architects of the Middle Ages.

In our modern society we are inclined to suppose that the scientific experience of men's minds really tells us something about the external order, because scientists corroborate one another, while we are inclined to suppose that the aesthetic experience of men's minds tells us nothing about the external order, because in this field there is no corroboration. Actually, however, the truth is the reverse of the popular opinion. It is one of the great merits of the philosophizing of Archbishop Temple that he has called attention to the point that science does not have the advantage over art which is so often alleged. "What scientific theory," he asks, "has the security of these works of art? The Newtonian Law of Gravitation seemed till yesterday to be assured beyond the risk of modification. Yet now, though the repute of Newton himself remains as well assured as that of Milton, his system is displaced by those of curvilinear space; while no amount of modern free verse displaces Milton's *Sonnet on his Blindness*. It takes longer for the aesthetic judgment to become stable than for the scientific, but when it reaches stability it also achieves finality as the other does not."[5] It is not maintained that there is ever *full* agreement concerning beauty, but there is far more than is often supposed, and there is far too much to be explained on purely subjective grounds, unless we are prepared to accept the miracle of coincidence.

We have mentioned especially the endurance of judgment about works of art, but the same could be said in reference to natural beauty. There is really no serious dispute about the beauty of the Grand Canyon of the Colorado or Yosemite Valley or the English Lakes. It is difficult to believe that the mere desire to be fashionable has been sufficient to take so many to Switzerland again and again. That there should be something considerably less than perfect agreement on the subject of beauty is what we should expect inasmuch as vantage points are so different. Indeed, if there were complete agreement, we should

[5] *Nature, Man and God*, p. 159.

suspect collusion. Years ago Lord Balfour gave us a figure of speech which explains why, on the hypothesis of aesthetic realism, there should be both the agreement and the disagreement which we actually find.

For we may liken ourselves to the members of some endless procession winding along the borders of a sunlit lake. Towards each individual there will shine along its surface a moving lane of splendour, where the ripples catch and deflect the light in his direction; while on either hand the waters, which to his neighbour's eyes are brilliant in the sun, for him lie dull and undistinguished. So may all possess a like enjoyment of loveliness. So do all owe it to one unchanging Source. And if there be an endless variety in the immediate objects from which we severally derive it, I know not, after all, that this should furnish any matter for regret.[6]

A final relevant consideration which leads to the conclusion that the subjectivistic interpretation of beauty is inadequate is that appreciation of beauty is found outside the experience of men, and plays a part in the lives of many animals. That men thrill to beauty in a thousand ways might, conceivably, mean nothing more than a human idiosyncrasy, something alien to the rest of reality and possibly pathetic, but if we find the response to beauty in various levels of nature, it is hard to avoid the conclusion that here we have a genuine insight into the nature of the real.

It has been sometimes suggested that the human love of music and painting originated in man's ancestors through the action of sexual selection and that this phrase explains the love of beauty as it now appears in lower orders. But this turns out, upon analysis, to give us no explanation of what most needs explaining, the fact that there was any appreciation of beauty in the first place. *For apart from an already existing appreciation of beauty in one sex, the possession or production of beauty by the other would not become a factor in sexual selection.* The taste is the cause of the selection, not the selection the cause

[6] Arthur James Balfour, *The Foundations of Belief*, p. 315.

of the taste. We are driven to the conclusion that love of beauty is an irreducible factor in large areas of the world. When we combine this with the fact that we *discover* beauty in still larger areas, we have reason to suppose that the approach to reality which aesthetics studies is a genuine and fundamental revelation.

We are not, of course, driven to the conclusion that all beauty that is experienced is objective. No human experience is purely objective, for we always see through colored glasses of some kind and try to objectify what is purely personal. Some of what we call beauty is, undoubtedly, a mere "projection," a finding of something that isn't there, but the considerations presented in the preceding paragraphs make the projection theory manifestly inadequate as a *full account* of beauty. We find, odd as it may seem, that beauty is something about which we can converse. It appeals both to our sensuous nature and to our rational nature, and it appeals to both together.

B. The Sense of Communication

Very seldom does the artist suppose that the beauty of his art is of his own making. The process is described as something far closer to *discovery* than to *invention*, but even discovery is not an adequate expression of the situation, since this word suggests that the artist is active in relation to a wholly passive environment. It is far more, we are told, as though the artist did not *choose*, but were *chosen*. The relation is not that of calm and deliberate choice, but of submission to a spell. The beautiful is not something I seek, but something which claims me. A. C. Bradley's penetrating analysis of the poetic experience is illuminating at this point. "Pure poetry," he writes, "is not the decoration of a preconceived and clearly defined matter: it springs from the creative impulse of a vague imaginative mass pressing for development and definition. If the poet already knew exactly what he meant to say, why should he write the poem? The poem would, in fact, already be written. For only its completion can reveal, even to him, exactly what he wanted. When he began and while he was at work, he did not possess his meaning; it possessed him."[7]

Composers, painters, poets, all these and many more know what it is to feel this claim and not to be their own masters any more. They understand the warning to Gareth which Tennyson puts into the mouth of old Merlin,

> Yet take thou heed of him, for, so thou pass
> Beneath this archway, then wilt thou become
> A thrall to his enchantments.

We find a similar and more haunting suggestion of how the seeker becomes the helpless listener in Coleridge's famous stanzas:

> He holds him with his glittering eye—
> The Wedding-Guest stood still,
> And listens like a three years' child;
> The Marinere hath his will.

> The Wedding-Guest sat on a stone:
> He cannot choose but hear;
> And thus spake on that ancient man,
> The bright-eyed Marinere.

The greatest lovers of beauty, including those who have been most successful in helping their fellows to see it or to see more of it, have repeated endlessly that, instead of their finding beauty, it has found them. It is like Francis Thompson's *Hound of Heaven*. "He on whom Beauty has cast her spell," concludes one of our ablest writers on aesthetics, "is not his own master, though in his bondage he finds freedom. He must listen and gaze till his release is given."[8]

It is this sense of the appreciation of beauty as being an imperious spell which makes most clear the notion of art as communication. The artist is convinced that he is spoken to, that

[7] A. C. Bradley, *Poetry for Poetry's Sake,* pp. 28, 29.
[8] William Temple, *Mens Creatrix,* p. 128.

he has learned something, and he proceeds, as best he can, to communicate to others what has been communicated to him.[9]

There is more than one way in which the humble searcher after reality may be rewarded by the sense of communication. One of the most striking ways is that of the recognition of truth. What we essentially mean by truth is the matching of our human minds with Something akin to them. When a scientist, working in his laboratory, thinks *truly*, his calculations and predictions are matched by the actual events as apprehended both by himself and others. Perhaps, therefore, truth is more an adverb than a noun. The fact that we can devise formulae which unlock secrets and facilitate new productions means that mind finds its counterpart in reality. The successful formula brings great delight, the same kind of delight we know when we master an ancient tongue and finally understand what the message is.

It is important to note that the sense of "kinship" which the mind experiences in what we call truth is not merely a recognition of a bare one-to-one correspondence. Beyond this is a sense of familiarity mixed with wonder. To be akin is not to be equal. That to which our finite minds are akin seems to be the controlling principle of the vast realm which we so inadequately know. As we come to understand something of the nature of reality we are increasingly conscious of our smallness and inadequacy, and yet we are not complete strangers. The lock is large and the human key is small, but sometimes the key fits and we cannot believe this is accidental. With the discovery that the counterpart of the principle of the mind's activity may be found beyond itself comes a sense of grandeur, but without bewilderment. Small as we are, we belong. In this con-

[9] The notion of art as communication is an old one, but it has received some of its most brilliant interpretations in modern times. The late T. E. Hulme showed promise of the development of a full aesthetic theory with this as the dominant note. "The essential element in the pleasure given us by a work of art," he wrote, "lies in the feeling given us by this rare accomplishment of *direct communication.*" *Speculations,* New York, 1924, p. 168.

nection it seems natural to appeal to Coleridge's famous aphorism: "In Wonder all Philosophy began: in Wonder it ends: and Admiration fills up the interspace. But the first Wonder is the offspring of Ignorance: the last is the parent of Adoration. The first is the birth-throe of our knowledge: the last is its euthanasy and *apotheosis*."[10]

The joy and wonder which men feel in the search for truth, including the quality of feeling of those scientists who think of themselves as materialists, is highly paradoxical if the real world they seek to know is unconscious matter or force, for it is the *same kind of feeling we know best when there is real communication between two finite minds.* The joy that comes in the effort to know the truth, and the reverence for it which makes good men spurn the temptation to deceit, are not intelligible if the only consciousness is at one end of the transaction, but they are completely intelligible if truth is the meeting of mind with Mind. We act as though the latter were the situation. We act as though there were an effort to communicate something to us, and that is why we say we understand. *It is hard to see how we can understand anything except another mind.*

One of the best reasons for considering truth and beauty together is that the pursuit of each of these gives the same intimation of communication, and thus a tentative conclusion is greatly strengthened. But the pursuit of beauty is the stronger partner in the logical enterprise. The communication in the recognition of truth is only *implied*, whereas the communication in the recognition of beauty is *experienced*. The apprehension of truth proceeds as if there were a universal Mind whose thoughts we feebly match; the apprehension of beauty reports itself as *direct communion with that same Mind.*

In his distinguished Gifford Lectures, *Theism and Humanism,* Lord Balfour rendered a great service by his insistence on

---

[10] Samuel Taylor Coleridge, *Aids to Reflection,* Aphorisms on Spiritual Religion IX.

communion as an aesthetic necessity. He considered, as many have, the situation in which there is a purely accidental combination of colors. By accidental we mean nonpurposive. Let us say we were to look at a color pattern produced by machinery, when this is something unintended by the maker of the machine. Or let us say that a dog's wagging tail dips into colors and splashes them on a near-by canvas. We might consider the result ingenious or striking, but we should not respond to it as we do to a work of conscious art. The reason is not the tiresome one that we must find a "lesson" in our art, but rather that there must be a matching of mind with Mind which is not possible when the cause of the production is accidental. "And this is not," says Balfour, "because we are unable to estimate works of art as they are *in themselves*, not because we must needs buttress up our opinions by extraneous and irrelevant considerations; but rather because a work of art requires an artist, not merely in the order of natural causation, but as a matter of aesthetic necessity. It conveys a message which is valueless to the recipient unless it be understood by the sender. It must be expressive."[11]

There is no way to enforce this observation except by appeal to actual experience of the reader. Let the reader consider his feelings in an art gallery, looking at a picture which baffles him though he cannot tear himself away. Finally, perhaps through the help of a friend, the picture ceases to baffle, and the observer says with deep satisfaction, "Oh yes. I see." It is then that the genuine *aesthetic* pleasure, as distinguished from mere sensuous pleasure, comes. The thoughtful observer, when he says, "I see," does not mean that the picture teaches some lesson which could be put into prose. The "meaning" of a work of .art, if it is good art, is not something that can be translated without loss in some other medium. What can be said in prose, ought to be said in it, reserving for poetry or for music or painting, what cannot really be said in any other way.

[11] Arthur James Balfour, *Theism and Humanism*, p. 67.

In any case, there is little doubt that the joy of *recognition* is essential to the appreciation of beauty in art, but recognition is meaningless apart from communication. The artist has a purpose and we understand his purpose. But his purpose must be of a special kind. If he is making a mere tool, if he is trying to be useful, he defeats his aesthetic purpose. In this connection Kant, as we might suppose, had a delicate insight, showing how beauty is distinguished from mere pleasure, on the one hand, and from *deliberate purpose or utility on the other*.

The artist must have a purpose, but he dare not have some ulterior motive. In order to express this important, but easily missed distinction, we may well adopt Kant's phrase used in another connection, "purposiveness without purpose." The man who tries to do us good or to modify our opinions has missed the aesthetic enterprise, though he may be a successful propagandist. The artist, on the other hand, is one who has seen something of such intrinsic worth that he is constrained to communicate it.

Does this interpretation of beauty, which receives so much justification in connection with human art, also find justification in the experience of natural beauty? Here we are on more difficult ground, for we already know that there is an artist responsible for the art, but whether there is an Artist responsible for natural beauty is what we are trying to determine. In this connection we are forced to rely on the reported experience of sensitive persons. How do those feel who have been greatly moved by the beauty of ocean and mountains and starry sky? Lord Balfour's own testimony is instructive:

The feeling for natural beauty cannot, any more than scientific curiosity, rest satisfied with the world of sensuous appearance. But the reasons for its discontent are different. Scientific curiosity hungers for a knowledge of causes; causes which are physical, and, if possible, measurable. Our admiration for natural beauty has no such needs. It cares not to understand either the physical theories which explain what it admires, or the psychological theories which explain its admiration. It does not deny the truth of the first, nor (within due limits) the sufficiency of the second. But it requires more. It feels itself belittled unless conscious purpose can be found some-where in its pedigree. Physics, and psycho-physics, by themselves, suffice not. It longs to regard beauty as a revelation—a revelation from spirit to spirit, not from one kind of atomic agitation to the "psychic" accompaniment of another. On this condition only can its highest values be maintained.[12]

If men do not feel this, it is hard to know what more is to be said, except that it has received the corroboration of other sensitive minds. Speaking of Balfour's testimony, Temple testi-fies as follows: "For what my own experience may be worth, it entirely confirms his interpretation."[13] As is well known this is also the interpretation of Wordsworth as expressed in his *Lines Composed a Few Miles above Tintern Abbey*. Words-worth was making his own testimony about natural beauty as genuine communion, which is not possible except between minds, when he wrote,

> And I have felt
> A presence that disturbs me with the joy
> Of elevated thoughts.

Here the poet, like the scientist, is not satisfied to rest with appearances, and delves deeper. The important fact about the testimony for our present purpose, however, lies not in Words-worth's personal testimony, but in the response which his poem has elicited. *Millions have added to the testimony by their satis-faction in the poem.*

The point we are making is greatly strengthened by the realization that, for many, the experience of natural beauty is almost indistinguishable from worship. The reverence which so many feel in noble scenes is not intelligible or defensible on any other than theistic grounds. There is nothing worthy of reverence about a *rock* or even a great pile of rocks. Indeed,

[12] A. J. Balfour, *Theism and Humanism*, p. 90.
[13] *Nature, Man and God*, p. 253.

the entire aesthetic experience is a cheat and a delusion unless beauty is a revelation from Spirit to spirit. If it is such a revelation it all makes sense. *In short, the aesthetic experience is what we should expect to find if theism is true.* But this is the essence of verification—to deduce consequences and then to discover that these consequences actually do occur.

C. THE AESTHETIC ARGUMENT

What we have already given in this chapter amounts to an aesthetic argument for the being of God, an argument which may stand parallel to the argument from nature, the moral argument, and the argument from religious experience. The wonder is that it is so seldom used in this connection. It is as though we felt more hesitation about placing reliance on aesthetic experience than on other experience. Even the able and brilliant apologetic of Professor A. E. Taylor in *Essays Catholic and Critical*, one of the best brief statements in existence, is only threefold where it might be fourfold.

Since the only kind of proof we know consists of the cumulative presentation of evidence, the probability being greater as the corroboration is greater, it seems a shame to use a rope of three strands when there might be four of approximately equal strength.

Why should we attribute less validity to the method of mind in art than we attribute to the method of mind in science? The aesthetic experience is extremely widespread, by no means confined to professional artists or critics, and has long been a central feature of culture. The oldest monuments to human genius indicate an early flowering of artistic ability. The same man is frequently an able scientist and an intense lover of beauty, and there is no reason to suppose that one of these approaches to reality is less revealing than the other. This becomes especially evident when we realize that the two methods actually support each other in that they point in the same direction.

Theology has been willing too long to limit its appeal to

certain conventional types of evidence, failing to take advantage of the support to be gained in other quarters. There may be vast productive fields waiting for the theologian to explore them. In any case we see that man experiences the real world in various ways, three of these being the scientific, the ethical, and the aesthetic. To each of these we have now devoted a chapter. Side by side with these is specifically religious experience, to which the next chapter will be devoted.

CHAPTER XII

THE EVIDENTIAL VALUE OF RELIGIOUS EXPERIENCE

"This array of testimony comes from many lands and from many generations. It comes from ignorant persons and learned, from saints and from those who would prefer to be called secular persons. It could be multiplied a thousand-fold."　　　—RUFUS M. JONES

Most of the arguments which have become classic in the support of the hypothesis of God as objectively real have been based on inference. We find, that is, that there are aspects of the world which are not understandable if theism is not true, but are understandable if theism is true. These arguments, as we have seen in an earlier chapter, are parallel to many used to arrive at scientific conclusions, the example given being that of the conclusion about the existence of atoms.

This kind of evidence is good evidence and can never be despised, inasmuch as we necessarily rely on it in so many areas of experience. Nevertheless, it is generally recognized that such inferential experience would be greatly strengthened if, in addition to it, there could be direct experience. If, in any situation, inferential arguments could show what logically ought to be the case, and if, furthermore, there could be a direct observation showing that the inference had the support of immediate experience, the impetus to believe would be very strong indeed. This is the procedure which has actually been followed in regard to certain astronomical discoveries, the most striking example being that of the discovery of the planet Neptune. The existence of the planet was first inferred as a necessary hypothesis in order to explain certain observed phenomena, and then by use of the telescope the inferred body was actually seen. It is conceivable that something like this may occur in regard to atoms, with the perfection of the new electron microscopes, which use electrical fields rather than light as their means of amplification.

The fortunate situation in the field of religious belief is that here the opportunity for the corroboration of inferential evidence by direct evidence is very great. One of the most amazing failures of historic theology has been the failure to employ, in the substantiation of religious belief, the same kind of empirical evidence which has long been used in support of scientific belief. The failure to make use of empirical evidence in religion is the more amazing when we begin to realize how abundant the evidence is, and how truly it has been the real basis of belief in actual practice. "I had heard of thee by the hearing of the ear, but now mine eye seeth thee," is echoed in every generation.

A. THE PRIMARY DATUM OF RELIGION

That fact that religious experience occurs is a fact with which every philosophy must eventually deal. The claim which such experience makes, the claim to actual contact, not merely with persons and things, but with the Creator and Sustainer of the universe, is so stupendous and so insistent that it cannot be neglected. Our philosophy must either explain it away or construct a world view consistent with it.

The reasonable procedure is to look at religious experience as we look at any other datum. It is the primary datum of religion, and it awaits analysis. If we are scientifically minded we approach experience without prejudice and with humility. The scientific temper demands that we neither *accept* the data of experience uncritically nor *reject* it uncritically. We do not know what any experience is worth in the verification of belief until we analyze it, subjecting it to all the appropriate tests available. The mere fact that millions have reported that they have known God directly is not absolute proof that they have really done so, but, on the other hand, to assume, prior to critical testing, that they have not really done so would be unscientific in the extreme.

It must be made clear that we are not referring to *belief* in this connection, but to *reported experience*. The two are different. Belief may arise from many sources, some of them intellectually respectable and some of them not respectable. There can be belief *because* of direct experience and there can be belief *apart from* direct experience. The point we are making is not that millions of men have believed in God, something almost too obvious to bother to mention, but rather that millions of men have reported and continue to report that they have known God with the directness and intimacy with which they know other persons or physical objects.

Not all religious experience is the same, but there are characteristic features which appear with astonishing regularity and which are not especially difficult to describe. Normally it is not some experience wholly separated from other experiences, but a particular way in which all reality is apprehended. It comes about most naturally in the mood of prayer or worship, but is by no means limited to stated times for these, either individually or collectively. Ordinarily religious experience has nothing to do with visions, ecstasies, raptures or other phenomena which are usually considered abnormal. It is true that some mystics have experienced these exalted states of consciousness or unconsciousness, but they are no part of *normative* religious experience.[1] It, on the contrary, is as unspectacular as breathing or sleeping. For most men and women religious experience has been a calm assurance of the reality of a relationship which gives meaning to existence.

The chief reason why the opinion has become current that religious experience is rare, and therefore of little evidential value, is that there has been a misunderstanding concerning

[1] Unusual mental states, such as "speaking with tongues," have frequently been minimized, even by those reporting them personally.

what is denoted by the term "religious experience." This misunderstanding has been created in large measure by certain writers, of whom Professor Leuba is characteristic, who have claimed to study the empirical phenomena of religion, but in doing so have limited their study to the *bizarre.* The result is that they have made the discipline known as the psychology of religion sound like a branch of abnormal psychology. Even William James in his brilliant book, *The Varieties of Religious Experience,* lent some credence to this interpretation or misinterpretation. Some critics have maintained that the only mistake James made, in this regard, was in the *title* of his famous book. The cases he presents are not really varieties, for they are all queer.

B. NORMATIVE RELIGIOUS EXPERIENCE

Interesting as may be the study of peculiar mental phenomena, that is no part of our present purpose. We are concerned with the logical structure of belief, and, for this purpose, we are interested in the unspectacular. This normative experience may be described by making certain definite propositions about it which are related to one another as steps in the progressive narrowing of the field.

(1) *Religious experience is perceptual.* By this we mean that experience, as reported, is not a matter of either speculation or imagination, but of something independent of the observer with which the observer has established contact. God might be either imagined or perceived, just as a tree might be imagined or perceived. We say the tree is perceived when the tree is experienced as external to the mind of the perceiver. Imagination is free to indulge in wishful thinking; perception is limited by the nature of the real as known. The point is that religious experience reports itself as so limited.

Perhaps it is necessary to remind the reader that perceptual and sensory are not identical concepts. Perception refers to a relation to an *object* and is thus distinct from *conception,* as well as from imagination. Sensation, on the other hand, refers to the kind of experience which comes through the instrumentality of end organs, of which ears and eyes are conspicuous examples. There can be nonperceptual sensation, as a blow on the head may easily demonstrate, and, unless normative religion is a delusion, there is a vast amount of non-sensory perception, i.e., real contact with a perceived object, *without* the instrumentality of the sensory end organs. If God is really known, as so many have claimed to know Him, it is clear that He is not known by means of our auditory, optic or tactual nerves. Sometimes the language of sense has been used in the reports of vivid religious experience, but nearly always such language is consciously figurative. This is well illustrated by the Psalmist's appeal, "O taste and see that the Lord is good." The very fact that men speak so often of an *inward* sense is evidence that they are not talking about the actual sensory apparatus. What they mean is that their awareness of God is *as vivid, as incontestable,* as any sensory experience ever is. One of the great seventeenth century interpreters of such experience attempted, in the following words, to tell his Dutch friend Heer Paets, what he meant by an "inward sense."

An example of an inward, supernatural sense is when the heart or soul of a pious man feels in itself divine motions, influences and operations, which sometimes are as the voice or speech of God, sometimes as a most pleasant and glorious illustration or visible object to the inward eye, sometimes as a most sweet savour or taste, sometimes as a heavenly and divine warmness or (so to speak) melting of the soul in the love of God.[2]

It would be stupid to minimize the value of expressions like those of Barclay on the ground that they are figures of speech. The more important any disclosure is, the more necessary figures of speech become. The necessity for figures of speech arises from the fact that intelligible language is used for the purpose

[2] Robert Barclay, *Truth Triumphant,* p. 897.

of making known what was formerly unknown, and this can only be done by establishing some similarity with what is already known. Thus we seek to make the experience of color understandable to the congenitally blind by comparing color with musical tone, though we are well aware that the two are not the same. Similarly, those who have tried to make religious experience understandable to others not conscious of it, have used the language of sense, while recognizing that it is not really sensory. They mean that it has the vividness, the certitude, the striking quality of that which impinges on ears, eyes, and other organs. An impressive testimony to this effect is that of Newman, when, speaking of his *inward conversion*, he affirmed years later that he was still more certain of it "than that I have hands and feet."[3]

It was, apparently, in an effort to emphasize the perceptual character of his own religious experience that the celebrated French mathematician, Blaise Pascal, used the word "Fire" in capital letters, as the central feature of the record of his life-shaking experience. This record, which Pascal's servant found sewed into the scholar's coat, at the time of his death, was made up largely of interjections, the normal language of assured contact. The word "Fire" was most emphasized, probably in the effort to show that what he perceived had about it the same indubitable quality that we find in the flame, which warms, lights, and even burns.

Perhaps there is need to remark in passing that when we speak of perception as *contact with an object*, we are not necessarily referring to a *physical* object. The object is that which is perceived, whatever it is. It would be both unphilosophical and unscientific to assert dogmatically that the only objects of perception are physical bodies. The kinds of object in which we must believe depend wholly on the kind of evidence which is available. The correct method is not to decide in advance whether or not there are nonphysical objects of perception, but

[3] John Henry Newman, *Apologia pro Vita Sua,* Everyman edition, p. 31.

rather to begin with the data of experience and wait to see to what conclusions we are led by the analysis of this experience.

(2) *Religious experience is cognitive,* in that it claims to be the kind of perception which gives the perceiver actual knowledge of God. In short it is possible, in religious experience, to go beyond Pascal's memorable hour, when there was certainty of contact, but little more. The prophets, in all generations, claim that their experience of God is such that they learn something about His nature, and His will for men. We are not discussing now the correctness of this knowledge, since such discussion should come later in this chapter; we are saying merely that the primary datum of religion includes a "knowledge claim."

Naturally it is not easy for men to tell others *what* they know, since language here becomes more inadequate than it ordinarily is, and poetry becomes inevitable, but this is not the important point. The point is that knowledge is claimed, though never perfect knowledge. The devout man in all generations says with St. Paul, "I know in part." It has long been recognized that men, in their knowledge of God, can touch no more than the hem of His garment. But to know in part, is to know something.

(3) *Religious experience is personal,* not in the sense that every devout man has consciously believed that God is a "Person," but that the experience characteristically recorded is of the kind which we normally associate with persons. The experience has about it, as aesthetic experience has, the augustness which we cannot expect contact with a mere "thing" to inspire. In many cases, and most strikingly in the experience of Jesus, the relationship is consciously personal. God is addressed in prayer as "O Father," and the second person is used when a pronoun is employed.

This personal aspect of religious experience becomes more clear when we note that what men try to describe is not so much a quest as a response to a revelation. If religion were a quest, we might seek our object as we seek a precious stone. All the personal qualities would be in *us*, not in the object sought and known. But it is not a mere quest. This seems to be the meaning of the ancient rhetorical question, "Canst thou by searching find out God?"[4]

Religion is not so much the thrill of discovery, as the awareness of being assaulted. The witness to this comes from testimonies as far apart as Francis Thompson's *Hound of Heaven* and Karl Barth's theology of crisis. Religion is not so much finding God, as reaction to the Reality which has found us. It is not so much man's bargain with God, as it is man's response to God's grace. But the point of all this, to which there is abundant testimony covering the greater part of three thousand years, is that this is the way we react to the tremendous, soul-stirring experience of *being loved. It is persons who do the loving*. Thus it is true to say that normative experience is personal, either explicitly or implicitly.

C. SUBJECT AND OBJECT

Assuming that the foregoing brief description of religious experience is sufficient for our present purposes, we can proceed to show the main structure of the argument based upon it. All that we know arises in experience. Our reason for believing that there is a physical order is the fact that millions of men report an experience of such an order. In a similar manner millions of men in all times and places have experienced God as the Sustainer of their lives. Therefore, God is.

The only reason for not accepting this forthright empirical evidence is the fact that experience can be delusory. Not everything that men experience exists. Two experiences given at a court trial and referring to the same event are sometimes contradictory. Though we cannot dispense with the ultimate appeal

[4] Job, 11:7.

to experience we cannot take experience at its face value. But this applies to sensory experience just as truly as it applies to religious experience. Why, then, are there so many who deny the evidential value of religious experience while they accept the evidential value of sensory experience? The fact that men may make mistakes about the interpretation of their sense perceptions does not lead the ordinary intelligent person to the conclusion that sense perception is a purely subjective affair, but the fact that some men have had religious experiences which we must regard as illusory has led a number of otherwise critical persons to the conclusion that religious experience is a purely subjective affair and no revelation of the real. It is indeed a curious leap to conclude, from the fact that men make mistakes, that there is no reality which they are making mistakes *about*.

This curious logic arises from an epistemological confusion, which in turn arises from an unrecognized metaphysical prejudice in favor of naturalism. Many theological writers have made the confusion easier by constantly referring to religion as an affair of the *inner* life. The consequence is that, for many, the serious question of the validity of religious experience is supposedly answered by pointing out that all religious experiences are mental—they are merely *in the mind*. How then, can they have evidential value? But all experiences are in the mind in this sense of the word. My perception of the bird in the tree is as much in my mind as is my perception of God. Strictly speaking every man is like Karl Pearson's imagined telephone operator, locked forever in his windowless exchange, but supplied with wires connecting him with what he takes to be an outside world. He cannot know for sure that there is an outside world at all. Even if he checks his messages by reference to the experience of another operator in another room, he has not escaped his "egocentric predicament" because this added evidence comes in what is merely another wire. Why should he trust his ideas about what purports to be a second operator any more than his ideas about the twentieth subscriber?

There are some persons who object to an empirical analysis which brackets sensory experience and religious experience, referring to the relation between them as an *analogy*. The facts to which we are now pointing show that this objection misses the mark. There is not an analogy between the two types of experience in regard to the subjective predicament; there is an *identity*. The notion that sensory experience has some advantage in certainty of objective reference turns out to be a mere superstition.

Many people appear to suppose that there is some *absolute* test of veracity in ordinary sense experience, but reflection shows that none exists. I see a flaw in the windowpane and the question arises whether this is just a figment of my imagination or is really there. Accordingly, I go over and touch the glass. But does this prove my original contention? All I have is another experience which, indeed, increases the presumptive value of my first observation, but I can never escape the circle of subjectivity.

When this particular confusion is dispelled the greatest barrier to a fair estimate of the situation is removed. To list an experience as inner or subjective is not sufficient to deny its objectivity, for on that ground there would be no objective world at all. Though all experiences are subjectively known, they may be *occasioned* by objective stimuli. Thus the assertion of subjectivity is no denial of objectivity. The chief question is the question of reference. Ideas *in the mind* may refer to what is *outside the mind*, in that it exists independently, so far as the individual mind is concerned. The concept of objectivity, one of the most advanced of which the human mind is capable, involves not only the ability to distinguish between the self which experiences and the world which is experienced, but also the ability to distinguish between what the experient wishes were the case, and what he is forced to believe is the case.

D. THE TESTS OF VERACITY

To know precisely what belongs to the objective order is a problem of the greatest difficulty, and one never fully solved in any extended area. We solve the problem, insofar as we solve it at all, not by the application of some special *means*, but rather by the humble process of noting converging lines of agreement with experience as known. If Karl Pearson's lonely telephone operator finds that fire alarms are coming in simultaneously on many of his wires and if the alarms refer to the same place, he is justified in believing that there really is a fire. When people, who differ in many ways, have substantial agreement about one item, we consider it more reasonable to posit objective status than to accept a miracle of coincidence. In this we may be wrong, but we have no suitable alternative.

The agreement, of course, must be of a particular kind to have any value. In testing the veracity of religious experience four tests are of especial importance.

(1) *Number of reporters.* Other things being equal an experience has more veracity if it is widely shared. One reason for doubting the objective status of the animals seen in *delirium tremens* is that those who see them are so badly outnumbered.

By the most conservative estimate the number of persons who have reported religious experience, not in the sense of ecstatic trance, and not in the sense of mere inference from the order of nature, but with a deep assurance of the divine undergirding, is many millions and, indeed, it is difficult to think of any similar data that are so numerous. The abundance of such reports in the Old and New Testament is enough to give us pause, but this is by no means the end of the story. When we think of the humble souls who have made their testimony in Christian lands in the intervening years, as well as many more quite outside the Christian tradition, we begin to see that we are dealing with one of the best attested experiences in the world. "The simple fact is," as Canon Raven has said, "that those who would explain away religion are hardly aware of the greatness of the task or of the qualifications necessary for it."[5]

The evidence upon which we can depend comes to us chiefly in three ways. (a) In the first place there is the vocal testimony, especially that which has appeared in gatherings similar to the Methodist "class meeting." Some of this can be discounted, especially when it follows the fashionable religious pattern of the day, but, taken as a whole, the vocal testimonies are so numerous and so sincere that it is impossible for a reasonable person to dismiss them as unworthy of attention.

(b) A second source of evidence is found in literary records, especially those of spiritual autobiography. This material, as is well known, is an important part of our literature from Augustine's *Confessions* to Newman's *Apologia* and beyond.[6] Even the Quaker journals alone make an impressive showing *and all of them were writen in order to provide the very data with which we are here concerned.*

(c) If these two sources were the only ones the evidence would be impressive, but they do not exhaust the data. The experiences of most people cannot be known by their own direct report, since they are too modest or are lacking in facility of expression. Accordingly we must learn what their experience is from the worship in which they share, the reading which they prize, and the prayers to which they turn for the expression of their own devotional life. Thus the Hebrew Psalms tell us something, not merely about the experience of the few persons who originally composed them, but chiefly about the experience of the millions, of all creeds, who have found in the Psalms the best expression of what they would like to say and cannot. The satisfaction found in the use of hymns, many of which are forthright testimonies to divine acquaintance, gives us similar evidence. The testimony implicit in prayer is similarly great.

[5] Charles E. Raven, *Jesus and the Gospel of Love,* London, 1931, p. 73.

[6] Reliable modern studies of this rich deposit are available in Gaius Glenn Atkins' *Pilgrims of the Lonely Road*, and Willard L. Sperry's Lowell Lectures, *Strangers and Pilgrims.*

We cannot know how many pray, but all will agree that the number is enormous. Anyone who believes in prayer is bearing witness thereby to direct contact between the human and the divine, inasmuch as God is supposed to hear our prayers. Of course this relationship need not be mutual, but the chief reasons for denying the objective reality of what devout men experience is already overcome, if there is the real contact which prayer entails.

Any thorough study of the number of the reports must include some reference to the fact that the report is not universal in the human race. There is not space here for an exhaustive treatment of this matter, but two relevant points can be made briefly. One is that *no* human experience, not even sight, is strictly universal, for experience depends in part on receptive powers. The higher we go, as in music for example, the less universal experience is. The other point is that failure to report experience has no evidential value, *unless* the individual concerned has met the appropriate conditions. The testimony of those who have not met the requirements has no logical weight and need not be seriously considered, whatever their qualifications in other ways. *The religious opinions of the unreligious are no more valuable than are the scientific opinions of the unscientific.*

(2) *The quality of the reporters* is more important than the numbers. Great numbers are not sufficient unless they include those who have qualitative fitness. The majority has frequently been wrong. Is there a substantial body of evidence coming from sensitive men, who are in command of their faculties, and properly qualified, on both moral and intellectual grounds, so that they inspire trust in that to which they bear testimony? We want to be sure of a substantial body of men and women of sufficiently good character not to engage in deliberate deceit and of sufficiently critical intelligence not to be self-deceived.

The answer is that there is a substantial body of evidence which meets these qualifications. That the great majority of reporters have been honest needs little support. It is not credible that the increase in personal effectiveness and power would come if men were consciously deceiving others in what they say on the deepest questions. This personal effectiveness is recognized even by those who reject the evidential value of the testimony. Furthermore, no serious reader can look at the written testimony of men like Pascal, Newman, and Fox and suppose that these men were engaged in a grand hoax.

The more important question concerns the sanity of the reporters and their capacity to resist delusion. Even if men are *honest*, their testimony is valueless if they are easily deluded. But the fact is that the reports come from a number of the most critical and sane persons the world has known, providing we use any standard test of sanity and critical power. How disturbing the testimony of Rufus M. Jones must be to those who want to equate mysticism with pathological states. All who know Dr. Jones recognize in him one of the most sane men alive. How disturbing the testimony of the late Professor Bennett of Yale must be, to those who seek to equate religious experience with gullibility. Professor Bennett's distinguished volumes, *A Philosophical Study of Mysticism* and *The Dilemma of Religious Knowledge*, indicate a mind which can out-criticize the critics.

The only way to avoid the weight of such testimony is to make religious experience an *evidence* of an unbalanced mind, but that is to beg the question in a flagrant manner. It is obviously true that some of those who have reported vivid religious experience have been mentally unbalanced, but this situation is by no means peculiar to religion. There are unbalanced people in every field. If some necessary connection between mental aberrations and religious experience could be demonstrated, the credibility of witnesses would be undermined, but no such demonstration is forthcoming. Undoubtedly there are some truths revealed to eccentrics which are hidden from the normal and prudent, but the overwhelming majority of those who participate in prayer are so sane as to be almost uninteresting. That is why their testimony so seldom finds its way into psychology books.

(3) *The agreement of the reports* is our third test of veracity. Even if the reports are numerous, and the reporters persons of proven integrity as well as critical judgment, the evidence is not good unless there is fundamental agreement in what is said. Part of the reason for doubting the objective reference to the animals "seen" by patients suffering from *delirium tremens* is that two or more patients do not "see" the same snakes.

Upon a superficial view, it is easy to conclude that the reports of the religious consciousness are more remarkable for their diversity than for their convergence. This conclusion is strengthened by the development of many sects. As we consider the matter carefully, however, we discover that the obvious differences, so easily recognized by the populace, refer chiefly to matters of organization and liturgical details, on the one hand, and to differences of creed on the other. It is when we concentrate on the actual record of experience that we are struck with the great degree of convergence in the testimony. There is, indeed, the most distressing divergency on all questions *about* religion, but not in the experience *of* religion. To use William James' familiar distinction, that on which men have argued is "knowledge about," and that on which they have agreed is "acquaintance with." The conclusion to which James came as a result of his long empirical inquiry was that there is "a certain composite photograph of universal saintliness, the same in all religions, of which the features can easily be traced."[7]

Such conclusions are enforced by a simple experiment. Take a number of records of direct religious experience, read them to listeners, putting all into the same tongue, and see what success the listeners have in separating and locating them. In many cases there is no way to identify the reports at all, and

[7] William James, *The Varieties of Religious Experience*, p. 271.

an ancient Hindu testimony is sometimes mistaken for a modern Christian testimony. "We need not trouble ourselves to ask," writes Dr. Inge, "and we could seldom guess without asking, whether a paragraph describing the highest spiritual experiences was written in the Middle Ages or in modern times, in the north or south of Europe, by a Catholic or by a Protestant."[8] As a specific test we may submit the following testimony:

And he hath many times refreshed my soul in his presence, and given me assurance that I knew that estate in which He will never leave me, nor suffer me to be drawn from all which he has graciously fulfilled; for though various infirmities and temptations beset me, yet my heart cleaveth unto the Lord, in the everlasting bonds that cannot be broken.

The saints all tell the same story and this is the story they tell. It is hard to see how this impressive agreement can be accounted for apart from the hypothesis that the object to which so many severally point is a genuine one.

(4) *The fourth and final test of the veracity of religious experience is the difference it makes.* It is not necessary to be a pragmatist in order to recognize that the pragmatic test is one among others. That there has been a new quality of life in countless persons as a result of religious experience is beyond serious doubt.

In religion we cannot reasonably look for a mark on photographic plates, but we can reasonably look for a mark on human lives. If the experience of God is what men claim it is, we should expect to see a general change in their character; we should expect them to walk with a new step. It is this that we can check abundantly in a way that should be convincing to the open-minded. The evidence of altered lives, including both new strength and new tenderness, is so great that only a small portion of it has ever been committed to print. Not all of those who have reported religious experience have demonstrated "the fruits of the spirit," but, in considering evidence

[8] W. R. Inge, *Studies of English Mystics*, p. 35.

of this kind, we are concerned not so much with what is universal as with what is typical. We can show the typical verification through moral strength, by pointing to characteristic experiences in different settings.

The sense of God's presence has been sufficient to make men courageous in the face of persecution, to sensitize their consciences to social wrong, such as that of slavery and poverty, and, above all, has suffused entire lives with joy. It was this last point, as noted earlier, which the scientific mind of Romanes was unable to explain away.

The pragmatic test of the veracity of religious experience has seldom been more vividly illustrated than in the letters of German pastors, which have been written in concentration camps during the last few dreadful years. The following expressions are characteristic:

"I cannot tell you how thankful I am for the inner experience I have been permitted to have in these days. Though I walk through the valley of the shadow, I fear no evil, for Thou art with me. This presence of God in such a situation becomes even now a precious reality. And how good it is that our faith may now manifest itself really as faith, not merely in words, but in deeds and in the attitude in which we stand ready to take upon ourselves unpleasantness for the sake of the faith, if God thus permits it that men oppress us for our faith's sake. No one will be able to say any more what formerly in foolishness was sometimes said: He merely talks that way because he is paid for it . . .

"God's ways are wonderful. And where He leads through dark ways, there one experiences his glory most. And again and again the experience is repeated: 'You thought to bring evil upon me, but God thought to turn it to good.' I am sure that all this, too, which we are now going through will serve 'only more for the furtherance of the gospel' in our congregation, without the congregation's needing to get into unwise (im-

prudent or reckless) agitation if our church services are for-
bidden.

"God has thrown us Christian people in our church to-day
out of all safe nests, out of all the nests of earthly security and
human calculations and plans, cast us out as it were into emptiness, into nothingness. In sudden shock and terror we may have
felt sometimes in these years as if we were plunging into a
bottomless abyss, sinking away into nothingness. What are we
now to do? Now we must fly if we do not want to be borne
away by the storms of oppression into the yawning chasms of
despair. But if we only really learn to believe, yes, learn really
to believe in God, and in firm belief and trusting prayer spread
our wings, then we shall experience—and how many times in
these years we have already experienced it with amazement and
awe—that we do not sink away; there is a power there which
holds us, we are borne by God's eternal father-arms, we are
sustained in the storms."[9]

What can we say in the face of testimonies so tremendous,
testimonies repeated in so many generations? Drugs and delu-
sions may sustain men for a time, but here is something which
wears out all opposition. It makes weak men bold and proud
men humble. Words seem impertinent and silence the only
adequate response. If that which sustains men and makes them
praise God in both bright and dark hours be not reality, where
is reality to be found?

Thus we see that the empirical evidence for the hypothesis
of God as real is the strongest evidence of all. It is the most
difficult to escape, especially in a scientific age when experience
is respected. We need, however, to integrate this evidence with
the other evidence which comes from our knowledge of nature
and of our own being. The full strength of each line of evidence appears, not in isolation, but in conjunction.

[9] From *Und Lobten Gott*, private translation of my colleague, Helena Nye.
The Student Christian Movement has brought out a translation, *I Was in
Prison*.

The conclusion to which we are driven is that in religion we have a situation in which the evidence of objectivity is even better than it is in natural science because the corroboration comes from such a long time and from such widely separated areas. The miracle of coincidence is so great that it is bound to be unacceptable to thoughtful persons. Yet what other alternative is there unless belief in God as objectively real is accepted? Herein lies part of the deep significance of the ancient saying that it is hard to believe, but harder still to disbelieve.

CHAPTER XIII

THE APPEAL TO HISTORY

"When we take history seriously, we shall find that we cannot regard religion as projection or illusion."　　　　—H. G. WOOD

Though the types of experience analyzed in the four chapters immediately preceding this one may be regarded as providing an adequate verification of the hypothesis we are examining, there are other types of data which are relevant and consequently must not be neglected. These supplementary means of verification are not sufficient to stand alone but, when related to the types of evidence already adduced, contribute to the total cumulative effect. The most important considerations of this kind are concerned, in some way or other, with history.

A. THE WITNESS OF HISTORICAL PERSONS

One such auxiliary evidence is that already outlined in Chapter V, in connection with the principle of authority. Our modern boast that we have outgrown the age of reliance on authority is sheer delusion. All things considered, there probably has never been a time when the authority of the expert loomed so high as it does now. Striking examples of such reliance are to be seen in medicine and in natural science. This reliance on the judgment of the expert, far from being anything of which we should be ashamed, is a mark of intelligence. Not only do we actually trust those who have better opportunity to know and who have shown themselves trustworthy, but we *ought* to do so. Otherwise, our life is impoverished.

There is no necessity of a full account of the argument here, since it has already received treatment in this book; but it is important, at this point, to show the relationship of the argument to the entire logical process upon which we are engaged. Nature, morality, aesthetic experience and religious experience are four separate witnesses who independently tell the same story; and this, as we have seen earlier, is what is meant by proof, which is always approximate. These make it reasonable for *us* to believe. But if we find, at the same time, that others actually do believe and that among these others are persons whose judgment we trust before our own, our private belief is greatly strengthened. This would be particularly true if those whose personal belief strengthens ours were acknowledged experts in the field of religion. The ground of their expertness would be their personal discipline, and the evidence of their expertness would be their standing in the eyes of their fellow experts. That it is possible to be an expert in the highest reaches of the spiritual life, as truly as in medicine or chemistry, will hardly be doubted, though the qualifications in each case are strikingly different.

The corroboration of our private belief by the belief of others sometimes takes the form of an appeal to the *consensus* of mankind. It is indeed true that the universality of religious belief in all races and periods known to us is an impressive fact and one that no sensitive person will be likely to dismiss lightly, but it does not impress us nearly so much as does the testimony of the few highly qualified experts, since the populace has often been wrong.

Now there is little doubt that the overwhelming majority of those generally considered religious experts have been believers in the sense defined earlier, and this is not because we beg the question by denying in advance the expertness of the unbelievers. There have, in fact, been religious experts who did not believe in God. So far as we can tell, this was the situation in which Gautama Buddha found himself. To take a modern illustration, Thomas Huxley had many of the qualifications mentioned in Chapter V as those of disciplined insight in the spiritual life, and yet he was not a conscious believer in the being of God. Romanes was already worthy of being called an expert while he was an unbeliever, though he later became a believer. We do not need to make any laborious tabulation, however, to see that such men constitute a distinct minority. The roster of those who have believed deeply and who have been worthy of the highest respect is long, and so illustrious that it must give pause to any thoughtful person. This is not proof, for good and great men have been wrong, but it is impressive corroboration.

It was this kind of corroboration which was used with such telling effect by the unknown author of the Epistle to the Hebrews in the famous eleventh chapter of that Letter. We are told, in a great crescendo, of the faith of Abraham, of Isaac, of Jacob, of Joseph, of Moses, and many more. Then comes the beginning of the moving climax: "And what shall I say more? For the time would fail me to tell of Gideon, and of Barak, and of Samson, and of Jephthah; of David also, and Samuel, and of the prophets." In like manner the modern apologist may well say, "For time would fail me to tell of Plato, and of St. Francis, and of Butler, and of Kant; of scholars, of apostles, and of martyrs." The list is long indeed.

Since we rely on genius in other fields, why should we not do so in religion? "It is impossible to see," writes Von Hügel, "why Plato, Aristotle, Leibnitz and Kant, and why again Phidias and Michelangelo, Raphael and Rembrandt, Bach and Beethoven, Homer and Shakespeare, are to be held in deepest gratitude, as revealers respectively of various kinds of reality and truth, if Amos and Isaiah, Paul, Augustine and Aquinas, Francis of Assisi and Joan of Arc are to be treated as pure illusionists, in precisely what constitutes their specific greatness."[1]

There is little doubt that this is the kind of evidence that is

[1] Baron Friedrich von Hügel, *Essays and Addresses on the Philosophy of Religion*, p. 38.

effective in practice, and it is especially effective when it is applied to the testimony of Jesus Christ. Here is the one who has most won the allegiance of men, so that all over the world men now live in the *Christian era*. Whatever our explanation of his unique appeal, there is no doubting the fact. Many who reject Christianity respond sympathetically to the teachings and career of Christ Himself. There is good reason to suppose that He plumbed the depths of the human spirit more fully than any who has ever lived. As the Fourth Evangelist so cryptically puts it, "He knew what was in man."[2]

The truth is that this Person, whom there is so much reason to trust, believed implicitly in the existence of God as His Father. This is attested in many ways in the Gospel narrative, but most convincingly in the use of the second person in prayer. "I thank *thee*, O Father." There is here none of the circumlocution which appears so prominently in the popular jargon of our time. So far as we know, he did not refer to "That great force whom men call God." The strong conviction about the reality of God's rule permeates all Christ's teaching and is the occasion of most of the parables. He turned to God in prayer as naturally as He turned to food when hungry or to men when lonely.

Whatever doubt was ever entertained about the historicity of Jesus is now allayed by the development of modern scholarship. There was a time when it was freely suggested that Christ was a mythical person, but such a suggestion is now out of date. Professor Henry J. Cadbury of Harvard, in his Lowell Lectures, *The Peril of Modernizing Jesus,* shows how modern historical and Biblical research, while they have undermined many preconceived notions of Jesus, have had the positive effect of making the actual historicity of Jesus more clear than ever before. We are fortunate in having, from the pen of Professor H. G. Wood of the University of Birmingham, a careful summary of the evidence for the historicity of Jesus in the volume,

[2] John, 2:25.

Did Christ Really Live?[3] The net result of years of co-operative New Testament study is well described by Professor Dodd in words as careful as the labor they summarize. "What matters most," he writes, "is that the more critical our study has been, the more sure we become that here is a real Person in history, many-sided, often perplexing, certainly too great to be reduced to any common type, and not fully intelligible to us; but, for all that, unmistakably individual, strongly defined in lines of character and purpose, and challenging us all by a unique outlook on life."[4]

When we think of the inexhaustibility of the character of Christ, of the mystery of His personality which has drawn so many men of letters to the task of retelling His life, we are not surprised that what He believed about God is still an important factor in contemporary belief. The fact that He lived long ago does not lessen the weight of His testimony, since there is no reason to suppose that the modern man has any advantage in the understanding of the deepest things. Perhaps the modern man has a genuine disadvantage, in view of the confusion of his life. In any case, countless people are influenced in their belief by the fact that Jesus believed. What is the chance, they ask, that He was wrong in that area of judgment in which He was most qualified and by which He set the greatest store? And the point we are making is that, from the point of view of logical theory, the corroboration of belief thus achieved is valid. To pay attention to the witness of the expert, and especially to the witness of the Supreme Expert, is not a sign of weakness or credulity, but a sign of rationality. If our grand hypothesis is true, it is reasonable to expect widespread belief among persons of spiritual sensibility, and above all, we should expect profound belief on the part of Jesus Christ. This is precisely what we do find.

[3] Published by the Student Christian Movement Press, London, 1938. For an equally reliable earlier volume on the subject, see Shirley Jackson Case, *The Historicity of Jesus,* University of Chicago Press, 1912.

[4] C. H. Dodd, *The Authority of the Bible,* New York, 1929, pp. 230, 231.

B. THE EVIDENCE OF HISTORICAL DEVELOPMENT

In spite of the fact that the chief roots of religion, at least so far as Western civilization is concerned, are found in Palestine, we have shown a curious reluctance to follow the spiritual genius of ancient Palestine in the intellectual support of religious faith. Among the conventional arguments for the existence of God, some, such as the cosmological argument and the teleological argument, are Greek, and some, such as the moral argument, are modern, but none is Hebraic or even early Christian. For long there has been a division of labor between Hebraism and Hellenism, with Palestine furnishing the inspiration in religion and Greece furnishing the intellectual superstructure. This has been true to such a degree that we experience mild surprise when we note the logic of belief which appealed to men in the ancient Hebrew tradition and in the beginnings of Christianity.

The chief evidence for the existence of Yahweh, according to His worshipers, was their own history. "Look at the record, and see for yourself," they said over and over. They were a despised people in bondage in Egypt, but Yahweh helped them to go free. He raised up leaders, while they were still a feeble folk, led them through the wilderness, helped them to cross the Jordan and set up their homes in a goodly land, in spite of violent opposition. Finally He aided them in establishing a kingdom of their own. In all this they were sure they had been guided to do better than they could have done for themselves. Of all of this the Exodus was the grand central symbol, and they were convinced that it was a sheer miracle of deliverance. Such people had no need of recourse to arguments such as the Greek thinkers encouraged, and the Israelites would probably have considered such arguments abstract or even tiresome. What was the need of arguing about your God if you could see that He had helped you?

This historical appeal is perhaps the chief key to the understanding of the Old Testament. It is no accident that so many of the books of the Hebrew Scripture are *historical*, since the entire compilation was originally conceived as a history of Yahweh's dealing with His people. In view of modern literary criticism we recognize that we owe the very existence of the Bible to the Hebrew notion that the crowning evidence of the being of God is to be found in history. The Bible as a whole is very little concerned with *ideas*, but very greatly concerned with *events*. There happens to be only one book specifically called "Acts," but the word could fairly be applied to most of the Old Testament and to the Gospels. "The crucial truths revealed in the Bible," writes President Mackay in a remarkable chapter, "are not timeless truths about God and man; they are rather historical truths, truths regarding events which took place in time but which were invested by God with eternal significance."[5]

Eventually the story was made to reach back to the origin of the earth and its inhabitants, but the most important part of the story covers only a few hundred years, reaching its climax in the glorious reigns of David and Solomon. Later events, dealing with exile and restoration, were naturally added to complete the story, while the books of the prophets furnished side lights on these events. The poetical and wisdom works were thrown in for good measure, on the supposition that they had been produced in the period before the decline of prophecy.

The history of Israel, as understood by the Israelites themselves, was far from a smooth progress to victory or success. On the contrary, this history was full of backsliding, disloyalty, and deceit. But those who heard and retold the story for posterity thought they could discern the guiding hand of God, chastising His people for unbelief and wickedness, and giving ultimate reward for faithful devotion. Thus the book of Deuteronomy makes Moses say:

Thou hast seen how that the Lord thy God bare thee, as a man

[5] John Mackay, *A Preface to Christian Theology*, New York, 1941, p. 93.

doth bear his son, in all the way that ye went, until ye came to this place.

Yet in this thing ye did not believe the Lord your God, who went in the way before you to search you out a place to pitch your tents, in fire by night, to show you by what way ye should go and in a cloud by day.

And the Lord heard the voice of your words, and was wroth, and sware, saying, Surely there shall not one of these men of this evil generation see that good land, which I sware to give unto your fathers, save Caleb the son of Jephunneh; he shall see it, and to him will I give the land that he hath trodden upon, and to his children, because he hath wholly followed the Lord.[6]

This might be very well for people who were in the midst of the deliverance as the associates of Moses were, but what about succeeding generations? When they should become curious, what kind of interpretation or apologetic should be given them to convince them? The answer was a simple one: Tell the old story again.

Then shalt thou say unto thy son, We were Pharaoh's bondmen in Egypt; and the Lord brought us out of Egypt with a mighty hand! And the Lord showed signs and wonders, great and sore, upon Egypt, upon Pharaoh, and upon all his household, before our eyes!

And he brought us out from thence, that he might bring us in, and give us the land which he sware unto our fathers.[7]

Here is a philosophy of history according to which events are shot through with purpose and with meaning. History is a theater of moral judgment, and the entire process points to the presence of a Guiding Hand. It was too wonderful, they supposed, to have happened otherwise.

Partly, no doubt, because they were still so largely under Hebrew influences, the earliest defenders of the truth of Christianity emphasized events rather than abstract ideas, sometimes speaking slightingly of the latter. It is interesting, in this con-

[6] Deuteronomy, 1:31-36.
[7] Deuteronomy, 6:21-23.

nection, to note the form of the defense of the first Christian martyr. Stephen began with the ancient story: "Men, brethren and fathers, hearken; The God of glory appeared unto our father Abraham, when he was in Mesopotamia."[8] And so the apology proceeds, telling always what God *did* for His people, ending with the coming of Christ and His rejection at the hand of Stephen's hearers. Paul of Tarsus, though obviously well educated as a man of the world, used the same kind of apologetic when he gave his great sermon at Antioch. "Men of Israel," he began, "The God of this people of Israel chose our fathers, and exalted the people when they dwelt as strangers in the land of Egypt, and with an high arm brought he them out of it."[9] Again the story was brought to a climax with the life, death, and resurrection of Christ. It is instructive to note that so great a portion of the Apostles' Creed deals with events which the creed asserts to have taken place.[10]

As we today consider this particular form of theological evidence, we are perplexed. We cannot think lightly of such an interpretation of history, but it seems to us that the ancient Hebrews were guilty of a vast simplification of the stream of events. Actually it is not so easy to see the marks of Providence in historical movements. Even though God may be conceived as using evil movements to serve as scourges and enforce a lesson, it is hard to see why the lesson goes on so long in some areas. The present is a particularly difficult time in this regard.

It was one of the very great marks of intellectual integrity in Cardinal Newman that he freely confessed his difficulties, and he reported that he felt especial difficulty on the subject of Providence. In the last chapter of his *Apologia*, Newman has a famous passage, conceivably the longest sentence in modern

[8] Acts, 7:2.
[9] Acts, 13:16, 17.
[10] I have dealt with the general subject somewhat less inadequately in an article, "Christianity as Idea and as Event," published in *Religion in Life*, Volume IX (Spring, 1940).

English, and therefore too long to quote, in which he expresses his sense of bafflement as he looks at the story of mankind. There may, he says, be tokens of a superintending design, but they are "tokens so faint and broken." At the conclusion he asks, "What shall be said to this heart-piercing, reason-be-wildering fact? I can only answer, that either there is no Creator, or this living society of men is in a true sense discarded from His presence."

Though all thoughtful people are bound to share, in vary-ing degrees, Newman's bewilderment, there is an important sense in which the theological claim of support from history is valid. It is no wonder that the Hebrews looked upon their sur-vival as an evidence of God's being and care. They *did survive* and have had a continuous existence to this day, whereas their contemporaries among the nations were lost, one by one. In view of the fact that it was through this people that the amaz-ing development of prophecy took place and that it was among this people that Christ was born, the conviction that a special people was kept alive for a special purpose is far from absurd. In one of his famous conversations, Disraeli was asked what reason he had to believe in God, and his reply was as brief as it was prompt. "The Jews," he said.[11] His answer has some-times been considered flippant, but it was not. "The Jews have survived as a nation," Professor Wood has reminded us, "not through faith in themselves, but through trust in God."[12]

We must remind ourselves that such a meaning in history, like any meaning, cannot be observed unless we look at long periods of time. The Jews have suffered terribly, but in the long run their faith has saved them. If we look at history in the large, there seems to be a real connection between sin and disaster on the one hand, and between faith and victory on the other. If this is true at all, we have new evidence that our world

[11] A similar story is told of the circle of Frederick the Great.
[12] H. G. Wood, *Christianity and the Nature of History*, p. 128.

is more than a set of mechanical forces and is indeed a Labora-tory of Purpose.

An example of how Providence may be seen in the long run, though it is not always evident in the short run, is seen also in the triumph of Christianity. That the Christian movement could have succeeded, so that the humble men who fished on the shores of the Sea of Galilee are today better known and more admired than the very Caesars who ruled the world of which their province was a despised part, is so amazing as to be incredible if we did not know it to be the case.

Frequently we can see a reason for events after they have occurred, though they are most baffling when we are in the midst of them. Even bad situations can serve good ends; good fruit does grow on evil trees. It is sobering to each succeeding generation of Americans, since the Civil War, to read the words in which Abraham Lincoln bore such eloquent witness to his own conviction that the hand of God can be seen in historical events.

If we shall suppose that American slavery is one of those offenses which, in the providence of God, must needs come, but which, having continued through His appointed time, He now wills to re-move, and that He gives to both North and South this terrible war, as the woe due to those by whom the offense came, shall we discern therein any departure from those divine attributes which the be-lievers in a living God always ascribe to Him?

There was a time when it seemed preposterous to suggest that a series of events which once occurred in Palestine might be of cosmic significance. That time is now gone; in our day we have come to have a reawakening to the revelatory value of history. The very conception of historical progress is a creation of Christianity, strikingly different from the cyclical conceptions which were dominant in the Greek and Roman world before the formulation of Christian thought. The specifically Chris-tian interpretation of history is that which stresses the dramatic character of events, and we now live in days which lend credence to this interpretation.[13]

In the philosophical tradition which was dominant in British and American reflective thought prior to the growth of realism in the twentieth century, time was something to be explained away. How much simpler the world is if it is transformed into a timeless reality in which succession is forgotten! The flux is so much easier to contemplate if it is treated as stationary. But absolute idealism escapes admission of the genuineness and irreducibility of the temporal experience only by recourse to what Professor Lovejoy has called "dialectical hocus-pocus."

One of the most curious phases of the former tendency to deny the ultimacy of temporality, by transmuting it into eternality, was the supposition that this somehow provided a support for religious belief. But whatever effect it had on the hope of immortality, it took away one of the chief means by which the reality of God is driven home to us here and now, the evidence of a persistent and unfolding Purpose, manifesting itself in time. The realistic insistence on time helps to provide an intellectual atmosphere in which the Judeo-Christian tradition is at home.

It is important to remember that the considerations put forward in this chapter do not stand alone, but must be understood in conjunction with the kinds of evidence presented in the chapters immediately preceding. "The truth of our religion, like the truth of common matters," said Butler, "is to be judged by all the evidence taken together."[14]

[13] Such an interpretation has been supported by Alfred Toynbee, in a monumental work, *A Study of History.*

[14] Joseph Butler, *The Analogy of Religion,* II, vii.

Part IV

DIFFICULTIES OF BELIEF

CHAPTER XIV

THE PROBLEM OF NATURAL SELECTION

"Philosophy means keeping hold of the main certainty, while going into all the difficulties." —BERNARD BOSANQUET

Now for the difficulties of belief and especially the difficulties of religious belief! The method we are following demands that we face, with intellectual honesty, any negative evidence that we can discover, as well as any problems relating to the positive evidence already presented.

That there are genuine difficulties in the path of theistic belief is not surprising. Butler's great principle that probability is the guide of life, a principle which we have seen reason to accept as true, has a number of important corollaries, one of which is the recognition that *no ultimate belief is likely to be free from difficulties and objections.* Along with the reasons *for* believing there are always some reasons *against* believing. This is true even of the Copernican hypothesis.

Since we cannot expect to find any ultimate position proved beyond a shadow of doubt, or utterly free from difficulties, our path of wisdom lies in a fair and honest comparison of the difficulties of rival systems. We have already noted some of the very considerable difficulties inherent in a naturalistic system; we should now face with equal frankness the difficulties inherent in theistic realism. Since the latter is the view which we see most reason to believe, we should face its difficulties in greater detail.

A recognition of the inevitability of difficulty makes the philosophical student careful about throwing over one belief until he has sought to discover whether there may be still more formidable difficulties involved in the alternative belief or beliefs. Accordingly it is quite possible for strong and intelligent belief to continue *in spite of* some objections. One of the many memorable utterances of Cardinal Newman bears directly on this observation, when he says, "Of all points of faith, the being of a God is, to my own apprehension, encompassed with the most difficulty, and borne in upon our minds with most power."[1] The notion that great believers, like Hooker or Butler or Newman, have been blindly credulous is far from the truth. They have felt certain difficulties, quite as vividly as atheists have felt them, but this does not mean that they have doubted the rationality of their belief. The positive evidence has been so great that the difficulties have been put in the minor place where they belong.

It is in the light of such principles that we examine certain problems in the next four chapters. The mere existence of the difficulties is not itself conclusive, but each must be examined separately to see what part it plays in the computation of the weight of evidence. Some difficulties turn out, on examination, to be trivial, and others more serious than they appear at first. Because of its historical importance, the problem of natural selection is the subject of the first of these four chapters.

A. THE DARWINIAN HYPOTHESIS

Of all the difficulties which hinder full acceptance of our grand hypothesis, the notion of natural selection is one of the most insistent and widespread. For countless honest people this helps to produce the reaction known as "yes, but." The evidence from nature and from the various aspects of man's higher life appears to be good evidence, but what if there is some principle which undermines it all, takes away the suppositions on which such evidence is based, and, consequently, makes it irrelevant? That the principle of natural selection is such a principle is widely supposed.

---

[1] John Henry Newman, *Apologia pro Vita Sua,* Everyman's Edition, p. 216.

It must not be supposed that the stumbling block we have in mind is the sense of conflict between the biblical stories of creation and the conceptions of the early history of our planet which have been drawn from a combination of geological and biological studies. There is no evidence that this conflict is widely or deeply felt. Whatever may have been the opinion in the past, the weight of opinion now is that the two accounts are not contradictory, or need not be. The biblical account may be respected for what it is—a brilliant insight concerning the probable order of creation,[2] and a statement of the profound faith that all natural objects find their ultimate explanation in supernatural Reality. The scientific account may be respected for what it is—a highly intelligent speculation on what occurred long ago, based on careful study of what can be observed in the contemporary world. There is no contradiction between the belief that the explanation of our earthly home is a purpose in the Mind of God and the belief that the first step in the development of our earth was the breakup of a star. If what we thus speculate actually occurred, it is not unreasonable to interpret the breakup of the star as part of the means by which the divine purpose was achieved.

All this seems so obvious to us that we have difficulty in believing that intelligent and competent men ever felt any real conflict. Yet we know that in the years immediately following the publication of Darwin's *Origin of Species*, there was a great uproar. But are we so sure that the uproar was about Genesis and evolution? As is well known, evolutionary theory is very ancient and was therefore known to educated men before 1858. It looks as though the uproar were somehow connected with

[2] The conception of creation given in the first chapter of Genesis is far from the naïve one it is vulgarly supposed to be. The wonder is not that it differs from the contemporary scientific account, but that the scientific account follows it so closely. It presents *light* as the first form of physical existence; it advances from the inorganic to the organic; it makes the appearance of man a late development in the process. The crucial points are seen to be three: the beginning of all things, the coming of *life*, and the coming of man's mind. These we see today as the greatest marks of discontinuity.

Darwinism rather than with *evolutionism* in general. Since Darwinism means chiefly natural selection, it will be helpful to see the argument for this principle in outline form. The main steps are:

(1) All plants and animals are engaged in a struggle for existence. The number of individuals born is, in every generation, much larger than the number who survive.

(2) Variations occur in all species.

(3) Some variations are well adapted to the situations in which species are, and others are not well adapted.

(4) Since most cannot survive, only the better adapted survive. Superior varieties ultimately extirpate the original species.

(5) The better adapted who survive, pass their special characteristics on to their descendants.

(6) New variations occur in the descendants and the process of natural selection continues.

It has been hard for any of the expositors of Darwinism to improve on Darwin's own summary in two sentences:

As many more individuals of each species are born than can possibly survive, and as, consequently, there is frequently recurring struggle for existence, it follows that any being, if it vary however slightly in any manner profitable to itself, under the complex and sometimes varying conditions of life, will have a better chance of surviving, and thus be naturally selected. From the strong principle of inheritance any selected variety will tend to propagate its new and modified form.

There can be little doubt of the immense appeal of this chain of reasoning. It brings simplicity and order into a vast realm of phenomena and seems, in great measure, to be nothing other than a combination of known facts. As stated by both Wallace and Darwin, in their studies produced independently in 1858, the theory seems actually *modest*. Professor Wallace's original conclusion does not seem startling: "We believe we have now shown that there is a tendency in nature to the continued progression of certain classes of *varieties* further and further from the original type—a progression to which there appears no reason to assign any definite limits."[3] "I am convinced," wrote Darwin at the end of the Introduction to his most famous work, "that natural selection has been the most important, but not the exclusive, means of modification."

In spite of this apparently modest beginning, the principle of natural selection was given the widest application, and gained popular appeal through Mr. Spencer's equivalent expression, "The Survival of the Fittest." It was an easy step for disciples to go beyond Darwin and hold that natural selection was the *exclusive means* of modification, and it was similarly easy, in spite of Wallace's explicit disapproval, to include all the higher life of man in the phenomena explained by the principle. Moreover the influence of Herbert Spencer, with his easy talk about *cosmic* evolution, made the application of the principle to the inorganic realm a natural one.

If we can bridge the gap between species, i.e., the different levels of the organic world, why can we not bridge, by the same means, the gap between the inorganic and the organic? Perhaps the first "life" was merely a spontaneous variation in some complex substance, a variation which was "better adapted" and therefore survived. Since the laws which regulate the production of a new species give as little evidence of conscious design as do the laws of chemistry, the unity of all phenomena seems to be a reality—a unity not of substance but of law and process. Moreover, since the value of undesigned variations can, supposedly, be applied to purely psychical factors, that which is *superior* to the organic seems to be brought within the system, just as does that which is inferior to the organic. Thus "biological evolution" becomes the key to *all* evolution, and the

---

[3] Alfred Russel Wallace, *Natural Selection and Tropical Nature*, London, 1891, p. 33.

doctrine enunciated by Darwin has the widest metaphysical significance.

B. THE DARWINIAN CONTROVERSY

There is hardly any chapter in our intellectual history which needs a more careful re-examination than that which deals with the Darwinian controversy. Unfortunately there is now a stereotyped account, taught to school children, which makes the situation grotesque. According to the stereotyped version, the theory of evolution was taught by Darwin and his associates, but they were opposed, in this high-minded effort, by ignorant clergymen who were more concerned with the verbal infallibility of Scripture than with the search for truth. The modern writers of intellectual history have succeeded in giving the impression that the trouble was all on one side, and that, if the controversy finally came to an end, it came to an end because the Christian opponents of Darwin realized their mistake. It was, then, a peace with victory and not a negotiated peace. Therefore the original opposition to Darwinism was merely stupid.

This stereotype is incorrect on several counts, of which the following are most important:

(1) The chief opponents whom Darwin and his associates had to convince were scientists rather than theologians. The doctrine of the fixity of species does not appear in the works of Christian Fathers, but first appears as a scientific conclusion of the seventeenth century. It has been pointed out that Francis Bacon knows nothing of it.[4] The conclusion arose from observations about the limits within which interbreeding is possible. There were distinguished men, such as Buffon and Lamarck, who renounced this modern scientific notion of the fixity of species, but it was not overthrown until the work of Charles Darwin and Professor Wallace appeared. Religious leaders had, indeed, accepted the current scientific theory, but it was still a scientific doctrine rather than a theological one

[4] Charles Gore, *The Reconstruction of Belief*, p. 6.

when the Darwinians attacked it. Darwin's strongest opponents were biologists.

(2) It was not the infallibility of Scripture that seemed to the ablest religious critics to be at stake in the controversy. The notion that the creation stories were allegorical was a very old one in Christian history. It is doubtful if the evolutionary theory would have been shocking even to St. Augustine. What was important, in the eyes of thoughtful Christians was not the letter of Scripture, but the grand principle which the Genesis account teaches. The Archbishop of Canterbury is correct when he says that "it did not take competent theologians long to appreciate the fact that the spiritual interest in the doctrine of Creation lies solely in the assertion of the dependence of all existence upon the Will of God, and that the first chapter of Genesis is a magnificent presentation of that truth."[5] This observation the Archbishop is able to enforce by reference to the teaching of his own father, Frederick Temple, formerly the Archbishop of Canterbury. To insist on the letter of Scripture might be stupid; but to insist that all existence is ultimately meaningless apart from reference to divine Will is not stupid. It was this deeper conviction which Darwinism, as popularly expounded, appeared to undermine.

(3) The most controversial part of the Darwinian doctrine was not the general theory of evolution, in which, as we have seen, Darwin had many predecessors, but the particular theory of the *causal factors* of that evolution. The general theory of evolution has, indeed, won the field; the evidence is great that all living beings have evolved (i.e., have been modified by descent) from earlier and simpler forms. But this is not *natural selection*, and it was the doctrine of natural selection that caused the gravest misgivings. It is interesting to note that these misgivings were not limited to a short time of violent controversy, but are felt today as strongly as ever. Natural selection, if

[5] William Temple, *Nature, Man and God,* pp. 48, 49.

accepted with complete faith, is as great a barrier to religious belief as it ever was.

Though evolutionism has won the field, the principle for which the Darwinians (as distinct from Darwin) were chiefly contending, has *not* won the field. In fact it was as extreme and one-sided in its way as was the principle of the Fundamentalists in their way. *The most violent adversaries were both wrong.* How little the notion of natural selection may now be regarded as the sole determinant in modification is judiciously stated by Geddes and Thomson, at the end of their valuable handbook, *Evolution:*

Natural selection remains still a vera causa in the origin of species; but the function ascribed to it is practically reversed. It exchanges its former supremacy as the supposed sole determinant among practically indefinite possibilities of structure and function, for the more modest position of simply accelerating, retarding or terminating the process of otherwise determined change. It furnishes the brake rather than the steam or the rails for the journey of life; or in better metaphor, instead of guiding the ramifications of the tree of life, it would in Mivart's excellent phrase, do little more than apply the pruning knife to them.[6]

The controversy of the third quarter of the nineteenth century now belongs to the history of ideas, but the major issue remains, and natural selection, even if it is assigned a relatively minor place by competent biologists, continues to be an obstacle to popular religious belief. That it may be a genuine obstacle, if taken seriously, is a true insight.

The notion that everything in the world, including the mind of man, has come about by the working of unconscious forces is a bold challenge to theism. This does not, it is true, constitute a denial of the being of God, *but it does eliminate many of the reasons for believing in God.* It would seem, in large measure, to make our grand hypothesis unnecessary. If the claws of the

[6] Patrick Geddes and J. Arthur Thomson, *Evolution,* Home University Library, p. 248.

tiger can be explained by the supposition that, among proto-tigers, there was an accidental variation according to which some had longer claws, and that these particular animals, having a positive advantage over their fellows, became parents, while those with shorter claws did not become parents, why may not every single development be so explained? Cannot man's love of beauty and his sense of moral integrity be accounted for in the same manner, understood as factors which have had survival value and have become established for that reason alone? If so, not only our evidence for the being of God which we find in nature seems to go by the board, but also that based on moral and aesthetic experience. The argument from religious experience would not be undermined, but all inferential argument would be undermined. Three of the four strands of our logical rope would be cut away.

The arguments from nature, from morals and from beauty, given in Chapters IX, X, and XI, are essentially similar in form in that each argues from effect to cause. In each case the effect is incompatible with a nonpurposive conception of reality; therefore the ultimate explanation of the world cannot be couched in nonpurposive terms. It is precisely this approach which natural selection appears to render inadmissible. Not merely the argument from design, but all inferential argument seems doomed.

This general effect may be illustrated by special reference to the design argument as conventionalized by Paley. The stock reference is to a watch which, if found, would lead the finder to posit an intelligence to account for its intricate accommodation of parts. But what if it could be shown that the watch was the result of another watch which kept time poorly, and that this poor timepiece had resulted from a mechanism that could hardly be called a watch at all, and so on back to the least intricate structure imaginable? What if it were possible, furthermore, to show that each of these changes was fully accounted for by a tendency in the structures to vary indefinitely, and that the environment were of such a nature as to facilitate the perpetuation of the more accurate timekeeper? Where, then, is the necessity of supposing a conscious intelligence as the explanation of the completed watch? *The result may be wonderful, but the reason it is wonderful is that it could not have survived if it had not been wonderful.*

C. THE LIMITS OF NATURAL SELECTION

When it is asserted, as has so often been done, that Charles Darwin made indefensible the inference of the being of God from the evidence of purpose in nature, the usual meaning is that chance variations, plus the success of the fortunate variations, will account for everything and therefore no appeal to divine Purpose is needed.[7] It is doubtful whether the evidence of design is so easily dismissed by these summary methods.

(1) *In the first place the natural selection principle does not account for the nonliving world* which, on Darwinian principles, plays so important a part in the evolutionary process, since most of the "environment" is nonliving, and it is the environment which determines the selection. The point is clarified by reference to the wingless beetles of Madeira mentioned prominently by Darwin and some of his successors. It is very windy on the islands so that the beetles which fly tend to be blown out to sea and destroyed. We must suppose that, during many successive generations, each individual beetle which flew least had the best chance of survival. But the chief factor here is the physical environment, and it is not "selected."[8] Only by the use of a lurid figure of speech can we apply the notion

[7] This reasoning is based on the principle of parsimony. Phenomena fully explained in one way require no other explanation.

[8] The question at issue is whether there are any facts, involved in the process of natural selection, which make the teleological conception unnecessary. Since natural selection does not account for all the factors, it alone does not have this supposed effect. For a vigorous argument to show that the principle of the survival of the fittest does not explain why the trend of evolution has been upwards, see A. N. Whitehead, *The Function of Reason,* pp. 4 ff.

of natural selection to the mechanical and chemical properties of inorganic matter. The marvelous "Fitness of the environment" for life, which Professor Henderson has so brilliantly presented, remains wholly unexplained by the naturalistic account.

(2) *In the second place the theory of natural selection does not account for variation.* The reason for this is that variation is the original material on which unconscious selection is supposed to work. Variations must exist before there can be selection among them. The unanswered question is why the favorable variations, such as those leading in the direction of scientific, moral, and aesthetic experience should ever have arisen. It is no sufficient answer to say that there were scattering variations in every direction and that, consequently, some such set of variations was bound to occur. Such an answer receives a certain plausibility from the known fact that scattering occurs, not only in games of chance, but in human life, making it possible, for instance, to conduct a life insurance business. But the fact that there are fortuitous variations in an unintelligent process does not mean that the variations give us *everything* of which we can think. What they cannot give is an intelligent order. Diderot to the contrary, it is preposterous to suppose that the random emptying and refilling of a case of type would some day, in the many possible combinations, give us the whole of the *Iliad*. So far as we can see, the case might be emptied through all eternity, and yet nothing even remotely resembling an epic poem emerge, for the particular kind of order which an epic poem represents is an intelligible order. The notion that random movement will eventually produce every conceivable combination of elements is a pure superstition, with no experiential basis. Professor Hocking has given a brilliant illustration of the weakness of the assumption that "given sufficient time all possible forms will be arrived at," by his picture of two squares with perfectly elastic particles in the corners, endowed with gravitational attraction for each other. If the four particles

are perfectly placed in the corners, they will move symmetrically back and forth through all eternity. If one is off the corner, ever so little, there will be irregular movements through all eternity, with no formation of a perfect square.[9]

As a matter of fact the variation which occurs and which natural selection employs is *not* variation in all directions. It is only variation in *some* directions, i.e., definite rather than indefinite variation.[10] There may be changes which suggest the throwing of dice, but the dice are loaded so that the changes point continuously in certain directions. "A whale," says Thomas Huxley, "does not tend to vary in the direction of producing feathers, nor a bird in the direction of producing whalebone."

(3) *A third difficulty is the naïve acceptance of the notion of chance.* A chance variation would seem to be nothing more than one concerning the causes of which we are ignorant. Unless we suppose that there are, or have been, some uncaused events, the present state of the world is the consequence of the *original variability of matter*. If the original constitution of the universe had been different, we might have no single combination of factors which now appears. From this it follows that natural selection in no way undermines the evidence of design in nature, taken as a whole. *If there is evidence of design apart from the hypothesis of natural selection, there is just as much when this hypothesis is accepted.* Design can be as evident in the combination of a million tiny variations as in a single leap in the same direction. Even natural selection itself becomes part of the evidence of God's purpose in the world, for it is the means of the sifting out of countless unsatisfactory forms and thus has helped to leave the stage relatively free for the development of those forms of existence which facilitate both the production and appreciation of value.

With the elimination of the conception of pure *chance*, the

[9] William E. Hocking, *Types of Philosophy,* New York, 1929, p. 113 f.
[10] See Geddes and Thomson, *Evolution,* p. 247.

supposed opposition between natural selection and teleology vanishes. As J. G. Schurman showed[11] there is no necessary connection between Darwin's brilliant observations on selection and the philosophy of chance with which his science became wedded. The *science* of Darwin is highly defensible, but the metaphysics of mechanism and fortuity is not defensible. The wise procedure would seem to be to keep the good science and let the bad metaphysics go. How bad the metaphysics is becomes apparent when we realize that if variations were genuinely fortuitous, they would not even be repeated except by another turn of pure chance. As Professor Schurman has said, "An action purely accidental—ungrounded, that is, in the nature of the being that performs it—would not, on the doctrine of chances, even be repeated by that individual, much less transmitted to its descendants."[12]

Such considerations show that natural selection, when accorded the modest place which modern scientists give it, does not, after all, undermine the empirical approach to theism. This approach infers from present experience a sufficient Cause for that experience. So long as we believe there are no uncaused events, this is a valid process, no matter how slow and laborious the steps are. If the present state of the world is a necessary outcome of its constitution, and if we find evidence of Mind in nature now, it follows that the original order cannot be explained without reference to Mind. It is not surprising for the key to the understanding of a process to appear late in the process. We do not see the reason for a thing until we see what it *becomes*. Mind has been inherent in nature all along, even though an outside observer a million years ago (if that were possible) would have seen little evidence of it. "Therefore," says Temple, "there is no insuperable difficulty in the view that the history of the universe is rational, though the ground of its

[11] *The Ethical Import of Darwinism*, New York, 1887, pp. 112 ff.
[12] *Ibid.*, p. 106.

rationality is only fully disclosed in its entire course, and though the element within it which supplies the unifying influence only appears late in that course."[13]

(4) *The inability to account for moral and aesthetic experience* is the fourth defect which keeps natural selection from being a sufficient explanation of evolution apart from the instrumentality of Mind. We have already noted, in Chapter VII, the degree to which a naturalistic metaphysics makes nonsense out of moral distinctions, removing any rational justification of praise or blame. It is relevant to point out now that natural selection, which is a crucial plank in the platform of philosophical naturalism, cannot show how ethical distinctions *ever came to be*.[14] Even the *appearance* of an explanation of the origin of morals depends on an ambiguity in the word "fittest," which is sometimes made to mean the same as "best." But it is abundantly clear that the difference between the two conceptions is very great. It was one of the chief contributions of Thomas Huxley that he clarified this point in his famous Romanes Lecture.

Fittest has a connotation of "best"; and about best there hangs a moral flavour. In cosmic nature, however, what is "fittest" depends upon the conditions. Long since, I ventured to point out that if our hemisphere were to cool again, the survival of the fittest might bring about, in the vegetable kingdom, a population of more and more stunted and humbler organisms, until the "fittest" that survived might be nothing but lichens, diatoms, and such microscopic organisms as those which give red snow its colour.

It may be doubted if the survival of the fittest can rationally mean anything more than the survival of the survivors, whoever or whatever they may be. In any case many forms of behavior, generally accounted excellent, and admired by professed nat-

[13] *Nature, Man and God*, p. 133.
[14] Evolutionary factors may account for some of the details of ethical development as the December, 1940, symposium of the American Philosophical Society indicated.

uralists, fail to survive in special conditions. A gentleman of high personal integrity has little chance in a society of gangsters. In an age which has produced unexampled means of spreading propaganda, it begins to look as though a highly adaptive form of behavior consists in the willingness to tell lies.

It is to the credit of Thomas Huxley that he fully recognized the sharp contrast between the ethical consciousness of men and the principles exemplified in subhuman nature. The central conviction of the great evolutionist's Romanes Lecture was the belief that man, in order to make social progress, must cultivate a spirit antithetical to much of what he finds in nature. The passage in which Huxley said this most explicitly and which can hardly be surpassed, is as follows:

As I have already urged, the practice of that which is ethically best—what we call goodness or virtue—involves a course of conduct which, in all respects, is opposed to that which leads to success in the cosmic struggle for existence. In place of ruthless self-assertion it demands self-restraint; in place of thrusting aside, or treading down, all competitors, it requires that the individual shall not merely respect, but shall help his fellows; its influence is directed, not so much to the survival of the fittest, as to the fitting of as many as possible to survive. It repudiates the gladiatorial theory of existence.

Though Huxley probably overstated his thesis there is little doubt today that his emphasis opened men's eyes. We now admit the fact that man really represents an *imperium in imperio*, that far from taking his moral conceptions from nature, he revolts against nature and judges nature. Instead of imitating the process of natural selection, man combats it.

The point to stress is that, if moral experience is based on something other than survival value and even contradictory to it, natural selection is powerless to explain the emergence of morals at all. There have been many attempts to interpret moral experience in Darwinian terms, but the authors of these attempts have either recognized their failure or have shown a most superficial knowledge of ethics. As an example of the latter we may point to Professor Copeland's effort to provide a handbook of practical ethics from the point of view of natural selection. How naïve such an optimistic effort can be is appreciated by considering the following sentences:

We have already seen that habits are subject to evolution; that good habits—good because they are beneficial, because they provide the prospect of surviving—survive and become widespread, while bad habits die out and are forgotten. The observance of ideals, of standards of conduct held by large numbers of men, involves all who share in the respect for these ideals in habits and customs of the same kind. Just as the habits and customs are subject to selection, so obviously, are the ideals also.[15]

Such a statement bristles with startling propositions. How amazing to find that bad habits die out. Perhaps the habit of war is an example. But of course they *must die out*, for the doctrine of survival demands it! How does such an interpretation of ethical experience account for the moral pioneer or the martyr who goes against the "standards of conduct held by large numbers of men"? "A bad or wrong ideal," writes the same author, "is clearly one the observance of which will lead people to improper conduct." This truism is hardly a revolutionary thesis, but the sentence which follows is startling indeed: "Improper conduct is such as lessens the prospect of survival." Again we read that "those guided by improper ideals perish." It follows that those who are still in existence are guided by proper ideals. Whatever is successful is right. By this standard the ideals of National Socialism in Germany must be moral to an intense degree. At this writing Hitler and his comrades are succeeding famously; they are surviving far more adequately than the Poles and French. Furthermore they are making as thorough preparation as possible for their long-time survival in the future as well as for the future decrease in their

[15] Edwin B. Copeland, *Natural Conduct,* Stanford University Press, 1928, p. 139.

competitors. *On the thesis of mere natural selection there is no rational basis for criticism of such conduct.*

The Hitler policy of violent conquest of neighboring peoples may eventually fail, and if it does fail, part of the reason for its failure may be the fact that the policy is morally wrong, but it seems needlessly perverse to say that it is wrong *because it fails.* If it is wrong at all, it is wrong *before it fails*, even while it is succeeding most fully. Anyone who recognizes the justice of such a remark is realizing that questions of ethics and questions of survival belong to different orders.

We have already mentioned an ambiguity in the use of the word "fittest." The use of the word "survive" is also ambiguous. When we speak of "survival value" we leave unanswered two extremely important questions. First, *whose* survival is at stake? What we universally call a good man may often be careless of his own survival, because he cares more for the survival of others. Second, *on what level* are men to survive? There are really a great many different ways in which survival is possible, some of which most of us reject as unworthy. We do not know anything about the moral excellence of "that which aids the prospect of survival" until we know the *level* of survival, and then we have introduced an ethical judgment such that natural selection is no longer the sufficient criterion.

The effort to explain the phenomenon of beauty solely by the action of natural selection is one of the most famous of Charles Darwin's endeavors. The key to the whole development of beauty and appreciation of it lay, Darwin supposed, in sexual selection. Beauty has survival value because the highly colored male is more attractive to the female, with the consequence that his advances are more acceptable to her than are those of his less favored competitors. Thus beauty in living things becomes progressive by inheritance.

That Darwin was here dealing with a positive factor in evolution can hardly be doubted. We actually see this kind of selection in contemporary operation. The important question, however, is not whether natural selection plays a part in the production of beauty, but whether it is an all-sufficient explanation. We must remember that it is only on the latter hypothesis that natural selection cuts away any of the logical ground from the argument used in Chapter XI. As we reflect upon the problem, we discover that natural selection fails, in several particular ways, to be an all-sufficient explanation of the presence of beauty in the world.

In the first place it does not account for the original appreciation of beauty. If creatures did not already respond favorably to it, its presence would have no effect upon survival. We must remember that there is no necessary connection between the possession of beauty and the appreciation of it. Furthermore it should be noted that brightness of color and beauty are by no means the same. To love brightness is one thing, but to love a harmony of colors is quite another. *Given aesthetic sensibility,* natural selection accounts for its spread in the animal world, but natural selection does not account for the sensibility in the first place or any of its qualitative refinements.

In the second place, natural selection does not account for the *amount* of beauty in the world. Obviously it has no bearing on the beauty of the inorganic world or on that of living things which are not reproduced sexually. The beauty of flowers, it has been argued, serves to draw insects to them and thus facilitate their fertilization, but why, then, should there be similar beauty among flowers not so fertilized? Throughout the world there seems to be a sheer abundance of beauty, far in excess of what survival would require, even in those forms of life where it has some bearing on survival.

We conclude that natural selection is not something which undermines inferential theistic argument, for the simple reason that natural selection is itself limited in scope. It is one of the factors which can help us to understand how the present world evolved into what it is, but it is by no means the only factor. The men who tried to erect it into the sole explanation were as bigoted and dogmatic as their evangelical opponents. More careful study has brought a measure of humility to all who study.

CHAPTER XV

THE PROBLEM OF WISH THINKING

"Above and beyond all things, the religious life is not a research after comfort."
—A. N. WHITEHEAD

The problem we have just considered, that of natural selection, is important because of its bearing on the first three forms of evidence for theistic realism. Unless it is solved satisfactorily, they are largely undermined. The problem to which we now turn stands in a similar relation to the fourth form of evidence, that of direct religious experience. Just as the theory of natural selection has been presented by some extremists as a sufficient explanation of scientific knowledge, moral experience and beauty, without reference to Purpose, so there are other extremists who claim that, as a result of modern psychological research, we can now make a full "explanation" of religious experience in terms of what is technically known as "wish thinking," thus making the concept of objective reference wholly unnecessary and therefore, according to the principle of parsimony, something to be rejected.

The difficulty thus raised demands particular attention, because the kind of explanation involved has caught the popular imagination. Whereas natural selection may be a stumbling block for the more thoughtful, the new psychology provides a stumbling block for the masses, partly because it has the appeal which usually goes with novelty. To counter some sober reference to the empirical evidence for the actual existence of God, with the remark, "But all *that* can be explained psychologically, you know," is to be modish indeed. The hypothesis in question is often put forward with such an air of assurance, and with such an impressive terminology, that the unsuspecting layman supposes he is dealing with demonstrated fact rather than mere theory, and submits accordingly. The hypothesis, we hasten to say, is by no means upheld by all psychologists and is specifically rejected by some of the most eminent.

A. THE HYPOTHESIS OF PROJECTION

The essence of what is sometimes called the psychological explanation of religious experience is the hypothesis that God is nothing more than the "projection" of human experiences. Men want to think they are not alone in the universe; therefore they believe in God. Men want to think there is purpose and meaning in the world; therefore they convince themselves that they see evidence of such purpose. Man is afraid, so he projects his fears on a cosmic screen.

Though this hypothesis is often presented as part of the "new" psychology, it is actually very old and was a commonplace among the Epicurean writers of antiquity, especially in regard to the projection based on fear. In modern times the most thoroughgoing exponent of this view of the matter has been Ludwig Feuerbach (1804-1872), the German sensationalist philosopher, the most important of whose books, the *Wesen des Christenthums*, was published in 1841.

Feuerbach's thesis may be stated briefly without significant loss. Religion, he held, is only the imaginative projection of human needs and hopes. Man supposes he has immediate contact with superhuman Reality, but he is only communing with himself. What men worship as gods are nothing but *Wunschwesen*, "wishbeings." Gods are *personified wishes*. Since men, when they worship and pray, are not conscious of the projection of their wishes, all religious experience is delusory.

When religion—consciousness of God—is designated as the self-consciousness of man, this is not to be understood as affirming that the religious man is directly aware of this identity; for, on the contrary, ignorance of it is fundamental to the peculiar nature of religion. To preclude this misconception, it is better to say, religion is man's earliest and also indirect form of self-knowledge. Hence, religion everywhere precedes philosophy, as in the history of the race, so also in that of the individual. Man first of all sees his nature as if *out* of himself, before he finds it in himself. His own nature is in the first instance contemplated by him as that of another being. . . . Hence the historical progress of religion consists in this: that what by an earlier religion was regarded as objective, is now recognized as subjective; that is, what was formerly contemplated and worshipped as God is now perceived to be something *human*.[1]

Feuerbach proceeds to his task by attempting to show that each item of religious belief or experience may be interpreted as man's effort to objectify some wish. Providence is the desire to believe we are important, the experience of God as personal is the effort to say that *our* personality is the highest form of being, prayer is our desire to converse with ourselves. Miracle is the very heart of faith, for though natural modes of dealing with human wishes and needs are satisfactory, miracle "satisfies the wishes of men in a way corresponding to the nature of wishes—in the most desirable way."[2] We love a miracle because, in it, we get what we wish right away—without any tiresome waiting.

Contemporary psychologists, who have upheld theories similar to that of Feuerbach, have not added materially to his evidence, but they have, by introducing psychoanalysis, and making use of questionnaires, appeared to give a scientific turn to the question. The chief contemporary advance, if any, has been made by researches into the phenomena of the "unconscious," and the "subconscious," possibly providing new data thereby. The study of abnormality has undoubtedly progressed in recent years and insofar as this sheds light on religious experience we have new information.

[1] Ludwig Feuerbach, *The Essence of Christianity*, translated by Marian Evans, Second Edition, London, 1881, p. 13.
[2] *Ibid.*, p. 129.

Professor Leuba, in his long study of mysticism, has given the subject a different turn than have the psychoanalysts. While they, like Feuerbach, have stressed the notion that religious experience may be accounted for in terms of *desire*, Leuba has held that religious experience may be accounted for in terms of *expectation*. Thus he accounts for the "sense of presence" so often reported. Leuba has likewise sought to explain certain phases of mysticism as erotomania.[3] An eminently fair and careful criticism of Leuba's thesis has been made by Professor C. C. J. Webb in his *Religion and Theism*, Chapter IV.

The work of Dr. Sigmund Freud, the most distinguished exponent of the hypothesis chiefly at issue, is work for which we shall long be grateful because of the new light he has shed on mental illness. His detailed evidence that many mental aberrations exist in a hidden form in apparently normal lives has contributed greatly to therapy. I have it on the authority of an eminent psychologist that Freud's followers are growing numerically, so far as mental hygiene is concerned, but they are becoming fewer so far as his religious theories are concerned.

Freud's major religious thesis is as follows: Religion is an attempt to provide a solution of the intolerable problem—the child in relation to his earthly father. Belief in God solves the problem, for God is the "Father-surrogate." The child feels helpless, he is full of emotional strain caused by the alternate admiration for his father and disillusionment about his father. This disillusionment he cannot bear, so, as he becomes a man, he imagines a Heavenly Father so perfect that he will never be disillusioned about Him. Freud's own synopsis of this doctrine is so clear that we can do no better than employ it at this point.

The libido follows the paths of narcissistic needs, and attaches itself to the objects that ensure their satisfaction. So the mother, who satisfies hunger, becomes the first love-object, and certainly also the first protection against all the undefined and threatening dangers of

[3] Cf. James H. Leuba, *The Psychology of Religious Mysticism*.

the outer world; becomes if we may so express it, the first protection against anxiety.

In this function the mother is soon replaced by the stronger father, and this situation persists from now on over the whole of childhood. But the relation to the father is affected by a peculiar ambivalence. He was himself a danger, perhaps just because of that earlier relation to the mother; so he is feared no less than he is longed for and admired. . . . Now when the child grows up and finds that he is destined to remain a child forever, and that he can never do without protection against unknown and mighty powers, he invests these with the traits of the father-figure; he creates for himself the gods, of whom he is afraid, whom he seeks to propitiate and to whom he nevertheless entrusts the task of protecting him.[4]

This theory is stated most fully in *The Future of an Illusion*, but is by no means unique to this volume. Indeed, this book is a restatement and amplification of Freud's many fugitive references to religion as well as his more extended treatment in *Totem and Taboo*. The careful reader naturally asks how Freud is able to suppose that he has shown religion to be illusory. What men want *could* be real. The child's helplessness *could be* a preparation for sensitive awareness of God who is really the Father of all men, just as it *could be* the sole and sufficient cause of belief in God. The clue to Freud's supposition that he can show religion to be illusory is found in the statement that, when the child grows up, he "finds that he is destined to remain a child forever." Because he remains a child, his judgments about objective reference in religion are as untrustworthy as are those of a child or of a savage. The civilized man, since he has only a veneer of the critical spirit, is not in a position essentially different from that of the savage who has faith in the objective validity of his tribal taboos.

The projection hypothesis is buttressed at all points by three kinds of illustrations, the pathological, the primitive,[5] and the infantile. Much is made, for example, of the fact that a lonely

[4] Sigmund Freud, *The Future of an Illusion*, pp. 41, 42.
[5] *Totem and Taboo*.

child is often observed to hold imaginary conversations with an imaginary playmate. Man is a grown-up child who creates in his daydreams an imaginary playmate, reports conversations with him, and calls him "God." The fact that men do not know that all this is a creation of their own fancy is not surprising, inasmuch as research into the subconscious has shown that people are usually unaware of the emotional sources of what is supposedly accepted on rational grounds. Theistic evidence, from the time of Plato on, is nothing but "rationalization" on a grand scale.

How faithfully the basic Freudian analysis has been followed by other psychoanalysts is well illustrated in the following paragraph from the pen of a physician.

The theological statement that God is our Father appears to be fully justified in a psychological sense. Both militant atheism and devout belief in God can be equally traced to the child's earliest reaction to his earthly father (or to the idea of a father when the actual one is missing). The attributes of omnipotence, omniscience, and moral perfection are invariably ascribed to the father at one stage or another during the young child's growth; they proceed at least as much from internal necessities as from any external example or suggestion. Various repressions to do with the idea of the father, together with his obvious shortcomings when judged by so absolute a standard, lead to the attributes of perfection being abstracted from him and incorporated in an intangible figure. This, in a couple of words, is perhaps the gist of the mass of knowledge we possess about the complicated development of the idea of God-head.[6]

Dr. Jung, in his later utterances, takes up a far less extreme position, but he still denies the possibility of determining, with any degree of accuracy, whether our religious experience has objective reference. "Religious experience," he says, "is absolute. It is indisputable. You can only say that you have never had such an experience, and your opponent will say: 'Sorry, I

[6] Ernest Jones, *Psycho-Analysis*, London, 1928, p. 74.

have.' And there your discussion will come to an end."[7] But if men are rational, it does not thus come to an end, for we learn to employ tests of objectivity. Otherwise the experience of a fool is as valuable as that of a wise man.

There is not much more to be said in expounding this particular attack on the veracity of religious experience, since no further "arguments" are presented. The fact that men turn to religion in times of strain and danger, such as wartime, is often alluded to, but this is no new observation and does not really add to the analysis already postulated. An effort is made to cast doubt on the testimony of each particular witness to the reality of contact with God by the assertion of emotional instability or personal strain. Since it is obviously impracticable to try to show this in each individual case, when so many are involved, the usual procedure is to resort to a generalization as follows: *When people are in the midst of religious experience they are wrought up. People who are emotionally wrought up are unreliable witnesses. Therefore all religious experience is worthless as evidence.*

B. WEAKNESSES OF THE PROJECTION THEORY

Inasmuch as considerations like those just presented offer real difficulties to many minds, causing them to doubt the force of evidence otherwise incontestable, it is important to analyze the situation as rigorously as we can. There are three chief weaknesses in the system, one *logical*, a second *dialectical*, and the third *factual*.

(1) *The first weakness of the hypothesis is that its supposed conclusion does not follow as a logical necessity from the evidence presented.* The explanation, it should be noted, is *consistent with* the notion that God is nonexistent, but it does not *prove* that God is nonexistent. All the phenomena presented as evidence are, in fact, *consistent with* the hypothesis of theistic realism. Even if Feuerbach is right in saying that belief arises

[7] Carl Gustav Jung, *Psychology and Religion*, New Haven, 1938, p. 113.

from hope, what we hope *could* be true, just as it could be false. In short, the reference to hope does not decide the question, and we must have recourse to some other method if we are to decide it.

The same is true of Freud's reference to unconscious emotional sources arising in childhood. Even if his observations are correct, there is nothing in his argument to oppose the theory that it is this very emotional disturbance which makes men sensitively aware of the objective presence of God. It was at this point that the late Professor Bennett's study of "psychologism" was so clarifying.

For all that psychology has to say, conversion might be what the convert thinks it is—the soul's discovery of God. Everything psychology has to say about the subconscious, of the "slow process of maturation" going on there and culminating in some invasion of the conscious, would still remain true within its limits. The one thing which as psychologists we could not do would be to prejudge the metaphysical issue by thinking of the subconscious as a place in the mind from which the saving impulses come, something that could be offered as a natural origin for so-called supernatural apparitions. In short, to say that "the subconscious did it" does not prevent one from saying "God did it." Both statements may be true at the same time. In conversion the deeps of the soul are stirred. True. But it is also true that an angel may have troubled the pool.[8]

Much has been made of the fact that many of those who have believed themselves in immediate communion with God have come to the experience with great expectancy, and this is frequently given as evidence that the resulting experience is illusory. But such a conclusion does not follow necessarily, since it is equally reasonable to assume that the mood of expectancy is one of the preconditions of actual revelation. Perhaps, apart from such expectancy, most men's sensibilities are not really aroused. *To ask why a man makes a proposition is not the same as to ask whether the proposition is true.*

[8] Charles A. Bennett, *The Dilemma of Religious Knowledge*, pp. 108, 109.

When we trace religious experience to infantile desires and then, on this account, deny objective reference to it, we are committing, in a glaring fashion, what is known as the "genetic fallacy." This fallacy is the assumption that *anything is what it comes from.* On this basis we should have to deny the objective reference of science, because science began with magic. But the fallacy is obvious when openly stated, and gets its only plausibility from the fact that it is usually introduced as a suppressed and unconscious premise.[9]

What the orthodox Freudian does is to make a new mistake while he corrects an old one. He is right in what he denies, but wrong in what he asserts. He is right in denying that desire gives any positive evidence of the reality of the desired object, but, not satisfied with this sober judgment, he goes on to assert that the existence of desire proves the alleged object to be illusory. It is difficult to see why this has any justification. *We are told that experience of God is illusory, and the reason given is that our nature leads us to be religious.* Why might not our nature lead us, just as well, to what is real? Religious experience, we are told cannot be "caused" by God as objectively real, since it is "caused" by man's nature. But only a person insensitive to *the fallacy of causal simplicity* could suppose that the existence of one cause denies the existence of other and quite different causes. Seeing is "caused" by eyes, but this does not mean that it is not also "caused" by light.[10]

(2) *The dialectical weakness* of the hypothesis under discussion lies in the fact that it proves too much. If religion is illusory because it is desirable to believe in God, everything else in which men believe is illusory, too. By the same procedure we should be forced to hold that science and art are likewise "projections." Man wants terribly to find order in the

[9] For a humorous and incisive analysis of the genetic fallacy, see Boris Bogoslovsky, *The Technique of Controversy,* pp. 153 ff. He cites the example of persons who will not eat apples grown in graveyards because they suppose they are thereby eating the corpses.

[10] Cause here means "necessary conditions."

world rather than chaos, so the great laws of natural science are merely formulations which are created to satisfy this desire, and they have no counterpart in the external world. All that we should need to do to clinch the argument would be to point to one or two scientists who finally went insane or were physically weak. Pascal was physically weak, we are told, therefore we cannot trust his analysis of his own religious experiences. By the same token we cannot trust his analysis of his scientific experiments such as that with the barometer.

Not the least of the absurdities to which a process leads is that of the self-defeat of the very principle which is so confidently put forward. If all our deepest convictions, supposedly supported on rational grounds, are nothing other than a projection of our irrational desires, how can the conviction that this is the case be free from the same taint? What irrational desires in the Freudians account for Freudianism? But a doctrine which, when rigorously applied, is self-destructive, has ceased to be a serious menace to anything. That which rules out everything, rules out nothing, for it has already ruled out itself.

Unless we can assume that men are sometimes normal and critical, we cannot even begin an inquiry into truth and falsehood, but if it is true that men are sometimes normal and critical, it is hard to see why some of those who have reported religious experience would not be in such a class. Even the fact that each person may have his foibles is no proof whatever that no person can be trusted about his deepest convictions. The transference of pathological concepts to normal psychology is illicit, but even insane people usually have areas of experience in which they are worthy of trust. To proceed from the observation that men are often deluded to the theory that they are always wrong is a *non sequitur* so glaring that it is reminiscent of the Irishman who, upon finding that one stove saved him half his coal bill, decided to buy two stoves and eliminate the bill entirely. The *non sequitur* is usually hidden by the introduction of jargon. The introduction of such a term as "Conversion Hysteria" is impressive to the layman.[11] What Freud does not tell us is that much conversion is not hysterical at all.

It is doubtful if those who follow Freud so gaily have any idea of how absurdly large is the assertion they are making. This assertion, as John Baillie has said, "would seem to mean nothing less than that all the world, except the few isolated souls who have definitely turned their backs on religious ways of thought, are in a state of mind not properly distinguishable from incipient madness."[12] To state the claim clearly is to discredit it.

(3) *The third and final weakness of the hypothesis, to which we shall point, is still more serious.* This is not a logical or dialectical weakness, such as has just been presented, but the fatal weakness of inconsistency with known fact. Whatever plausibility the supposed "explanation" achieves comes from the assertion that, in religious experience, what men claim to experience is in accordance with their wishes, desires, and expectations. The reference to wishes was the keystone of Feuerbach's structure and has likewise been that of the Freudian analysis. Freud speaks of the notion of a self-revealing God, and adds that "it is very odd that this is all just as we should wish it ourselves."[13] If it could be shown that the religious experience of men is frequently *at variance with their wishes*, the teeth of the difficulty would be pulled. Now, as a matter of fact, so far as we *ever* know fact, this is the case.

The testimony is that the individual tries to escape from God's presence, but cannot. This, of course, is the point of Francis Thompson's interpretive poem, *The Hound of Heaven.* That this poem has been so greatly loved is evidence that it expresses a widely recognized experience. In the story of *Jonah,* one of the most brilliant and profound in all Hebrew literature, it is noteworthy that the prophet tried to flee from the presence of the Lord, though in the end he found he could not

[11] *Psychopathology of Everyday Life,* English translation, p. 310.
[12] John Baillie, *The Interpretation of Religion,* New York, 1928, p. 163.
[13] Sigmund Freud, *The Future of an Illusion,* p. 58.

really escape.[14] Jonah tried to escape because his religious experience *forced* him to believe what he did not *want* to believe. The demands which the experience involved were too hard.

Far from helping men to have a good opinion of themselves, normative religious experience makes them despise themselves. When they see themselves in the light of God's presence they realize that their supposed righteousness is filthy rags. Note that in the classic account of the prophetic experience in the sixth chapter of *Isaiah*, the prophet, having "seen" the Lord, says "Woe is me."

It is not surprising that Pascal, who knew the spiritual life so deeply and so well, could write, "Men hate and despise religion, and fear it may be true."[15] Life would be so much easier and simpler if there were not the moral demands which religious experience involves.

The blunt truth is that the upholders of the doctrine of *Wunschwesen*, from Feuerbach to Freud and beyond, do not know what they are talking about. They have spun a theory without bothering to check the evidence, most of which is never seen in clinics or laboratories. That there have been men whose alleged religious experience has been highly comforting, wholly in line with their desires, none doubts, but to assert that this has been the universal experience or even the characteristic one is to reveal gross ignorance. If this dogma were true we should expect all prayer to be self-seeking, but instead we find the recognition of a demand for the most rigorous self-denial and self-sacrifice. Those who have claimed to know God best have found that He demands things almost impossible to perform. How, on the hypothesis of *Wunschwesen*, did the notion of the *Cross* ever enter the world? Pascal seems to be addressing men of our time when he says: "Let them at least learn what is the religion they attack, before attacking it."[16]

Religious experience in its simpler forms often gives a cer-

14 *Jonah* I, 10.
15 *Pensees*, 187 (Brunschvicg).
16 *Pensees*, 194.

tain comfort, but, as it becomes more advanced, the note of tragedy enters. The maturity of Christianity, as a religion among other religions, is indicated by its stress on this tragic note. If the haunting words, "Let this cup pass away from me; nevertheless not as I will, but as thou wilt," can be interpreted as expressing a desire for comfort, the word comfort has become so ambiguous as to lose whatever explanatory value it ever had.

Not only has the nature of God, as revealed in religious experience, been different from what men have *desired*; it has likewise been different, in many cases, from what they have *expected*. St. Paul's experience on the Damascus Road is a vivid illustration of a revelation which was *neither* desired nor expected. The prophets were taught to expect one kind of experience, but they actually had another. Therein lies the possibility of progress. The whole prophetic movement reaches its climax in the words, "Ye have heard it said, but I say unto you."

It is likewise erroneous to suppose that men invariably think of God as a larger exemplification of themselves. That there is some anthropomorphism, no one doubts, but, with the development of insight, devout men recognize that God is "other" than themselves. The classic expression of this conviction is the sentence put in the mouth of God, "My ways are not your ways, nor my thoughts your thoughts."

In conclusion we may say that the hypothesis of wish thinking, if critically examined, is a valuable one. Though the hypothesis, as presented by Freud, goes far beyond the evidence he has assembled to support it, it is highly salutary for all who believe in the objective reference of religious experience to recognize the degree to which they may be deluded. Anything which makes men less dogmatic, recognizing the frailties of human nature and the many ways in which our critical judgment may be clouded, is a wholesome discipline in humility. But the Freudian, if he is consistent, will also eschew dogmatism. And when he does, his theory ceases to be an absolute barrier to belief in the objective reference of religious experience.

CHAPTER XVI

THE PROBLEM OF NATURAL LAW

"These 'laws' are merely abstractions devised by us for our own guidance through the complexities of fact." —LORD BALFOUR

The difficulties to which we turn in this and the following chapter, differ from the difficulties just considered in two respects. The difficulties just considered belong, for the most part, to restricted periods in the history of thought, but the two difficulties to which we now turn are perennial. The problem of natural selection was felt most keenly in the latter part of the nineteenth century and the problem of psychological explanation has been felt most keenly in the twentieth century, but the problem of natural law has bothered men for several centuries and the problem of evil has been of major importance since man began to think reflectively at all. A second difference between the difficulties just considered and those remaining to be considered is that the former refer to particular intellectual disciplines whereas the latter have no such specific reference, but are concerned, rather, with many kinds of experience. Natural law is involved not in one science, but in all, and evil is to be found both in the natural order and in the moral order.

A. THE NATURE OF THE DIFFICULTY

The difficulty about natural law is one which concerns the practical as well as the theoretical aspects of religious belief. It touches men in the more intimate phases of their devotional life and becomes a real barrier. The notion of natural law most often entertained is that there is a fixed system of natural sequence, a sequence such that religious experience seems to be an intruder. Three specific beliefs are thus affected.

(1) The first specific religious belief to be affected by the problem of natural law is the *belief in prayer*. Prayer is the very heart of religion as distinguished from mere intellectual affirmation. It is the conscious response of man to the love of God as dimly or clearly known. It includes thanksgiving, praise, communion, petition, and intercession. It is the central religious fact both in individual experience and in group experience, whether formal or informal. The earliest religious practices of which we have historical evidence are those of prayer, often extremely crude, and the most highly developed form which religion takes in sensitive persons is the sense of spiritual communion with God. If there is something which rules out all this, making it impossible for the truly thoughtful man, the difficulty placed in the way of religious belief is really crucial.

The greatest difficulty is felt in connection with petition and intercession. Men have long prayed for rain, but how can this be done with intellectual honesty when we realize something of the nature of meteorology? Men have long prayed for the restoration of the health of their loved ones, but how can this be done by honest persons who know something of the action of germs? When a patient has pneumonia what is needed, it would seem, is not prayer, but sulfathiazole. Such considerations do not, of course, prevent recourse to prayer, but they hinder it. Most fathers, it is probable, would pray for a child in danger of contracting infantile paralysis, but many would wonder, in doing so, if they were acting rationally. The trouble is not that men cease to pray, but that so many cannot pray "with the consent of all of their faculties."

The difficulty felt is most obvious when the time factor is important. If a person receives a letter and, before opening it, prays that the letter may not contain bad news, the prayer has no justification. Whatever is in the letter is there already, and nothing under heaven will change it. In other words, such a prayer is self-contradictory. It asks that what is be something other than what it is. But the same difficulty remains in less obvious situations. Prayer about the letter is pointless at any time after it is written.

Much of our uneasiness in regard to other areas, such as the physical and the biological, arises from the conviction that the situation is already as fully determined by natural laws as the contents of the letter are already fixed by the writer. Whether there will be rain is already on the cards. But if this is true for one day, why not for a million? In the same way, the ravages of a disease seem to be already determined by the introduction of germs. In short, it is always too late.

Perhaps, then, prayer is merely an irrational survival of a superstitious and anthropomorphic age. In that case, it will eventually cease with the growth of critical intelligence or continue as a sentimental gesture, but nothing more.

(2) The second specific belief which the concept of natural law seems to rule out is the *belief in miracles*. Miracles, in the sense of striking evidences of divine Power in the ordinary course of the world have been reported from the earliest times and the reports have been widely believed. Many miracles have been extremely well attested, and have been accepted as valid by thoughtful persons. The life of Christ, for example, has been considered miraculous by countless millions. This refers not only to His supposed deeds, but to His very existence and to His triumph over death. Even when we make due allowance, as we must, for the unreliability of oral transmission and the natural human desire to enlarge upon stories, there remains a core of historical evidence for such a miracle as the resurrection which meets adequately the tests used in historical research. But an increasingly large number of people find they cannot believe such a miraculous account, not because the historical evidence is not good, but because they have a conception of natural law which rules such events out as *impossible*. From what we know of natural laws, they say, a body *could not* come to life after it had been dead more than two days. In the same way, they say, the physical amount of food *could not* be in-

creased as it was alleged to have been in the story of the feeding of the five thousand. It is often admitted that apparently miraculous healings might occur, since so many diseases have a psychical basis, but actual physical changes are, they suppose, in a different category.

This rejection of miracle, which seems inevitable, is very serious for theism. If we find ourselves unable to believe in miracle, we may still think of God as the Author of the universe, including its natural laws, but such belief is almost valueless for practical religion. There does not seem much reason for worshiping a God who has made a world such that He is effectually shut out from participation in its management. Religious experience in the sense of communion appears to be still open to those who reject miracles, but, as we shall see later, this rests upon a misunderstanding of the radical alteration in world view which rejection of miracles must entail.

(3) *Providence* is the third belief which seems to be hindered by a belief in natural law. It is, indeed, comforting to think that our lives and destinies are overshadowed by divine care, but how can this be? If a man jumps off a precipice, will Providence step in to annul the law of gravitation? If an epidemic breaks out, will Providence destroy the germs? Or would it be better to take advantage of medical knowledge? Does God really care for a righteous nation, guiding its destinies over many years and protecting it from enemies, as the ancient Hebrews believed, or was Napoleon correct when he said God was on the side of the largest battalions?

Whenever there is apparent evidence of providential care we are bound, if we adopt the position just stated, to hold that the situation is a mere *coincidence*. Thus we might seek to explain the apparently providential act by which the grain of the Mormon pioneers in Utah was saved, when a sudden incursion of sea gulls destroyed the pests which were about to destroy the grain. The mother of the philosopher, Josiah Royce, recorded really amazing providential guidance and protection in her journal of the trek of the Royce family to California, but if we believe in natural law, we tend to conclude that the Royce family was merely lucky.

B. TWO KINDS OF ORDER

What we mean, fundamentally, when we say that natural law reigns is that ours is an *ordered* universe. There are only two genuine alternatives, so far as we know, to such a conception. One alternative is that the world is fortuitous, proceeding, in whole or in part, on the basis of *chance*. It is hard to make this conception even intelligible, and far harder to find any adequate support for it. Though there are a few subatomic phenomena which now suggest such an interpretation,[1] we know that, in many former instances, what at first appeared as fortuitous was discovered later to be such that it could be included in a causal nexus. The other alternative to the conception of an ordered universe is one subject to continual *whim* and *caprice*. A great deal of the belief in divine intervention has been on no higher level than this. But this is nothing other than the naïve spiritualism which, as we have suggested earlier, cannot honestly be defended. A capricious God would not be worthy of reverence.

If *chance* and *caprice* are the only alternatives to a law-abiding system, no others having been presented in many centuries of reflective thought, our choice is clear. Unless ours is an orderly system, it seems difficult to know how we can proceed with anything. Apart from this hypothesis, not only would practical science be impossible, but a good part of the reason for believing in God (that presented in Chapter IX) would be discarded.

The great question before reflective thought is not *whether* ours is an ordered system, but *what kind of order* it represents. And it is in answering this question that we find the most hope of dealing adequately with the difficulty presented at the begin-

---

[1] These are the phenomena interpreted by the Heisenberg principle of uncertainty.

ning of this chapter. Though many different kinds of order may be imagined there are two which have been presented with especial conviction, one of these being a *mechanical* order and the other an order of *purpose*.

(1) *The belief in a mechanical order,* fixed and uniform, has been at the heart of most of our difficulty about prayer and natural law. It can be stated simply without distortion. The thesis is that there is fundamentally one kind of causal sequence in the world, that found in mechanical systems. This may be illustrated by the weather. The impact of air currents on one another is fully describable in mechanical terms, providing we have the time and patience. Wishing obviously does not affect the motion of the clouds nor are they self-moved. There are orderly ways in which material aggregates move, ways which we can learn, but cannot alter. If the weather is determined already, as most of us suppose, for the next twenty-four hours, why is it not determined for the next million years? We chiefly assume that the official forecasters, when their predictions fail to come true, have overlooked some determinants and that, with more care or more skill, they could have succeeded.

It is customary to speak of this alleged system of nature as a "closed" system and Professor Whitehead shows, with admirable conciseness, why this is the case. "We cannot wonder," he says, "that science rested content with this assumption as to the fundamental elements of nature. The great forces of nature, such as gravitation, were entirely determined by the configurations of masses. Thus the configurations determined their own changes, so that the circle of scientific thought was completely closed."[2] That there is such a closed system has been the orthodox creed of a great part of modern science since the seventeenth century. It has appeared to have a full justification by the pragmatic test, for it has actually worked and produced results. But grave intellectual difficulties have long been apparent in the system.

[2] Alfred North Whitehead, *Science and the Modern World,* p. 71.

(2) *The belief in a purposive order* is the belief that nature cannot be explained except as the activity of Mind expressing itself through process. Nature, when interpreted in terms of purpose, is not a self-running mechanism, an enormous perpetual motion machine, but a subsidiary system created and sustained for a *reason*. This *reason* gives dependability, since purpose is as strongly opposed to chance or caprice as mechanical determinism can possibly be. The purposive conception of law does all that the mechanical conception does, in that it points to the regularities of nature, but it also does more, in that it presents a rational explanation of the regularities. The world, according to this hypothesis, is not rational because it is a system of natural law; it is, rather, law-abiding because it is the expression of a transcendent Reason.

Whereas the mechanical conception of natural law is entirely monistic, the purposive conception is dualistic or pluralistic in that it admits the existence of both minds and bodies, though both find their ultimate explanation in the reality of God. Purpose is the larger conception, since it can include mechanism, and mechanism cannot include purpose. The purposive systems we know best, i.e., human beings, include mechanical levels which operate alongside the levels of consciousness and, though they follow different laws, can be used in the service of purpose. In short, a purposive system is a personal system and our hypothesis involves the frank effort to understand the universe in personal terms.

It is unfortunate that this effort has so often been misunderstood and lampooned, even by persons of good general intelligence. Many are apparently unable to distinguish between a crude anthropomorphism and the assertion that personality best explains the world order we actually observe. A striking illustration, all the more important because it does not come from the pen of a professional philosopher, is afforded by one chapter in the late Hans Zinsser's remarkable autobiography. The sad truth is that the superficial judgments which Zinsser made are characteristic of a fairly wide public.

And the conception of a God so constituted that we are, as individuals, of direct concern to Him appears both presumptuous—considering our individual insignificance in the scheme as a whole—and unnecessary for that feeling of helpless reverence in face of the universal order which is the essence of religious experience. Moreover, palaeontologically considered, one would have to assume that such a personal God existed long before the evolution of man. . . . Yet reward, punishment, immortality of the soul in the theological sense, could have no meaning whatever until there had developed creatures possessing a nervous organization capable of abstract thinking and of spiritual suffering. One cannot imagine such a God occupied through millions of years, up to the Pleistocene, with personal supervision, reward and punishment, of amoebae, clams, fish, dinosaurs, and sabre-toothed tigers; then, suddenly, adjusting his own systems and purposes to the capacities of the man-ape He had allowed to develop.[3]

Though the reader is disarmed by the fact that the chapter heading under which this paragraph occurs includes the sentence, "A discussion of religion quite devoid of philosophical value," it remains true that this statement shows extremely confused thinking. What is most amazing is that a person who could think so carefully within his field could think and write so carelessly out of his field. There is no logical difficulty in the notion that God *was*, long before the advent of man as a creature able to discern, ever so dimly, something of His eternal purpose. Why should there be anything irrational about the appearance late in a series of the event which finally gives a hint to the meaning of the series? This happens frequently in poetry. That which is highest in value could be deepest in nature, to use Montague's excellent phrase, long before the emergence of creatures able to appreciate value. Do those for whom Dr. Zinsser has spoken seriously suppose that the fact of evolution,

[3] Hans Zinsser, *As I Remember Him*, pp. 72, 73.

if it is a fact, really denies meaning to the universe? By recourse to what prejudice do we conclude that a meaningful creation must come all at once? Zinsser's reference to God's sudden adjustment to man is particularly inappropriate, if we assume, as we do, that all the prior steps in the evolutionary process were steps in the same direction, and that the major reason for the whole process was the production of the kind of environment appropriate to the emergence of creatures capable of determination by the apprehension of the good.

When we suggest a way in which an ordered whole may follow laws and yet be dominated by purpose, we are not suggesting something unfamiliar to our common experience. The best illustration of how experience can be orderly and yet nonmechanical, is found in moral experience, where we see the self-expression of a *constant* and constantly developing character. In character we observe an order which is flexible, but not capricious. We cannot predict the details of a man's moral actions as well as we can predict the weather, but we can do something far more important, we can predict the general character of his actions. When a man has a well-developed and trustworthy character, we do not know *which* of several particular alternatives he will choose, but we can be sure that he will *not* choose something ignoble. The reason for this is that moral actions are determined, not by efficient causation, but by the good as apprehended. The guide to conduct is not any one of several particular actions proposed, but something permanent which finds expression in them. In short the conception of an ordered system in which the causal sequence is nonmechanical is not some wild speculation, but is already known in the moral experience of all men.

C. EXAMINATION OF THE MECHANICAL THEORY OF LAW

If the mechanical conception of natural law, which refuses to admit conscious purpose as a causal factor in the world, can be shown to be the actual principle on which reality, insofar as we know it, is organized, we must accept the situation with humility, following the truth where it leads, giving up our practical religious belief as well as our faith in the freedom of choice. Before we do this, however, we should examine the mechanistic theory of law to see whether it is really so certain. Above all, we must ask whether there are any aspects of reality as known to which this conception of natural law does not apply.

At the outset it is pertinent to note that law, understood in the mechanical sense, is both speculative and abstract. We realize that it is speculative when we note that the complete uniformity, which the mechanical picture suggests, is not actually found in experience. Physicists are not agreed on the extent to which our laws are statistical in nature, but it seems clear that many are to be so understood.[4] The conception of natural law which is a barrier to religious belief is one which tells what *must* happen, but, as we become more critical, we realize that we do not know anything about "must" in the natural order. It is hard enough to know what is, without attempting to dogmatize about what is *necessary*. What we find, in scientific research, is evidence that there are certain uniformities and rhythms which the creation displays. "Laws" are merely the abstract and largely conventional statements of what is thus found. The laws do not exist apart from the instances from which they are known.

Here, in this more modern approach, we have something strikingly different from Laplace's "Law of Nature." We are not so awe-struck by reference to natural law if we realize that laws, as used in modern science, are nothing but *modes of action, uniform or nearly so*. The person who holds this less dogmatic understanding of law is not forced to deny an excep-

[4] For an able presentation of this matter see Bernard Bavink's chapter, "The Demolition of the Mechanistic World Picture." The English title of the book in which this chapter appears is *Science and God*, New York, 1934.

tion when he observes it; instead he accepts it with what Alexander and Morgan call "natural piety." Statistical laws are not "broken" when exceptions occur, for the concept itself includes the possibility of exceptions in rare cases. Outrageous runs of luck do not invalidate the laws of probability. Although the statistical interpretation of law is largely contemporary, fifty years ago Balfour was already seeking to free men's minds from a superstitious reverence for natural law, as the quotation at the head of this chapter indicates. Laws, he held, possess neither independent powers nor actual existence. Balfour was pioneering in the modern tendency to be realistic about law in words like the following:

And if we would use language with perfect accuracy, we ought, it would seem, either to say that the same cause would always be followed by precisely the same effect, if it recurred—which it never does; or that, in certain regions of Nature, though only in certain regions, we can detect subordinate uniformities of repetition which, though not exact, enable us without sensible insecurity or error to anticipate the future or reconstruct the past.[5]

When we say that natural law, mechanically interpreted, is abstract, we mean that most of what seems valuable to men is left out when we make the formulae called laws. All the flesh and blood of actual experience is gone, and nothing remains but a skeleton picture. Any law, because it is a generalization, omits the reality of individuality, which we have reason to prize so highly. We cannot suppose that a law, which can be expressed in a mathematical equation, by marks on a blackboard, represents more than a single aspect of reality.

One way in which the orthodox conception of natural law involves a distorting abstraction is that so vigorously criticized by Bergson, when he refers to the tendency to explain things in spatial categories. The distortion of nature involved in intellectual "spatialization" arises from the notion of simple loca-

[5] A. J. Balfour, *The Foundations of Belief*, p. 299.

tion, according to which the interpreter of an event makes it manageable by eliminating the factor of time. This is an example of what Whitehead calls the "Fallacy of Misplaced Concreteness." The concept of simple location, inherent in the mechanical theory of natural law, makes induction particularly difficult, as Whitehead shows in the following passage:

For, if in the location of configurations of matter throughout a stretch of time there is no inherent reference to any other times, past or future, it immediately follows that nature within any period does not refer to nature at any other period. Accordingly, induction is not based on anything which can be observed as inherent in nature. Thus we cannot look to nature for the justification of our belief in any law such as the law of gravitation. In other words the order of nature cannot be justified by the mere observation of nature.[6]

The price of the abstraction inherent in the mechanical conception of natural law is that it fails to give adequate expression to the richness and variety of the world. In short, it is too simple. Emergent evolution, which has become such an important element in modern thinking, is a revolt against the oversimplified view of reality as ultimately reducible to one kind of order, namely, the lowest. Why, it asks, should we not pay as much attention to the kind of order found in organic wholes and the kind found in purposive behavior, as we do to the kind found in merely material aggregates? Among modern philosophers who have been particularly insistent on this point have been Lloyd Morgan, A. N. Whitehead, and Arthur O. Lovejoy. Professor Lovejoy represents this entire revolt against the oversimplification of reductive naturalism when he writes:

The union of the conception of evolution with the conception of reality as a complex of which all the parts are theoretically deducible from a very small number of relatively simple laws of the redistribution of a quantitatively invariable sum of matter and of energy—this union the "emergent evolutionist," if I may so call him for short,

[6] Alfred North Whitehead, *Science and the Modern World*, pp. 72, 73.

now declares to be a *mésalliance*, of which the progeny are hybrid monsters incapable of survival.[7]

It is important to ask what kinds of novelty there might be, which, if they should appear, would make the hypothesis of reductive naturalism invalid, and would, accordingly, uphold the contentions of the emergent evolutionists. Professor Lovejoy has analyzed these for us as follows:

They would consist in the appearance at certain points in the history of some system of (a) *qualities* not previously found anywhere in that system; or (b) *types of objects or events* not previously existent therein, not merely combinations of anything previously existent, and characterized by new qualities; or (c) *laws,* i.e. modes of uniform action, not previously exemplified by any entities in the system.[8]

That such kinds of novelty do appear in the evolutionary process the studies of Lloyd Morgan, Jan Smuts, and others have shown. The chief point to stress now, however, is that the third kind of novelty mentioned by Professor Lovejoy is fully as important as the others and even easier to substantiate. Without arguing the question whether the new "objects," such as organisms, are merely combinations of previous existents, or are *genuinely novel*, it is at least clear that there are new laws. The question whether mind and matter are fundamentally the same *substantially*, seems beside the point when they so obviously follow different modes of action. The distinction between the "mental," as that which is private to consciousness, and the "physical," in the sense of an independent system of entities or events having those causal relations which physical science seeks to describe, was one of the first of man's philosophical acquisitions, and one which is still necessary for rational thought and action. Whether nature is bifurcated is a debatable question, but

[7] Arthur O. Lovejoy, "The Discontinuities of Evolution," *University of California Publications in Philosophy,* Volume V, p. 177.
[8] *Ibid.,* p. 178.

that experience is bifurcated is not a matter of reasonable doubt. Dualism, both psychophysical and epistemological, has been the main intellectual tradition in the Western world since the time of Plato, and modern attempts to discredit this tradition have not been conspicuously successful.[9]

Many have set their hands to the task of showing the radical difference between the two kinds of being whose existence is almost universally admitted, *bodies* and *minds*, but few have done better service in this connection than Professor Webb of Oxford who insists that all men do, in practice, distinguish between one set of qualities, such as extension and motion which we attribute to bodies and another set of qualities, such as those of thinking and feeling which we attribute to minds.[10] If we are going to be empirical accepting the world as we find it, we must somehow find room for both sets of qualities. The truth is that a rigidly mechanical system cannot account for the second set of qualities, except in an epiphenomenal sense. The point must be stressed that the contemporary rejections of monism are based on the observation that the one-level conception of natural law does not cover all the facts. Since we actually find different levels of law in the experienced world, our notion of natural law must be enlarged and enriched to include phenomena radically different from those observable on the mechanistic plane.

Among the modern analyses of the problem of natural law as related to the philosophical basis of theism, that of F. R. Tennant is especially thorough. This is found in the first two chapters of the second volume of his *Philosophical Theology*. Professor Tennant's chief contribution is his insistence that the mechanical view of natural law is wholly abstract. It deals with "inert identicals" and these are separated from actuality. Meta-

---

[9] Professor Lovejoy's book, *The Revolt Against Dualism,* is an account of the attempt to dislodge the dualistic tradition, along with his defense of both kinds of dualism.

[10] C. C. J. Webb, *Religion and Theism,* New York, 1934, pp. 100, 101.

physically speaking, an abstraction is nothing. "Mechanism," Tennant writes, "is not a phenomenal aspect; it is abstractive description: and, as such, it is neither universally applicable nor in any single instance exhaustive."[11]

D. THE WORKING SOLUTION OF THE PROBLEM

When we turn to the alternative principle of order, that which is produced in the interests of an enduring and unfolding Purpose, we find what we seek. Not only is this conception free from the strong criticisms which have long been felt in regard to a mechanistic order,[12] but new positive advantages are involved. Above all it accounts for the delicate combination of regularity and novelty which experience reveals. The *regularity* of natural laws is explained, if God is self-consistent in character and His actions not capricious. The *novelty* is explained by the fact that an intelligent motivation is always adapting itself to changing situations.

If the purposive order already described is really the order of the universe, it is reasonable to suppose that events in the world show thoughtful adaptation to circumstances, something that cannot be expected if the mechanical conception of universal law is the true one. Constancy of purpose must often exhibit itself by a *change in procedure*. The parent may have the constant purpose of the advancement of the child's real welfare, but loyalty to this purpose entails apparently contradictory behavior at different times in the life of the child. The order which comes from Purpose has, thus, a unity of aim and variety of method.

Exceptions to the general rule would be fully consistent with a purposive order though the reality of the Purpose would insure that exceptions would be rare. Exceptions for a good rea-

---

[11] F. R. Tennant, *Philosophical Theology*, Cambridge, 1930, Vol. II, p. 50.
[12] The criticisms have been made by laboratory scientists as well as by philosophers of science. See R. A. Milliken, *Evolution in Science and Religion*, Yale University Press, especially pp. 13, 14.

son, such as the welfare of the human race, would not be "breaks" in a purposive order, but would, instead, be necessary elements in such an order.

If the system of laws studied in physics and chemistry is only one system in a larger whole concerned with the carrying out of the purpose of God, it is wholly reasonable that the subsidiary system should be dependent and that, at times, its ordinary procedure should be superseded. If the world is really the medium of God's *personal* action, *miracle is wholly normal.* What we call *a miracle is a situation in which constancy of purpose makes necessary a conspicuous adjustment of means.* "When there is no sufficient reason for variation," writes Temple, "none will appear. And for the vastly greater part of Nature's course there is, so far as we can tell, no reason at all for variation, and much reason for uniformity."[13] A miracle is an event in which there is a *reason* for variation. In short, a miracle, far from being a mysterious event, as is popularly supposed, is really *an occurrence which can be understood.*

Such a conception makes miracles a reasonable feature of the world system. This is a distinct intellectual gain, since there has long been good evidence for the existence of miracles, but many have found themselves forced to reject the evidence, *a priori,* solely because they supposed a belief in natural law made belief in miracles impossible. The notion of a purposive order sets minds free from the bondage of such dogmatism. Unless we have a superstitious reverence for natural law in the nineteenth century sense, we do not decide in advance the question of the actual occurrence of apparently miraculous events, such as the resurrection of Christ, but decide on the basis of the available evidence. We do not talk easily about what *cannot be,* for we should need to be very wise to know that.

When we first begin to think about them, prayer, miracle, and Providence seem to involve separate and distinct problems, but, as we consider them more fully, we see that they all refer

[13] William Temple, *Nature, Man and God,* p. 268.

to the same problem. All of them have been widely believed in by devout people, but all of them have seemed partially unsupportable by a logical approach to reality. The chief reason for the difficulty in every case has been a "block universe," a closed system of nature to which men's minds as well as their bodies belong and which permits no teleological adaptation. That such a rigid system is the actual system of the world does not appear to be self-evident and the arguments which many have advanced against the proposition make it appear improbable.

If, on the other hand, the order of the world is accounted for by reference to the constancy of divine Purpose, the obstacles to belief in both prayer and Providence, as well as miracle, are removed. Prayer and Providence are merely special kinds of miracles, obvious evidence, that is, of the direct effectiveness of purposive causality. Prayer means conscious participation in the purposive order in particular situations; Providence means the continual evidence of Purpose, both in the lives of individuals and the whole world. It is a corollary of belief in Providence that history, instead of being a mere sequence of events, has a *meaning.*

In a wholly mechanical order prayer could not be efficacious, *even in the life of the individual who prays.* Not only would it be impossible for A to influence B's action or destiny by prayer; it would be impossible for A to influence A's action by prayer. Even the crude conception of auto-suggestion is ruled out, since a fully mechanical system involves *epiphenomenalism*, either consciously or unconsciously. By this term we mean that thought, if it exists at all in a fully mechanical order, exists as an impotent observer and not as a causal agent. Certainly mechanism cannot admit God as a causal agent. Countless people have comforted themselves with the thought that their prayer might be privately effective even though it had no intercessory value, but there is no rational justification for such a faith. Apparently there is no half-way house between belief in a purposive order,

which makes any noncontradictory prayer a reasonable procedure, and the rejection of such an order which rules out *all*
prayer as delusion.

We come here to one of the most important decisions that
men can make about their theory of reality. The essence of the
mechanistic view is that it is totalitarian, seeking to embrace all
of reality in a system of mechanical determinism. It is undermined whenever we can point to experience which cannot be
understood on the mechanical level. This we have done in
earlier chapters of this book. But the experience of reality in
prayer is part of the evidence which shows the inadequacy of
the closed system. It begins to look as though we must finally
decide between what is only a metaphysical prejudice on the
one hand and a living experience, on the other, which is attested by the testimony of countless persons whom there is
reason to trust.

Prayer, you say, cannot change a situation when once disease
has set in. How do you know? We know very little about our
amazing world, far too little to engage rashly in the use of
universal negatives. The testimony to the value of prayer is so
great[14] that when a metaphysical system is a barrier to it, it is
reasonable to doubt the credibility of the system rather than the
prayer. So long as one really believes in God, no ethically sensitive petition need be ruled out. If the figure of speech which
makes our relation to God a filial one has any adequacy at all,
it seems perfectly proper for us to pour out our desires before
God without anxiety as to what is a scientifically permissible
request. God does not need to *change* the laws of nature in
order to answer prayer, if the laws themselves, as there is good
reason to believe, are dependent upon a divine Purpose, and
are relatively constant only because God's will is constant.

In view of recent developments in thought, those who have
reason to believe in prayer need not be apologetic or hesitant.

[14] As an example of such testimony see T. H. Somervell, *After Everest.*

The central question is the old question of mechanism, and it is really not so formidable. Unless the world is a closed mechanistic system, there seems no reason to doubt the efficacy of prayer, but we know that it is not such a system, for there are men in it. A world in which thought can move matter is a world in which it is wholly reasonable for prayer to affect destiny.

The publication, a few years ago, of the volume *Scientific Theory and Religion*, from the pen of E. W. Barnes, was an intellectual event of great importance, as many readers have discovered. Part of the significance of this event is the fact that Bishop Barnes is that rare creature, a genuine expert in widely separated fields. He is as little the amateur in quantum theory as in philosophy and theology. Accordingly his forthright statement about prayer deserves frequent repetition and becomes a suitable conclusion to the present chapter:

I myself, of course, have no doubts as to the value of prayer. A merely mechanical theory of the Universe I reject. God rules the world: the laws of Nature are His laws and in no way constrain His freedom. Thus there is no reason to believe that God cannot grant favourable answers to the crudest petitionary prayers: our experience alone can determine whether He thus acts as we seek His aid. I should even hesitate to affirm dogmatically that petitions for rain or fair weather were necessarily unavailing: until we have proved that the physical cosmos is a closed system, there is no theoretical reason why God should not hearken to such prayer. I would pray for a friend's recovery from sickness with the knowledge that such prayers are often of no avail and yet with hope that God in His goodness would grant my petition. With great confidence would I pray for strength against temptation, whether I myself or some other was in need.[15]

[15] E. W. Barnes, *Scientific Theory and Religion*, New York, 1933, pp. 612, 613.

CHAPTER XVII

THE PROBLEM OF EVIL

"The greatest theoretic difficulty against all Theism lies in the terrible reality of Evil; and yet the deepest adequacy, in the actual toil and trouble of life, of this same Theism, especially of Christianity, consists in its practical attitude towards, and success against, this most real Evil." —BARON VON HÜGEL

The problem to which we now turn is the most persistent and the most difficult which the mind of man knows. In a study such as we have undertaken it cannot be escaped, but, at the same time, there is no hope of a really satisfactory solution. The area of difficulty can be reduced though it cannot be eliminated. It can, in fact, be reduced sufficiently so that it is not an absolute barrier to theistic realism, and that is all we really require, since intelligent belief is compatible with the recognition of some difficulty, as Newman and others have insisted. Perhaps no belief in the world is ever utterly free from difficulties. Certainly no great religion pretends to provide a perfect solution of "the riddle of the universe."

Professor Montague, in a much quoted passage, has spoken of the problem of evil as one half of the "Prolegomena to Every Possible Theology," the other half being the problem of good.[1] It seems more suitable, however, to consider the problem of evil near the end of our study, rather than as a part of the prolegomena, for the very good reason that the problem does not arise except derivatively. *If there were not good evidence for the being of God, the problem of evil could not even occur.* Even if men believed in God, but did not believe that God is *good*, the problem would not occur. It is thoroughly pointless to in-

[1] In *Belief Unbound.*

clude, in a philosophical treatise, a chapter on the problem of evil, unless the treatise also includes a consideration of that view of the nature of reality without which there is no such problem.

It is a highly significant historical fact that, in spite of the Greek genius for philosophical inquiry, the classic statement of the problem of evil should have appeared, not in the Hellenic tradition, but in the Hebraic. The Greeks were slow in arriving at ethical monotheism.

If there is no God, if reality consists of a series of events wholly devoid of meaning and purpose, we should be perplexed, but the presence of evil in the world would be in no way alarming and would demand no special explanation. The fact that the demand for an explanation of evil is so nearly universal is one of our best indications of how widespread theism really is. The fact that this evidence is unconscious and indirect is what makes it so impressive—it is not something adopted for the sake of appearances. But what is thus implied by the general recognition of the problem of evil, is also implied by the other problems we have already considered. The problems raised by natural selection would not even occur to men if there were no evidence of Purpose; the problem of psychological explanation is no problem apart from religious experience; the problem of natural law demands no answer apart from prayer. The widespread recognition of all these problems, and the interest they arouse, constitute a significant part of the evidence of belief which we have already mentioned.

A. THE NATURE OF THE PROBLEM

The problem of evil is that which arises in any rational mind when the widespread tendency to believe in the goodness of God is challenged by the patent fact that the world is imperfect. The world has in it, not only a vast amount of good, both potential and actual, and not only a vast amount of beauty, but also a vast amount of evil or negative value. This array of evil includes suffering, error, imperfection, and sin. Even the most unphilosophic mind, when aware of the widespread presence of evil in the world, which there is reason to believe is the workmanship of a loving and omnipotent Spirit, recognizes a dilemma. Either God wills to remove the evil and is not able, or God does not will to remove it. If we accept the first horn of this dilemma, God cannot be considered omnipotent and there is some doubt whether we have a genuine monotheism, for other powers, equal to God or superior to Him, are recognized.

Without the supposition of other and contending powers, it would be necessary to hold, as Hume suggested, that God was *incompetent*. Perhaps this world is the work of a mere amateur. This world, for all we know, says Hume, "is very faulty and imperfect, compared to a superior standard; and was only the first rude essay of some infant deity, who afterwards abandoned it, ashamed of his lame performance; it is the work only of some dependent, inferior deity; and is the object of derision to his superiors; it is the production of old age and dotage in some superannuated deity; and ever since his death, has run on at adventures, from the first impulse and active force which it received from him."[2] If, however, we accept the second alternative, God is no longer worthy of our love and trust. He would, indeed, be morally inferior to some of His creatures, a situation which is hardly credible.

Both of these alternatives have been widely recognized as unsatisfactory, and there has been a continual effort to find a third alternative, logically consistent with the facts as known, which will make it possible to believe in One who is both all-powerful and all-good. The effort to find this third alternative is an enterprise which fills many volumes and even has a special name, originated by Leibnitz. Such an effort to vindicate the justice of God in permitting natural and moral evil is a *theodicy*. The first mature theodicy was the Book of Job.

[2] David Hume, *Dialogues Concerning Natural Religion*, Part V.

The problem of the justification of evil, after it has appeared, is closely connected with the problem of its origin. If God is the Creator of the world, He would seem to be responsible for everything in it. But sin and suffering and other forms of evil are in it. Therefore God must be the author of sin and evil. The amount of squirming that has been done to avoid this conclusion is very impressive, but little of it is really convincing. On the other hand, if there is something in the world which God did not create, how are we to account for it? As we have seen above, Mind is the only ultimate explanation of anything. Must we therefore posit an eternal Evil Mind as well as an eternal Good Mind? If so, we are landed in the intolerable difficulties of ultimate dualism.[3] We are not greatly helped by adopting the Manichaean heresy.

All this suggests that the reasonable procedure is one in which we try to choose the path of least difficulty, realizing that no path is wholly clear. In this connection it is important to remember that giving up the problem does not provide an easy path, either. That would mean a retreat to the naturalism which is so unsatisfactory because it is unable to account even for its own truth. In addition, the formidable problem of good would be quite unsolved.[4] To overcome a difficulty about the meaning of the world by adopting a hypothesis according to which nothing has meaning, is a bold step, but it has not seemed to most men a particularly reasonable one. The adoption of pantheism likewise does not diminish, but actually increases the theoretical difficulty "since the world as it stands, and not an Ultimate Reality behind it, is here held to be per-

[3] It should be noted that, though we have seen reason to support both epistemological dualism and psychophysical dualism, consistency does not demand that we accept metaphysical dualism, which deals with another question. The convictions that the "knower" and the "known" are independent entities, and that "minds" and "bodies" have different qualities and follow different laws, are wholly consistent with the thesis that God is the ultimate bond of unity and that there is a single comprehensive order in which all find their place.

[4] Cf. *supra*, Chapter VII.

fect."[5] John Bennett has introduced a fresh note into the discussion by pointing out that, if there were no evil, the very absence of evil would constitute a problem since there would be nothing to jar us out of an attitude of self-sufficiency.[6]

Our predicament, then, is this: the problem of evil cannot be wholly solved, but it, likewise, cannot be avoided with intellectual self-respect. One way is open—to see how much of the problem can be whittled away.

B. PROPOSED SOLUTIONS OF THE PROBLEM

It is worth while to list, in outline form, the chief solutions of our problem which have been seriously put forward. In this we shall limit our list to those proposals which are supposedly consistent with theism, since the other proposed "solutions" merely give up the problem instead of solving it. Though hosts of suggestions have been put forward, many have no novelty other than the novelty of terminology and the fundamental proposals may be reduced to five:

(1) *The first proposal is the wholly naïve suggestion that suffering is a direct result of sin* and a just recompense for it. This is the theory presented by Job's friends and is the chief metaphysical foil in the wonderful dialogue which is named for the man who rejected this view. The theory may be either that the suffering is visited directly on the sinner or that it is visited on others, especially his descendants. Both forms of the theory were rejected by Christ.[7]

How widely this theory is held it is impossible to know, but there are frequent indications that it is never quite discarded, especially in the popular mind. Each great earthquake brings out some pronouncements about the wickedness of the city that has been shaken, pronouncements reminiscent of Sodom and Gomorrah. But in any case the theory is wholly unsatisfactory,

[5] Baron Friedrich von Hügel, *Essays and Addresses on the Philosophy of Religion*, p. 94.

[6] John Bennett, *Christian Realism*, New York, 1940, p. 164.

[7] Luke, 13:1-5; John, 9:1-3.

and that on three counts. (a) In the first place it does not account for the sin, which is a far greater evil than the suffering it allegedly causes. We are no nearer a solution of our fundamental question, which is how we can avoid making God the author of sin. (b) In the second place, the theory is not in accordance with observed phenomena. The Psalmist may say he has never seen the righteous forsaken, but most other men have seen that deplorable sight. With the modern revival of the strategy of terror and the widespread employment of physical as well as mental torture, the evidence for a disparity between what men deserve and what they get is particularly abundant. Natural evils, such as earthquakes, do come to "wicked" cities, since all cities are wicked, but why do they not come to the other wicked cities? Are we to suppose that San Francisco was especially wicked in 1906 and Tokyo especially wicked in 1923? (c) In the third place, the theory is not consistent with the goodness of God. Not only does it, in its usual form, involve suffering to wholly innocent children, but also its only virtue is an abstract justice, with no suggestion of love.

(2) *A second proposal is that all evil is really illusory.* Such a doctrine is popularly represented by the teachings of Christian Science and is academically represented by certain versions of absolute idealism. The theory gets its chief factual support from the observation that what *seems* like evil often turns out not to *be* evil, especially when viewed in a larger context. The upshot of this is the essential identification of evil and error. Frequently it includes the notion that all evil experience is purely subjective and, since it exists only in the mind of the observer, is not part of the objective reality.

Though this suggestion is less inadequate than the first proposal, it is gravely unsatisfactory as a solution of our problem. Even if the hypothesis be accepted as true, we are still faced with the question of how the *appearance of evil* is to be explained and how it originated. The illusion of pain is undoubtedly almost as unpleasant as "real" pain, whatever that may be. Why is not illusion itself a genuine evil? A world in which so many persons are made so that they are "deceived" about anything which seems as real as unmerited suffering, needs a vast amount of explaining. A world of dupes is hardly preferable to a world of suffering sinners.

The hypothesis of illusion is upheld philosophically only by what we are forced to call metaphysical hocus-pocus. We are told that all evil disappears in the Absolute, just as temporal sequence is somehow transmuted into eternality or timelessness.[8] But this kind of dialectic is increasingly unconvincing. It is not even religiously satisfactory, since the Absolute thus arrived at is utterly different from God as known and worshiped.

A still more formidable objection to this theory, from the practical point of view, is that it would cut the nerve of moral effort if it were taken seriously. If all evil, whether moral, natural, or intellectual is truly illusory, we are foolish indeed to *fight* it; it would be far preferable to *forget* it. Accordingly it is hard to think of God in moral terms if there is no genuine evil to fight. If there is no genuine evil, if there is nothing in the universe that has *negative* value, our only moral task is to realize that this is the case. In the face of such notions, there is something wonderfully refreshing about the words of L. P. Jacks, when he asks the question, "How shall we think of evil?" and answers it by saying, "We shall think ill of it." But we cannot think ill of it if it doesn't exist. "For my own part," writes Dr. Jacks, "I would rather live in a world which contained real evils which all men recognize than in another where all men were such imbeciles as to believe in the existence of evil which has no existence at all."[9]

[8] For example, F. H. Bradley says that "since in ultimate Reality all existence, and all thought and feeling, become one, we may even say that every feature in the universe is thus absolutely good." *Appearance and Reality*, p. 412.

[9] L. P. Jacks, *Religious Foundations*, p. 105.

Whatever else we do we must avoid any supposed solution of the problem of evil which makes men think well of it or in any way "reconciles" them to its existence so that they do not seek to overcome it.

(3) *A third, and far more important proposal is that which sees evil as a necessary defect in a good plan.* This does not deny the reality of evil, but it does hold that some forms of evil enter into the formation of a larger good or are the necessary concomitants of a good process. The strength of this solution lies in the fact that it can be illustrated abundantly from many levels of experience, some of which will be mentioned more fully later in this chapter.

Evil is a necessity in high moral endeavor, since a world which had no evil in it would not present the moral decisions which are the necessary means of developing moral strength. Though suffering sometimes crushes the sufferer, there are many times when the final result is more glorious than would be conceivable in any other kind of world. It is our duty to rid the world of disease and persecution and many other evils, but we must admit that some of the grandest chapters in human life are made possible by these very evils which men learn to bear nobly or fight bravely. It is hard to avoid the conviction that any other kind of world than an imperfect one would be an everlasting tea party, and that its inhabitants would inevitably be soft.

It is the truth that many of the goods we value most highly are those which owe part of their excellence to the difficulty of attaining them. We like that which costs something, but how could any goods be costly and dangerous apart from the presence of evil in the world? Dr. Temple has provided a brilliant illustration of such a good in his discussion of victory, which is a conspicuous form of good. "A world in which there was no victory," he writes, "would be, so far, an inferior world. But if there is to be victory, there must be opposition. To demand the good of victory without the existence of an antagonist is to demand something with no meaning."[10]

Persuasive as are these arguments to uphold the theory of evil as a necessary condition of the good, the theory is easy to lampoon. The form in which it was most widely held in the eighteenth century was savagely lampooned, as is well known, by Voltaire in *Candide*. The notion of which Voltaire was making fun was not, it should be emphasized, a notion that minimized evil. Far from it. The philosophical optimist frankly recognized the reality of evil, as well as its wide distribution, but *the point was that the world contained the proper amount of evil*. It was this, and not the entire absence of evil, as is popularly supposed, which made distinguished men speak of ours as the "best of all possible worlds." It was a world, many contended, which had just enough pain to make possible the good of patience, just enough danger to make possible the good of courage. If there were any less evil, it would be a worse world, rather than a better one.[11]

In practice this doctrine has not actually tended to cut the nerve of moral effort, but this is because the logic of the situation is not followed to the bitter end. If it is really true that there is *exactly* the right amount of evil in the world, it would be a great mistake to remove any of it and thus make the world worse.

The theory we are now presenting has some superficial resemblances to the theory that all evil is illusory, and the two have sometimes been identified in popular thought, but they are fundamentally distinct. According to this third proposal, the evil in the *part* must be real, else the good of the whole is impossible. One does not develop great virtue by combating *fancied* ills. The theory has much to commend it, and the basic

[10] William Temple, *Mens Creatrix*, p. 268.
[11] See A. O. Lovejoy, "Optimism and Romanticism," Publications of the Modern Language Association of America, Volume XIII (1927).

insight on which it rests must be part of any moderately satisfactory view of the matter; but it has a serious fault in regard
to the *amount* and *distribution* of evil. That *some* evil is the
condition of the highest good, seems clear, but why should
there be so much of it? Would not a more modest amount suffice? Moreover, the evil does not seem to be spread in such a
way as to achieve the highest moral ends. Some people have
too much suffering, and some too little. And the theory seems
to be most earnestly espoused by fairly comfortable people who
point out to others how much worse their lives would be if
they had less to combat.

> The toad beneath the harrow knows
> Exactly where each tooth-point goes;
> The butterfly, upon the road,
> Preaches contentment to the toad.

How easy it is to lampoon the argument, L. P. Jacks shows in
the following passage:

I read the other day a book intended to justify the ways of God
to man, which argued that if men are to have teeth at all they must
have teeth that can ache. There must therefore be such a thing as
toothache. Quite so. But what if the number of aching teeth in the
world at this moment is a hundred times as great as it need be? And
why should the aching be as violent as it is? Would not a milder
and more endurable form of the malady satisfy the requirements of
the argument? And why should my teeth ache rather than yours?[12]

(4) *The fourth fundamental way in which men have sought
to solve the problem of evil is by a frank admission that God's
power is limited.* This proposal admits that the popular dilemma
presented above is genuine and therefore inescapable. We must
conclude, either that God is not wholly good or that God is
not wholly powerful. Almost any sensitive mind will choose

[12] L. P. Jacks, *op. cit.,* p. 103.

the latter hypothesis,[13] and Dr. Rashdall has shown us the rational justification for such a choice of belief. To believe there is a limit to God's goodness would be to deny utterly the notion that the Good is our ultimate principle of explanation, whereas to believe that there is a limit to God's power is only to continue a line of thought which no person really escapes. All admit that God cannot change the past, and this, says Rashdall, is wholly consistent with a really intelligent conception of omnipotence. "God possesses all the power there is."[14]

The notion that God is limited and thus, in some sense, *finite,* has received strong support from various quarters, but it has likewise received strong criticism. L. P. Jacks' brilliant essay, "How Shall We Think of Evil?" an essay which seems to have attracted surprisingly little notice, accepts the notion of the limitation of divine power with gusto. Jacks refuses to recognize as God any being with whose "goodness" evil can be "reconciled," but he can recognize as God the Source of all opposition to evil. God *opposes* evil and we, insofar as we oppose it, have a point of contact with Him. Though Jacks does not say so explicitly, he is bound to hold, as truly as did the standard eighteenth century optimists, that ours is *the best possible world*, though he may have a different reason for upholding the proposition. Our world, according to the limitation doctrine, is the best world possible, because God made it as free from evil as He could. There is something about evil, it is suggested, which even God cannot conquer at will. Hastings Rashdall, as intimated above, gave to this doctrine the backing of his great name.

Among American writers who have declared themselves as

[13] Some readers may wonder why we do not list the notion that God is not completely good, i.e., the first horn of the dilemma, as one of the proposed solutions. We do not because it is not really a "live option." Suggestions of it appear in primitive religion, but it is not seriously proposed in advanced thought.

[14] Hasting Rashdall, *Philosophy and Religion,* New York, 1910, p. 83. See also *The Theory of Good and Evil,* Vol. II, pp. 287-288.

convinced of the limitation of God are men as representative of different metaphysical systems as E. S. Brightman and W. P. Montague. Professor Brightman's ambitious work, *A Philosophy of Religion,* receives its distinctive flavor, in contrast with other volumes on the same subject, by the careful treatment of the question, "Is God Finite?" Theistic absolutism and theistic finitism are carefully analyzed and contrasted, but Professor Brightman accepts the latter as the more satisfactory explanation of the facts, particularly the facts of evil. In distinguishing between God and the Given, Brightman reminds his readers that he stands in the tradition of Plato, for God, as depicted in the *Timaeus,* is not the omnipotent Creator, but the Demiurge or Cosmic Artisan. When faced with the criticism that theistic finitism, according to which God is *potent*, but not *omnipotent*, is inconsistent with the spirit of true religion, Brightman defends his position by pointing to five specific religious values which finitism safeguards:

(a) There is greater assurance of divine sympathy and love.
(b) There is something awe-inspiring about the magnificent cosmic struggle.
(c) Finitism furnishes incentives to co-operative endeavor.
(d) Belief in a finite God affords ground for belief in cosmic advance.
(e) It is more natural to pray to a finite God, who may be moved by our infirmities.[15]

John Bennett has recently espoused a variant of this view[16] though he knows that the sentence "God cannot" sounds blasphemous to many persons. Bennett quotes Brightman with approval. As evidence that God faces limited possibilities, Profes-

---

[15] E. S. Brightman, *A Philosophy of Religion,* New York, 1940, pp. 327, 328.
[16] In an article published in the *Journal of Religion* for October, 1938, and reprinted in *Christian Realism,* New York, 1941.

sor Bennett points out that God cannot create an interdependent community of persons without having a world in which evils spread.[17]

Such an emphasis is largely an extension of what has often been said in traditional theology. It has long been recognized that God is at least limited by the laws of logic, especially the law of noncontradiction. It is obvious that God could not make round squares, for such a statement is strictly meaningless. But is it not equally true, though perhaps less obvious, that God could not make created beings without the dangers inherent in createdness? Gilson, writing in conscious harmony with the main theological tradition of the Middle Ages, which reached its climax in St. Thomas Aquinas, notes especially that "these very limitations and mutabilities for which nature is arraigned, are metaphysically inherent in the very status of a created thing as such."[18]

Gilson and other thinkers of his persuasion are careful, however, not to say that createdness necessitates evil. Mutability may be a necessary consequence of the very existence of finite spirits, but evil is not.[19] That which is a part, of course, cannot be the whole, but why could not the "mutable" parts be fitted harmoniously together without mutual hostility? "As far as the inequalities in creatures are concerned," says Gilson, "to call them evil would seem an abuse of terms."[20]

Though there is this much in common between the fourth proposal in regard to evil and Catholic philosophy, the agreement is soon exhausted, since the Catholic thinkers pronounce strongly against the notion of God as finite. The fundamental characteristic of God, according to Thomistic philosophy, is Being, and the concept of Being leads to both perfection and

[17] *Christian Realism,* pp. 173, 174.

[18] Etienne Gilson, *The Spirit of Medieval Philosophy,* New York, 1936, p. 113.

[19] At this point I think John Bennett makes a wrong inference when he says the same principle is involved. See *Christian Realism,* p. 174.

[20] *Op. cit.,* p. 113.

infinity. The only kind of limitation which St. Thomas admits is a logical limitation and does not mean, it is contended, that there is some power, external to God, which He cannot handle as He will.

Anyone who has some notion of the degree of sophistication which characterizes Thomistic thought cannot lightly oppose such a clear testimony. Perhaps the doctrine of limitation, as a solution of the problem of evil, is too simple, too much of a short cut. There is something both courageous and honest about throwing oneself on one of the horns of the dilemma, but we must admit that the great tradition has involved the refusal to do so. The great tradition has been the refusal to give up either God's goodness or His omnipotence.

Dr. Temple represents this reluctance to accept finitism while, at the same time, recognizing its value. He sees that Rashdall's hypothesis is "immeasurably superior, alike on theoretical and practical grounds, to the doctrine that evil can be dismissed as an illusion."[21] But he thinks that the acceptance of finitism really means throwing up the sponge and admitting that the search for rational explanation of the universe is a failure. If goodness is the only self-explanatory principle and if we find in the world something beyond the good, called the given or by any other name, our search for explanation has failed. Perhaps this is the best we can do, but we can at least conceive something better. If there is something external to God, in the "nature of things," which imposes a limitation upon Him, we are far from full ethical monotheism. The God of Plato's *Timaeus* is not very exciting, and the truth is that he is not the Judeo-Christian God at all.

(5) *The fifth proposal is the answer of childlike faith*. This is essentially the working solution at which the unknown author of the *Book of Job* finally arrived, and it has always been part of the solution for those deeply religious, whatever their additional views might be. Many of those who have defended one

[21] *Mens Creatrix*, p. 264.

of the first four proposals have admitted some perplexity at the end, and supplemented their theories with the one we are considering now. The positive contribution of the *Book of Job* comes in the "Speeches of the Lord" which give Job something better than that which is provided by the feeble remarks of his friends. The essential point of these final speeches is that the problem is too great for the finite mind, that Job sees only a small segment of reality, and that his criticisms are accordingly inappropriate. How can Job *know* that either God's power or goodness is limited? His knowledge of temporal things is admittedly slight; his knowledge of eternal things is still more slight. The conclusion of the book[22] is Job's recognition of his own humble status with the consequent mood of childlike trust. The trust, if we interpret as intentional the juxtaposition of texts, is not blind credulity, but the consequence of the direct vision of God. (Job, 42:5, 6.)

It seems clear that this fifth proposal, though it has little metaphysical value, must always be part of any satisfactory "solution." The position need not be, it should be noted, merely a deduction from ignorance, which is always logically suspect. The point is that the humble worshiper *already* has abundant reason to believe in God in the full theistic sense. If, then, he runs into some difficulty, even a difficulty as great as the problem of evil, he does not, for that reason, give up his faith. *The reasons for his faith are so great that they can weather a few storms.* Religious insight makes us believe that there *is* a full solution of the problem of evil though we are too ignorant and dull to understand it.

C. THE REDUCTION OF THE AREA OF DIFFICULTY

While we recognize that we are not likely to find a completely satisfactory solution, we are nevertheless eager to whittle down the problem as best we can. Since we cannot expect

---

[22] Disregarding the wholly inconsistent appendix apparently added in the interests of mistaken piety.

to present some new proposal, wisdom would seem to lie in combining the valid insights of other proposals, insofar as they are consistent with one another. The lesson of Job may be assumed to be a part of any working solution and is consistent with any in which a sense of perplexity remains. Since, however, this is not really a proposed solution so much as a working faith that there is a solution, it needs no further elaboration. The first and second of our five proposals, the theory of evil as direct reward and the theory of evil as illusion, hardly deserve serious discussion. Then the proposals which remain are only two: the theory of evil as the necessary condition of good and the theory that God is limited in power. It is desirable to combine the parts of these which can be defended, omitting, if possible, the parts which cannot be defended, and, above all, keeping the practical attitude toward evil which makes us seek to overcome it. Since it is the practical overcoming of evil in countless moral struggles which gives us our best clue to its theoretical explanation, we must be extremely careful not to adopt a theoretical explanation which in any way undermines this clue.

At this point our study is facilitated by dealing separately with moral evil and natural evil. By moral evil we mean that which arises in or as a result of *sin*, and sin is possible wherever there is a creature sensitive to moral values. Natural evil is that which arises when self-consciousness is not a factor. Most actions of beasts are presumably in the latter class.

(1) *Moral evil* is far more serious than natural evil and yet it is the more easily understood. Discussions of the problem of evil often begin by reference to earthquakes, floods, and epidemics, but these are almost trivial in their effects when contrasted with the unmerited suffering which comes as a result of the actions of wicked men. An earthquake may destroy life, but it does not torture. Much of the worst of human suffering is mental anguish, and this is caused far more by evil men than it is by the forces of nature. Human beings can, if they

choose, move away from known volcanoes or earthquake terri-
tory, but they can hardly escape the society of their fellow men.
Moreover, many of the supposed natural evils are chiefly trace-
able to human greed or other moral turpitude. Floods are frequently the result of an irresponsible policy of lumbering which
takes away from the hills their natural means of holding back
the rain water. Epidemics may be accentuated by the overcrowd-
ing which is one result of a lust for financial gain, irrespective
of the human cost.

In attempting to find some explanation of moral evil, we
must explore more carefully the notion that God is limited. It is
instructive to note that all who discuss the matter seriously agree
that *there is some limitation.* The only question is *where* the
limitation begins. The Catholic writers who oppose finitism all
agree that God is limited logically, and those who agree with
Professor Brightman merely hold that the limitation is greater.[23]
There is some indication, however, that a great deal of the argument is purely verbal. It is interesting to note that the illustrations given by the upholders of finitism are illustrations, not
about the "nature of things," but about the "nature of goodness" or the "nature of personality." The illustrations already
quoted from John Bennett's valuable paper are all of this kind.
Many of Professor Brightman's observations are similar. Furthermore, these are like the limitations admitted in traditional
theology since they are based on the principle of consistency.

What we suggest is that there is really a tacit agreement
among most thinkers in that they combine the third and fourth
proposals already outlined. They actually hold that God is
limited, but limited in a special way, namely, that He is limited
by the conditions of goodness. This may not be the best possible world, but it is, so far as we can see, the only kind of
world consistent with the Purpose we dimly glimpse.

[23] Why God should be limited by the laws of logic and no more is not
as clear as it once seemed. If He is limited by laws of logic, He is, presumably, also limited by the laws of mathematics. But physics is largely applied
mathematics. Are physical limitations therefore to be excluded *a priori*?

If we begin with the notion which we cannot give up—the belief in the absolute goodness of God—we must suppose God has a wholly good purpose. Judging by the hints which evolution gives, that purpose is the production of other centers of consciousness capable of spiritual determination which may be defined as "determination by what seems good as contrasted with determination by irresistible compulsion." Perhaps man as we know him represents only a very low form of such spiritual determination, but men at least understand what it is. Now choice would be an absolute essential in such an enterprise. God's purpose would be defeated if goodness were compelled; moreover it would not be genuine goodness. The goodness of a machine, which has no alternative, is, of course, not goodness at all. A creature who chose the good voluntarily would be superior to one who could not do otherwise.

If the possibility of goodness involves choice, it also involves the possibility of evil; and, if the possibility is genuine, it will sometimes be realized. Therefore, the conditions of the occurrence of evil are identical with the occurrence of the higher aspects of the moral life. It cannot be said God directly wills sin or evil desire, because it is not *necessary* that we sin. The sin is *our* fault, not God's, though God made us so that we might sin, because otherwise the best in life could not be. Temple makes a fine distinction at this point which will, no doubt, seem to some readers evasive and to others convincing. "We cannot doubt," he says, "that God foresaw the issues of conferring selfhood upon finite beings, so that sin falls within His purpose, and is even part of it, though it cannot be said that He directly willed or wills it."[24]

Such an interpretation receives impressive support from the devotional writings of that great scholar and saint, Lancelot Andrewes. Perhaps the problem is easier to solve devotionally than philosophically. In his private prayer Andrewes says:

[24] William Temple, *Nature, Man and God*, p. 369.

> Two things I recognize, O Lord, in myself:
>   nature, which Thou hast made;
>   sin, which I have added:
> I confess that by sin I have depraved nature;
> but call to remembrance, that I am a
>   wind that passeth away,
>   and returneth not again;
> for of myself I cannot return again from sin.
> Take away from me that which I have made;
> let that which Thou hast made remain in me.[25]

Here we have the abiding Christian paradox of sin. We are to blame for it, but *we* cannot heal it. God did not cause it, but He can forgive and overcome it.

Heresy has come from supposing either:

a. The power to cause implies the power to overcome or
b. The power to overcome implies responsibility for sin's existence.

i.e., Heresy comes from any denial of the paradox.

The kind of sin which is most serious is man's own; it cannot be attributed to animal inheritance or to the demands of the flesh. Most of the moral evil concerned with animal appetites is comparatively superficial, but that concerned with self-centeredness may be both profound and far-reaching in its effects. The center of our trouble is not the turbulent appetites, but the personality as a whole. "It was not the body that made the spirit sin," writes Gilson, "it was the spirit that brought death to the body."[26] Adam and Eve, according to the legendary story of Genesis, were really both advancing and "falling" in that they made, at the same time, a step which enables us to rise to great heights and to sink far lower than any beast. The same self-consciousness which is the necessary condition of remorse is also the means of vicious self-centeredness.

There is very little evil in the animal creation, in spite of the

[25] *The Devotions of Bishop Andrewes*, Volume II, Introduction.
[26] Etienne Gilson, *The Spirit of Mediaeval Philosophy*, p. 114. See also Temple, *Nature, Man and God*, p. 367.

fact that large animals eat small animals. The necessity of food getting involves moments of terror, but the modern students of wild life suggest that the older picture of nature "red in tooth and claw" was sentimentalized. Actually there seems to be a great deal of enjoyment of life in the animal creation. It is with man that the hard problem arises, and this, it would seem, is because man is a creature who is personal as the animals are not. Evil is the price we pay for moral freedom.

It is such considerations as those just mentioned which make it reasonable to maintain that the limitation on God's working, which accounts for the presence of evil, is due, not to the *nature of things*, but the *nature of goodness*. We can take a step farther, however, by showing that the limitation is inherent in the *nature of personality*. A person is a being whose acts are determined, not by external compulsion, but by an appeal to the apprehension of the good. This theory supports the Christian doctrine that God works with men by *Grace* and it interprets the Cross as a revelation of the way in which God is always reaching out to win men.

This highly convincing notion has been the chief theme of John Oman and those consciously influenced by his thinking.[27] The book in which Oman has especially developed the notion that personality necessarily involves risk is *Grace and Personality*. In this important volume the point is carefully made that it is impossible to play safe in dealing with persons, since they cannot be manipulated, as things can be, without doing violence to their essential nature. If God, being personal, desired the existence of finite persons in the world, it was necessary that they should be free to fail, since to *force* them into goodness would involve a severance of personal relations. If one is truly a person he must keep his own house in order with no one to compel him. "In that task," says Oman, "God, no more than man, can help us except through our own purpose, guided by

[27] See, for example, William Wilson's Swarthmore Lecture, *Our Response to God*.

our own insight, dealing with our own world; and, only as grace works in that personal way through ourselves, is it God's dealing with us as His children."[28] Again it is the concept of noncontradiction which is the ruling principle. That God should deal *personally*, and yet compel the avoidance of evil, would be as meaningless as the production of round squares.

It is freely admitted that the "solution" offered is not wholly satisfying, but it does solve part of the problem and give a modicum of mental peace. It absolves God of the authorship of evil; it gives a rational account of why evil is necessary; and it avoids extreme finitism by showing that the limitation is inherent in God's own character, rather than in some intractable area outside God's power. It does not show why the exact amount and distribution of evil are necessary, but it does make us see that suffering of the innocent is part of the price that must be paid if we are to be really personal beings. We are not personal unless we choose, and men who make bad choices are bound to harm others. In spite of the horrible suffering which choice involves, most of us would prefer such a world to its alternative. Moreover, the very presence of evil tells us something important about the character of God, something which we otherwise might not know. If God, desiring good, nevertheless permits evil, this shows that He is a God of love, using persuasion rather than compulsion. This, indeed, is the way love works.

Perhaps what we chiefly need is a new conception of omnipotence. If omnipotence means ability to do *anything*, then surely God is not omnipotent, but this is a purely childish notion. A. C. Turner, who was killed in France in 1917, has left one of the best suggestions we have in this connection. It was his conviction that the problem of evil is eased by a more mature theory of omnipotence. "Love," he wrote, "is omnipotent because it can always in any circumstance give a perfect expression of itself. It has no need to manipulate history, because it

---

[28] John Oman, *Grace and Personality*, Cambridge, 1919, p. 51.

is always sufficient to meet any situation. The activity of love is self-giving; it can afford to give itself away, and no reception which it may meet can be either a limitation or a real defeat. If divine love is the author of all existence, it follows that nothing can exist wherein love cannot find expression."[29]

Here is a suggestion which raises the discussion to a new plane and opens new vistas of future thought. Perhaps the trouble all along is that men have taken too seriously their spatial and physical metaphors. These do not really apply to a loving Spirit.

(2) *Natural evil* is far less important in the modern world than moral evil, but it is harder to explain. Evil may be the price of moral freedom, but natural evil does not seem to have such a clear connection with anything good. The nearest we come to this kind of connection is in the observation that many of the finest traits of character emerge in the struggle against disease and other dangers. The peril of safety is really greater than is the peril of danger. One of the most persuasive elaborations of this theme is to be found in a series of essays, written by C. F. G. Masterman, with the general title, *In Peril of Change*. The essays were published in 1913, on the eve of tremendous change, with the complete disappearance of the tranquil life which Masterman so much feared. He saw the beginning of a time when most of the evils of nature were curbed and when there was a prospect of the final elimination of disease. "The general view of Nature which this new race is cultivating," he wrote, "is that of a well-ordered watering place which is the sole experience of most of them: a cleaned beach, breakwaters to temper the rough onslaught of the sea, with promenade and pier and safe playing-ground for the children."[30]

Such a prospect did not please Mr. Masterman, because he

---

[29] A. C. Turner, "Faith, Prayer, and the World's Order," in *Concerning Prayer*, London, 1916, p. 421.

[30] C. F. G. Masterman, *In Peril of Change*, London, 1913, p. 168.

recognized that the best things in human life are reserved for some tremendous crisis. "The times of disorder and unsettlement when men suffered from oppression, trembled in terror before vague and inexplicable forces, were ravaged by great plagues and lived always in uncertainty, were the times which produced the highest developments of art and the finest flower of human character."[31] That this is true we cannot doubt, though it does not carry us far enough. The good life demands that nature include *some* dangers, but it is hard to see why the good life requires the *particular* dangers which exist.

A similar approach to the problem of natural evil is afforded by a consideration of accidents, which bring such sharp anguish. For the most part we cannot conceive how there could be an ordered world inhabited by free agents and accidents not occur. If knives are sharp enough to do good work, they are sharp enough to cut the fingers which guide the work. If automobiles go fast enough to work efficiently, they go fast enough to destroy the lives of those who ride in them. There are real barriers to belief in the love and power of God, but accidents are not among them.

Though part of natural evil can be thus explained, not all of it can be. We do not need earthquakes to keep life from being dull, and we do not need cancer or infantile paralysis to keep men from being oversatisfied. Even the heroism of rescue squads and the patient labor of research in these maladies are not sufficient to balance their harm. It is facts like these to which we refer when we say the problem of evil is not solved, though it is reduced.

In the face of such failure there are three pertinent remarks to make, which may well bring this chapter to an end. (a) First, God may have other purposes than those which directly concern human life. He makes the rain to fall, as the author of *Job* reminds us, "on the wilderness where no man is." What works evil for us may work good for some other part of the

[31] *Ibid.*, p. 170.

creation which we do not know. Our vision is so narrow that what seems to us inexplicable might seem fully understandable if seen with the eyes of God. (b) Second, there is the strong hope of immortal life, and this may provide new means of overcoming evil, of which we cannot even dream in our present state. So far as we can see, only in the light of immortal existence could a final rectification be achieved. (c) Third, whatever our theoretical conceptions may be, the practical task of overcoming evil remains. It is open to all men and women to join what Dr. Albert Schweitzer has called "The Fellowship of those who bear the mark of pain."[32]

[32] Albert Schweitzer, *On the Edge of the Primeval Forest,* pp. 173 ff.

CONCLUSION

CHAPTER XVIII

THE BELIEF IN IMMORTALITY

"We have this treasure in earthen vessels." —St. Paul

No introduction to the philosophy of religion can leave out some consideration of immortality, and yet this is a subject which does not fit easily into the pattern we have been following in this book. We have sought, thus far, to be faithful to the spirit of scientific method in that we have presented data, outlined a central hypothesis, sought possible verification and faced relevant difficulties. Desirable as it might be to continue this pattern of inquiry in regard to the belief in immortality, the truth is that this subject does not lend itself to such treatment. It is not merely that immortality cannot be *proved*. Complete proof, as we have indicated frequently, is never known. The trouble is that when we test validity of belief in immortal life, there seems to be no satisfactory way of calculating the "weight of evidence." Belief in immortality is not, on this account, to be judged irrational, but it is a belief which does not lend itself to impressive justification. The many books on the subject largely repeat a very few arguments, because there seems to be nothing more to say.[1]

Immortality is further distinguished from other subjects in the philosophy of religion by virtue of its peculiar relationship to theism. Immortality does not fit into Part III of our study along with the reasons for believing in God, because it is not

---

[1] The Ingersoll Lectures at Harvard University, which have been given annually for almost half a century, are instructive in this connection. The famous lectureship has been held by many distinguished thinkers, but these men have not been able to present new evidence for the immortality of man, though many have offered freshness of treatment.

such a reason. Belief in God may lead to belief in immortality, but belief in immortality does not lead to belief in God. Moreover, it does not fit into Part IV along with the difficulties in the path of belief. Whatever else it is, immortality is not a *problem*. For these reasons we shall treat the subject now before us somewhat differently from others, as well as more briefly. The best that can be done is to describe the situation as clearly as possible, and there let the matter rest.

The contrast between the reasons for belief in God and the reasons for belief in immortality is very great. Belief in God is rationally supported by the combination of several lines of converging evidence, each having nearly the same importance. They amount to a much closer approximation to proof, when considered together than could be supposed by considering them separately, since, as Butler said in an aphorism already quoted, "Probable proofs, by being added, not only increase the evidence, but multiply it."[2] This situation does not obtain in regard to immortality. The strands of the rope of evidence are so unequal in strength that Butler's principle has practically no application. Instead of supplementary evidence we have separated intimations, but some of these are very precious.

Immortality may have many meanings, but there is only one that is really worth discussing, *the survival of personal individuality,* after the shock of physical death. What so disturbs us, making death a part of the problem of evil, is the waste which the destruction of personality would entail, if it is final as it appears to be. Personality, as we have described it earlier, is the most precious manifestation of reality known in the world. It is infinitely superior to *things* or to *abstractions.* The one phenomenon which gives a hint as to the meaning of the evolutionary process is that of free spirits able to apprehend the good and, in a measure, to be guided by it. The production of such a level of experience would be a meaningful purpose for the world, no matter how much else the purpose might include.

[2] Joseph Butler, *The Analogy of Religion,* II, vii.

*Now the belief in immortality has most commonly meant the
belief that physical death cannot frustrate this evident purpose.*

It is wholly unprofitable to alter the common meaning of
immortality so that we refer to the future of the race or to a
depersonalized continuation of "Spirit." In regard to the latter
it is doubtful if depersonalized spirit has any meaning at all.
What we prize is not spirit in general, which may be a complete abstraction, but *spirits*, i.e., concrete individuals. Just as
God is best understood, not as "Love" or "Good," but as "an
independent centre of consciousness," having "a differential activity of his own,"[3] so what is precious among men is the particular focus of spiritual life which each represents. It is conceivable that this is destroyed when our bodies disintegrate, but,
if so, the notion that history has a meaning is largely undermined, and the immortality which most people desire for those
they love is nonexistent. Even if a depersonalized immortality
does have any meaning, it is hardly worth discussing, and is
certainly not desirable. What we are really concerned about is
the kind of belief which refers to something which is exciting
and momentous, *if true.*

It should be made clear at this point that the endless life of
the human race is no substitute for the plain man's conception
of immortality. That our earth will one day be wholly unfit
for the continuation of our enterprise is as certain as any of
our predictions can be. No less an astrophysicist than Professor
Eddington has compared favorably the evidence for the law of
increasing entropy with that of all other physical laws. Some
day, if our present judgments are at all correct, the works of
man will be as though they had never been. The fact that this
will not happen for a very long time does not alter the main
fact, namely, that the race does not provide a reasonable hope
for immortality at all. If there is no survival of physical death,
the mere continuation of life on this earth for a few million
years does not provide an escape from the ultimate frustration

[3] C. A. Bennett, *The Dilemma of Religious Knowledge,* p. 50.

of apparent Purpose. Professor Montague has described the situation with blunt honesty by saying: "However desperate the chance for individual survival may be, the chance for collective survival in the sense of an endless material continuance of its race and its culture is more desperate by far."[4]

The belief in individual survival has been so widespread as to be actually universal in some communities, particularly primitive ones. Primitive man, for the most part, looks upon survival as evident. Indeed, doubt of immortality is something of a modern innovation. But the fact that the belief has been widespread does not, of itself, constitute evidence. What we seek is something which can substantiate or destroy this widespread belief, according to the direction in which the search for the truth takes us. Possible corroboration has come chiefly in three separate ways, which we may consider in order.

A. EMPIRICAL EVIDENCE

We naturally turn, in the first place, to the kind of evidence of immortality which is consistent with the method of science. Can we point to any empirical evidence that can pass the tests of validity? There seems little doubt that primitive man considers himself in possession of such evidence. He does not suppose that his belief in the continued existence of his friend or enemy is a mere inference; he has, he thinks, experienced direct contact with the departed one, perhaps in dreams.

Civilized man tends to judge this primitive experience as worthless because the reporters of the experience are not critically alert to the distinction between subjective and objective factors in the experience. Can we, then, find some empirical evidence less crude? We have already seen that the argument from direct experience is by far the strongest of the cumulative arguments for theism. If all we had to depend upon were speculation, belief in God might still be more reasonable than disbelief, but the fact that we can point to actual experience, which

[4] W. P. Montague, *The Ways of Things*, p. 545.

passes the tests of realism, puts the matter in a wholly new light.

The belief in immortality, it must be agreed, does not have similar support. Whereas millions of otherwise trustworthy men have reported experience of fellowship with God, we do not have more than a trickle of such evidence of life after bodily death. Perhaps the very situation precludes such evidence of life after bodily death. What we are talking about is our own future and that we cannot experience, while we are still in the present. The experience of God, on the other hand, runs against no time barriers.

It is conceivable, of course, that we might have some intellectual commerce with other mortals who have survived bodily death, much as our rude ancestors supposed. Here is our only chance of empirical evidence. That such evidence is available is the contention of certain groups interested in psychical research. We ought to attend to all such supposed evidence with open minds, sitting down before the fact, here, as elsewhere like little children, and refusing to judge the case in advance.[5] The truth is, however, that the supposed empirical evidence for survival is not generally convincing. Particularly does it appear unconvincing when contrasted with the empirical evidence for theism which we have presented in outline in Chapter XII of this book. The "spiritualist" evidence is unimpressive, not only in the number and quality of the reporters, but far more in the content of the "messages." It is fair to expect some remarkable insights to be made available through communication with those "on the other side," but our expectations in this regard are vain. A. E. Taylor expresses what many have recognized when he says the alleged messages "display a distressingly low level of intelligence." "They are mostly," Taylor continues, "a medley of sentimental gush and twaddling sermonizing. If their authors

[5] So thoroughgoing was the empiricism of William James that he prepared for the possible reception of messages from himself after his decease. He asked his brother, Henry James, to remain in Cambridge a few months to receive communications if he should succeed in transmitting them.

are, as it is often alleged that they are, the great moral and intellectual heroes of our past, it would seem that the brightest prospect the unseen world has to offer is that of a gradual declension of mankind into an undying society of trivial sentimental bores."[6]

The phenomena of necromancy are likewise suspect because of the lack of moral effects, such as we have a right to expect from experiences so moving. The "fruits of the spirit," often so obvious in communion with God, are not, in necromancy, observable in any unusual way at all. Furthermore, when we consider the amount of conscious and unconscious fraud in such matters, as well as the amount of unrecognized communication between living persons, we are justified in the conviction that very little of the supposed facts is left to explain.[7] Even what is left permits of more than one explanation; the communications *might* be demonic.

There are some who maintain that the resurrection of Christ is a significant piece of empirical evidence for immortality.[8] But it is difficult to see why this should be the case. The resurrection of Christ was alleged to be a physical event and what chiefly concerns us is a nonphysical event, viz. the continuation of conscious individuality when the unity of the body is destroyed. If the Resurrection actually occurred, it would seem to be not so much evidence of immortality in general, but rather of Christ's uniqueness. It is an indication, not of what occurs in the lives of other men, but of what does *not* occur in the lives of other men.

[6] A. E. Taylor, *The Faith of a Moralist,* Volume I, pp. 259, 260.

[7] Stanford University has had for many years a generous fund set aside specifically for the study of psychical phenomena, including those which are sometimes alleged to prove immortality empirically. Among the supposed communications which have been studied by the scholars assigned to this task some have been attributed to fraud and others to delusion, but no single case has been judged free from both.

[8] For a careful estimate of the historical evidence for the Resurrection, see *Essays Catholic and Critical,* edited by E. G. Selwyn. The essay on the Resurrection is by the editor of the volume.

B. INTIMATIONS FROM THE NATURE OF MIND

A far more promising approach is that which is frankly inferential. Most philosophers who have tried to deal intelligently with the subject, recognizing the lack of scientific data, have contented themselves with showing *what is reasonable to suppose*. They have analyzed the nature of mind, shown its sharp contrast to the body, and then have concluded that the same fate need not befall both. They have found in man's mind, including his logical, aesthetic, and moral experience, hints of another order to which he belongs. Our life is meaningful, it has long been argued, only on the supposition that it is the beginning of something uncompleted here which is somewhere to be completed. Josiah Royce was in the main philosophic tradition when he wrote, "Of this our true individual life, our present life is a glimpse, a fragment, a hint, and in its best moments a visible beginning."[9]

The classic use of this method is that of Plato, particularly in *The Phaedo*. In this remarkable dialogue, personal immortality is upheld with great confidence, and a number of reasons are brought forward. If we eliminate the arguments which now seem to us fanciful or naïve, all that are left refer, in one way or another, to the notion that man *already*, in this life, carries hints of an eternal order about him. Plato's psychophysical dualism, which has been the main tradition through most of the succeeding generations of reflective thought, provides a suitable groundwork for such observations.

The heart of Plato's argument is that we actually do find, in the midst of a world that is wholly mutable, another kind of existence, with definite marks of stability. The farther we get from the body, with its appetites and the falsifications of sensory experience, the closer we get to the truth. Our real life seems not to be a physical life at all. Therefore the philosopher wel-

[9] Josiah Royce, *The Conception of Immortality*, p. 76.

comes release. "The seen is the changing, the unseen is the unchanging."[10] But it is the body which is akin to the seen.

This way of dealing with the fact of death gains as we dwell on the strangeness of human life in its earthly setting. Human life promises more than it attains, and, if death ends all, is a mere fragment. Now when we find a fragment of a vase, it seems a fair guess that the rest of the vase is in existence, even though we do not see it. Man's life seems to be not only fragmentary, however, but truncated. The truncated part seems, thus, to give us some idea of the nature of the part which is unseen, but without which the part that is seen has little meaning.

Man's mind is always something of a stranger to bodily existence, as though it is a pilgrim from another realm. The soul is "simply fastened and glued to the body" until philosophy sets the soul free. Being free, the soul recognizes that its true destiny lies elsewhere and prepares for that destiny. The emancipated soul "will calm passion, and follow reason, and dwell in the contemplation of her, beholding the true and divine (which is not matter of opinion), and thence deriving nourishment. Thus she seeks to live while she lives, and after death she hopes to go to her own kindred and to that which is like her, and to be freed from human ills."[11] Death seems to be reasonable as the portion of the body, but it looks like an intruder in the spiritual life which has a different lineage.

There is not much to be added to this argument. To some it is convincing and to some it is not convincing, and that is all. Modern authors have been able to do little more than to restate the conviction of Plato in contemporary language. How attractively this may be done is shown in the publication of Professor Rufus M. Jones' West Lectures, *Spirit in Man*. What Professor Jones does is not so much to speculate about the future as to examine the spiritual life we already have, here and now, to see

[10] *Phaedo,* 79.
[11] *Phaedo,* 84 (Jowett).

whether there is anything worthy of deathless existence. Like a true disciple of Plato, Professor Jones emphasizes man's relative independence of time and space, and, above all, his "imaginative dominion over experience." "We reach," he says, "through the veil of what we call matter and are in a higher World which is kin to our minds and to which, as great amphibians, we really belong. In fact we lie open-windowed to it and partake of it."[12]

A similar approach and one fundamentally similar to the Platonic one is the Kantian inference from moral experience. Again we pass from something in man's mind to the kind of world which must be, if what is in man's mind is a clue to reality. The moral argument for immortality points out that we are impelled to seek moral ends and that the destruction of human personalities would make these moral ends unattainable. Since the moral obligation cannot be fully realized in this life, that obligation is a delusion unless there is a wider plane of existence on which further realization of the obligation is possible. It would, Kant argues, be a curious world indeed if man were obliged to do what he cannot do. But only on the hypothesis of immortality is there a possibility of the fulfillment of the obligation. Obedience to the moral law, says Kant, requires endless progress, but endless progress is only possible "on the supposition of an *endless* duration of the existence and personality of the same rational being." Immortality, Kant supposed, can be shown to be a *necessary postulate* if moral experience is to be taken seriously.

This argument has been given an impressive treatment by A. E. Taylor in Chapter VII of his book, *The Faith of a Moralist*,[13] but he is careful to point out that it is not a demonstration valid for everyone, but only valid for those who believe in the absolute objectivity of moral obligation. Rufus Jones

[12] Rufus M. Jones, *Spirit in Man*, Stanford University Press, 1941, p. 58.
[13] Taylor's succinct statement is, "that since the moral law can rightfully command us to live as aspirants to eternity, eternity must really be our destination" (p. 281).

states the case in one sentence when he says, "If we are to have values of the intrinsic and eternal type, we must take by faith as real the kind of world in which they *can* be."[14]

All such arguments are met in the modern mind with a strong objection to the effect that the higher things of the mind, including moral experience, are wholly dependent upon the body. This was known long ago and received its classic expression from Lucretius. There are, in fact, no new arguments against immortality, although we have been able to present the classic objection in enormous detail. However, no modern objection is really any more weighty than that which Plato used in the *Phaedo*, putting it in the mouth of Simmias. Simmias was in full agreement about all that was said concerning the wonder and glory of the spiritual life, but he could not see that this wonder and glory was itself an evidence of continuance. To make his point clear he used the illustration of the lyre and the wonderful harmony it produced. The harmony, he said, is something superior to the lyre; it is invisible, incorporeal, perfect and divine, whereas the lyre and the strings are material, composite and earthy, just as the body is. When someone breaks the lyre, however, the harmony is gone, wonderful as it was. In fact the harmony is gone sooner than the crass materials which made up the lyre. "The thought, Socrates," said Simmias, "must have occurred to your own mind that such is our conception of the soul; and that when the body is in a manner strung and held together by elements of hot and cold, wet and dry, then the soul is the harmony or due proportionate admixture of them. But if so, whenever the strings of the body are unduly loosened or overstrained through disease or other injury, then the soul, though most divine, like other harmonies of music or of works of art, of course perishes at once; although the material remains of the body may last for a considerable time, until they are either decayed or burnt."[15]

---

[14] Rufus M. Jones, *Spirit in Man,* page 46.
[15] *Phaedo,* 86 (Jowett).

This is the modern objection exactly. The modern man is often willing to admit that there is a real difference between body and mind, but he sees so much evidence that the mind is dependent upon the body that he cannot see how the glory of the mind is itself an evidence of its going on. The things that matter most seem to be at the mercy of the things that matter least. Our treasure is very great, but how can it be kept if the earthen vessel which contains it is broken. Just as a change in the materials of the lyre affects the harmony produced, a change in glandular balance or some disease of the central nervous system may alter radically the functioning of the individual mind. We now know enough about brain surgery to be sure that the noblest of mental and moral characteristics may come to an end, not merely at death, but as a result of purely physical changes before death.

The answer of Socrates, according to Plato, was the rejection of the analogy of the lyre. The soul, he said, is not like a harmony, for a harmony is purely passive, unable to initiate anything. Man's soul, by contrast, is wonderfully *active* and often dominant. Though the condition of the body affects the mind, this is not the whole of the story, since, by means of thought, we deliberately curb or change the body, as well as external objects. As William James maintained in his Ingersoll Lecture, the body seems more like an instrument than anything else—a tool which the mind uses to attain its ends. The amazing ability of some men and women to rise above physical weakness provides part of the evidence for the truth of this thesis. The extent to which the tired body can be driven in pursuance of some cherished aim makes it clear that, if we are to use any analogy at all (which is probably inevitable) it would be far better to represent the mind as a charioteer than as a harmony. The mind frequently denies the body its natural satisfactions, especially when a moral obligation is recognized. Hunger and imprisonment are often chosen when dishonor is the alternative. The refusal of Socrates to flee is the classic illustration of such experience. The notion that the soul *leads* and thus cannot be understood as passively dependent upon the condition of the body is, no doubt, the heart of Plato's argument. We discover, he says, the soul "leading the elements of which she is believed to be composed; almost always opposing and coercing them in all sorts of ways throughout life, sometimes more violently with the pains of medicine and gymnastic; then again more gently; now threatening, now admonishing the desires, passions, fears, as if talking to a thing which is not herself."[16]

The question of the absolute dependence of the mind on the brain is still an open question. The data, as James insisted, are still amenable to more than one hypothesis. Though this recognition is an important factor in our study, we must note that it is only a negative factor. It gives no positive argument for immortality, but only *leaves the way open* for such positive argument if any is forthcoming. Indeed, the whole philosophical approach to the question is inconclusive, giving little help unless something is added. Why, we may reasonably ask, does the presence of a fragment give evidence that there is more to come? Because, it may be replied, the world would otherwise be unreasonable. But how do we know it is not unreasonable? The world, indeed, is far more intelligible if what is most precious is not wantonly destroyed, but what is the ground of belief in intelligibility? Certainly the mere existence of a material structure gives no such ground; a material structure might be fundamentally unintelligible. As we have seen in Chapter IX, the whole notion of an order, which science explores, implies a genuine matching of mind with Mind. Thus the basal assumption of science that the universe is intelligible is really the assumption of theism.

Apart from theism or some similar belief, the Platonic and Kantian evidences for immortality have no cogency. The reality of God is the only assurance we have of ultimate rationality. To one who believes in God as the cosmic support of moral

[16] *Phaedo*, 94 (Jowett).

obligation the Kantian argument has cogency, but it has such cogency for no others. Unless God is the author both of our moral nature and of our total environment, there is no reason to posit a fundamental harmony between them. On the other hand, if there is good reason to believe in God, as we have seen that there is, the arguments of Plato and Kant become valuable in a secondary way.

We are driven to the conclusion that immortality is best approached, not from the point of view of science, and not from the point of view of philosophy alone, but from the point of view of religion. Professor A. E. Taylor supports this conclusion strongly when he says, "Apart from an adequate doctrine of God it is, as I believe, impossible to find any secure foundation for a doctrine of human immortality or any ground for thinking the prospect of such immortality attractive."[17] Thus we are pointed forward to our third and final approach to the subject of immortality. The scientific evidence for immortality is practically worthless, the philosophical argument is inconclusive, but the religious argument may prove to be fruitful.

C. THE COROLLARY OF FAITH

One of the apparent paradoxes concerning immortality is the fact that the subject of life after death is often of far less concern to the deeply devout man than it is to the unbeliever. A nontheistic thinker like McTaggart may face anxiously the old question, "If a man die, shall he live again?" but to the majority of those who believe in God, experiencing reality in worship, the subject is an incidental one. It is instructive to note how small a part any argument about immortality played in the thought of Jesus, if we may judge by the Gospel narrative. He dealt briefly with the question of the Resurrection when the Sadducees insisted, but He based His faith on the logically prior faith in God. "He is not the God of the dead, but of the living," was the sufficient answer. The reality of

---

[17] A. E. Taylor, *The Faith of a Moralist,* Volume I, p. 256.

God, Jesus intimated, is the sufficient guarantee of the continuation of what is precious, even though we do not know how the continuation occurs. We do not need to know. Faith in the conservation of personality does not stand alone, for the religious man, but is a corollary of faith in God. Consequently it is right that the primary faith should receive the major emphasis.

If God is the author of evolution and if men are, as Jesus taught, God's children, creatures toward whose existence the long effort of creation has been pointing, then we may rest secure about our futures. We do not know what the future holds for us, but belief in God convinces us that the general world order is not an irrational one. What is fundamentally precious will not be wasted, and the human spirit will somehow be conserved. This is the real faith which has sustained most devout men; the reason that they have argued so little about immortality is that they do not need to; once the reality of God is sufficiently sure, the subsidiary question is also largely solved. It is reasonable, in the philosophy of religion, to deal as carefully and thoroughly as possible with the theistic hypothesis, and then to say very little about immortality, for there is really very little to be said.

The faith on which alone a truly rational hope of immortality rests is the faith which is understandable to the humblest worshiper. Accordingly, it is not surprising that one of the most adequate expressions of the religious approach to immortality is found in the profoundly simple lines of Whittier.

> I know not what the future hath
> Of marvel or surprise,
> Assured alone that life and death
> His mercy underlies.

Beyond this we cannot go. If God really is, such faith, though it is the faith of a little child, is wholly reasonable. If God is not, the world has no ultimate meaning anyway, and the question about immortality is not worth asking.

SUGGESTIONS FOR READING

The field of study with which this volume is concerned is so vast that no student can expect to cover it fully and no bibliography which can be presented is really adequate. All that an author can do is to point out to the serious student some of the acknowledged classics and influential modern works, thus suggesting literary points of departure. It would be easy to make a bibliography so extensive as to be practically worthless, since it would not tell the student where to begin. To avoid this pitfall an author must make selections, some of which seem arbitrary. The books mentioned are ordinarily found in a good university library and are limited to those written in the English language or translated into English. Wherever possible, mention is made of the specific section of a book which bears on the problem under consideration.

The suggestions for reading fall into two classes, determined in each case by the student's purpose. First, the student may be expected to wish to go farther with the subject of each chapter and to have some guidance in selecting the relevant literature. Accordingly, Appendix A gives suggestions by chapters. In the second place, the student may be expected to write a paper on some particular problem which seems important to him. Thus he may gain confidence and learn much in general by a fair degree of thoroughness in one inquiry. To facilitate this purpose, Appendix B gives subjects for term papers with preliminary book lists in each case. These are intended, not as sufficient bibliographies, but as means by which the student can make a start. After he begins the reading he will be able to make his own bibliography, each book leading to others. These subjects and book lists have proved useful in my own teaching and the presentation of them here may save the instructor's time.

A. Bibliography by Chapters

Chapter I

One of the most valuable books of recent times, dealing with the subject of this chapter, is *Science, Religion and Reality,* edited by Joseph Needham. Among the most striking contributions to this volume is the Introduction provided by Lord Balfour and the chapter by John Oman, "The Sphere of Religion." See also, in the same volume, Malinowski's "Magic, Science and Religion." Important observations on the relationship between art and religion, presented from the point of view of the philosopher, are found in William E. Hocking's *The Meaning of God in Human Experience.* Bernard Bosanquet's *Science and Philosophy and Other Essays* deals carefully with the subject of the present chapter from the point of view of the Absolute Idealist. An important statement of the difference between philosophy and religion is to be found in *Mens Creatrix* by William Temple, especially in the Prologue. This is a valuable book and should be read entire. An inspired volume, interpreting science in its relation to the other expressions of the human spirit, is Professor Whitehead's *Science and the Modern World.*

Chapter II

The most ambitious of contemporary discussions of the chief problems raised in this chapter is *The Nature of Thought,* by Brand Blanshard. Chapters XXV, XXVI, and XXVII are especially commended to the reader. Professor Blanshard upholds the coherence theory of truth. *Knowledge, Belief and Opinion,* by John Laird deals at length with the contributions of various modern philosophers to the problems considered and this is highly recommended to the reader who is anxious to understand more of the historical background. For the reader who wishes to have a critical introduction to pragmatic thought, there is value in *What Is Pragmatism?* by James Bissett Pratt, even though the volume is not strictly new. Professor Pratt shows how pragmatism tends to see religion, neither as a divine revelation nor a philosophical construction, but as a human product which receives its justification from its human usefulness.

Chapter III

The books on logic are numerous indeed, but three modern ones may be mentioned, representing three important approaches. The best account of classical logic is *Logic*, by H. W. B. Joseph. The chapter on "Induction" is especially brilliant. A second important volume is *A Modern Introduction to Logic*, by L. Susan Stebbing, whose book has literary charm as well as obvious competence. A third choice is *An Introduction to Logic and Scientific Method*, by Morris R. Cohen and Ernest Nagel. Chapter XVII of this volume gives a careful account of the nature of historical evidence. John Henry Newman's *Grammar of Assent* is still challenging after many years, having able chapters on formal and informal inference.

Chapter IV

A good starting point for further reading on the subject of this chapter is *The Will to Believe*, by William James. This essay is now generally criticized in a negative way, but has been the starting point of many important developments. It shows the value of faith as a way to knowledge, but does not meet the charge of wish-thinking. Chapter VII of *The Interpretation of Religion*, by John Baillie is one of the most dependable accounts of the subject from the point of view of one who accepts a central position similar to that upheld in this book. Chapter I of *Pathways to the Reality of God*, by Rufus M. Jones, deals with the necessity of faith, with emphasis upon religious experience. A new note has been introduced into the discussion by Harold A. Bosley, *The Quest for Religious Certainty*, who deals carefully with "tentativeness." See especially Chapter VII.

Chapter V

The question of authority has received many able treatments in our time, one of the most provocative being that of Walter M. Horton, "Authority Without Infallibility," published as one essay in *Religious Realism*, edited by D. C. Macintosh. This is an attempt to define religious authority in terms agreeable to those who accept the authority of the expert. The most ambitious work of modern times on the subject is that of James Martineau, *The Seat of Authority in Religion*. Valuable insights may be found in Lord Balfour's *Foundations of Belief* and Charles Gore's *The Reconstruction of Belief*, Book III, Chapters V and VI.

The distinction between authority and infallibility made by Professor Horton is also upheld by A. E. Taylor in *The Faith of a Moralist*, Volume II, Chapter V. Since a great part of the question of authority in modern thought refers to the Bible, we are fortunate in having a thorough book on the subject from the pen of C. H. Dodd, *The Authority of the Bible*. The author, accepting as valid the modern critical approach to the literature of the Bible, nevertheless presents the Bible as authoritative for men. Its authority is presented primarily as the authority of the men of religious genius who speak in it.

Chapter VI

The most ambitious of the older attempts to depict, in a critical way, the philosophy of naturalism is that by James Ward, *Naturalism and Agnosticism*. This is difficult reading, but most rewarding. William E. Hocking, in his *Types of Philosophy*, has given a good brief account of naturalism though he is critical of it. For a contemporary exposition of naturalism, on the part of one interested in ethical theory and who upholds naturalism, see John R. Reid, *A Theory of Value*. James Bissett Pratt's *Naturalism*, as the text indicates, is an exposition of a point of view which is not identical with naturalism as usually understood and proposes to give something of a middle way. *A Common Faith*, by John Dewey is an attempt to outline religion on naturalistic lines.

Chapter VII

The exposition of the inadequacies of naturalism have been numerous in contemporary thought, but some of the best of these are as follows: James Ward, *Naturalism and Agnosticism;* C. C. J. Webb, *Religion and Theism,* Chapter II; A. J. Balfour, *The Foundations of Belief,* Part II, Chapter I. For a single chapter packed with pertinent criticism it is hard to think of one which surpasses

Chapter I in *Some Problems of Ethics*, by H. W. B. Joseph. The title of the chapter is "Ethics and Natural Science."

Chapter VIII

The historical development of theistic realism, especially in its relationship to Greek thought, is admirably presented by Etienne Gilson in *God and Philosophy*. The works of another Catholic thinker, Jacques Maritain, may well be consulted in this same connection. Even more valuable for the general reader, however, is the work of Baron Friedrich von Hügel, *Essays and Addresses on the Philosophy of Religion*. The first four chapters are especially important. One of the most thorough accounts of the fundamental theistic hypothesis is that of W. R. Matthews, *God in Christian Thought and Experience*.

Chapter IX

The argument for the existence of God from the facts of nature is today something more than the classical arguments, because it puts so much stress on the fact of science. Two important thinkers who have been especially constructive in this regard are Professor Tennant and Archbishop Temple. Tennant's great work, *Philosophical Theology*, should be consulted, especially Volume II, Chapters III and IV. Perhaps the most easily readable of Tennant's contributions to this subject is the essay "The Being of God in the Light of Physical Science," published as Chapter II in *Cambridge Theological Essays*. *Nature, Man and God*, Archbishop Temple's Gifford Lectures, often quoted in this book, takes the facts of science and of evolution and presents them in their religious aspects in a remarkable way. Note especially Chapter V. For a single essay presenting the argument from nature along with other arguments, it is hard to surpass "The Vindication of Religion," by Professor A. E. Taylor of the University of Edinburgh. This appears in *Essays Catholic and Critical*, edited by E. G. Selwyn.

Chapter X

The moral argument for theism has received its most extended and careful modern treatment in the Gifford Lectures of W. R.

Sorley, *Moral Values and the Idea of God.* Note especially Chapter XIII. Paul Elmer More, in his *The Sceptical Approach to Religion*, presents the moral argument as the chief one, though he presents it briefly. The argument is given in outline by W. R. Matthews in *Studies in Christian Philosophy*, Lecture IV, and by Hastings Rashdall, *Philosophy and Religion,* Lecture III. This lecture shows that the objectivity of our moral judgments logically implies belief in God. To go along with the discussion of freedom included in this chapter, see Nicolai Hartman's *Ethics* (English translation), Volume III, pages 80 ff.

Chapter XI

One of the most inspired accounts of the aesthetic approach to reality is that by the late Clutton-Brock in the essay "Spiritual Experience," published in the volume entitled *The Spirit*, Chapter VIII. Lord Balfour's well-known aesthetic interest is expressed carefully in the *Foundations of Belief*, Part I, Chapter II. His *Theism and Humanism* should be read entire by all those who have any special aesthetic interest. An interesting brief treatment of the subject is that of E. W. Lyman's *The Meaning and Truth of Religion*, pages 194-202. Professor Tennant's estimate of the aesthetic argument is given in a few closely packed pages in *Philosophical Theology*, Volume II, pages 89-93.

Chapter XII

The validity of religious experience has been the subject of a number of modern volumes. The present author's book, *The Knowledge of God,* which is an extended treatment of the argument for religious experience, includes a bibliography of the problem of objective reference in religious experience and readers may wish to consult this bibliography. The phrase "religious experience" owes its present vogue to William James's Gifford Lectures, *The Varieties of Religious Experience.* This book should be consulted, but it does not go seriously into the question of validity. One of the most trenchant criticisms of the argument of religious experience from the point of view of the theistic thinker is Hastings Rashdall's *Philosophy of Religion*, Lecture IV. My Swarthmore lecture, *The Trustworthiness of Religious Experience,* is a brief answer to the kind of argument which Rashdall presents. One of the most careful analyses of the various forms of religious experience is provided by Charles E. Raven in *Jesus and the Gospel of Love*, especially Part I.

Chapter XIII

One of the most thoroughgoing studies of the historical nature of Christianity is Charles Clayton Morrison's *What is Christianity?* The nature of Christianity is, in this volume, largely identified with its history, and a study of this interpretation is a valuable preparation for the theistic argument from history. For a brief statement of the historical argument, see Charles Gore's *Reconstruction of Belief*, Chapter VII. John Macmurray, in his *The Clue to History*, has shed important light on the entire subject. Also bearing on the material of this chapter is the bibliography for a term paper on "The Religious Significance of History" as given in Appendix B.

Chapter XIV

A frank consideration of some of the leading hindrances to religious belief appears in H. H. Farmer's *Experience of God*, Part II. For important light on the special problems which the concept of evolution raises for the religious or ethical interpretation of the world, one of the best treatments continues to be that of J. G. Schurman, *The Ethical Import of Darwinism*. Though published in 1888, it is still pertinent. The most penetrating study of evolution, from the point of view of the philosopher, is, I believe, that of H. W. B. Joseph, "The Concept of Evolution" which is Chapter XI of *Ancient and Modern Philosophy*. The author asks most embarrassing questions. A brief presentation of the entire problem from the Christian standpoint is found in E. W. Lyman's *The Meaning and Truth of Religion*, Chapter XII. The series of essays edited by B. H. Streeter, under the title, *God and the Struggle for Existence*, continue to be relevant.

Chapter XV

The careful student should begin by reading the works of Sigmund Freud mentioned in the text. There have been many thorough treatments of the logical issues raised, one of the most thorough being that of Cyril H. Valentine, *Modern Psychology and the Validity of Christian Experience*. Important briefer treatments are those of Macintosh, *The Problem of Religious Knowledge*, Chapters IV and V; C. C. J. Webb, *Religion and Theism*, Chapter IV; and Charles Raven, *Jesus and the Gospel of Love*, Chapter III. Chapter VII of my book, *The Knowledge of God*, is on the same subject.

Chapter XVI

No author in our time has dealt more brilliantly and penetratingly with the problems raised in natural law than has Professor Tennant. See especially his *Philosophical Theology*, Volume II, Chapters I and II. These chapters are entitled "Conformity of the World to Law" and "Law and Mechanism." John Oman's much quoted book, *The Natural and the Supernatural*, is an extended treatment of the subject, whereas valuable brief treatment is given in Baron von Hügel's *Essays and Addresses on the Philosophy of Religion*, Chapter XI. For a study of prayer, providence and miracle taken altogether, see H. H. Farmer, *The World and God*. Appropriate to this chapter also is the special bibliography for a term paper on miracle, found in Appendix B.

Chapter XVII

The appendix to *Christian Realism*, by John Bennett, which appeared separately in the *Journal of Religion*, October 1938, has been mentioned in the text and is highly recommended. One of the most interesting treatments of the problem is that by A. E. Taylor, *The Problem of Evil*. This is brief but pithy. William Temple's most interesting insights on the subject are found in *Mens Creatrix*, Chapter XX, and *Nature, Man and God*, Chapter XIV. Professor Tennant's treatment is in *Philosophical Theology*, Volume II, Chapter VII. The relation of the problem of evil to the hope of everlasting life is presented in an interesting way by G. A. Johnston Ross in his West Lectures at Stanford University, "Behavior and Destiny; A Christian View." Mention is made of Professor Brightman's proposed solution in the text, a study of which should be matched by a consideration of the argument put forth by Charles Hartshorne in *Man's Vision of God*. This volume presents a somewhat different kind of limitation theory.

Chapter XVIII

All of the Ingersoll Lectures deal directly with the subject of immortality and there are chapters on it in most books on the philosophy of religion. Among the most provocative of the Ingersoll Lectures are those of Josiah Royce and William James. An ambitious treatment of the question is that of A. E. Taylor in *The Faith of a Moralist*, Volume I, Chapter VII, "The Destiny of the Individual." Definitely Christian approaches are those of Harry Emerson Fosdick in *The Assurance of Immortality*, William Adams Brown, *The Christian Hope*, and F. R. Barry, *The Relevance of Christianity*, Part II, Chapter XI. *Spirit in Man* by Rufus M. Jones is a contemporary treatment of importance, written by a man who has thought long on the subject and is influenced by Greek as well as specific Christian considerations. A full-length treatment of enduring worth is *And the Life Everlasting*, by John Baillie.

B. Term Papers in the Philosophy of Religion

Term papers might well be written on any of the subjects of chapters. In that case the bibliographical notes of Appendix A may prove useful. Some of the subjects listed below are similar to parts of chapters, but none is identical with the subject of any chapter of this book.

THE KINDS OF AGNOSTICISM

Bosley, Harold A., *The Quest for Religious Certainty*, Willett, Clark & Company, Chicago, 1939, Chap. IV.

Macintosh, D. C., *The Problem of Religious Knowledge*, Harper & Brothers, New York, 1940, Chap. XIV.

Pringle-Pattison, A. S., *The Idea of God*, Oxford University Press, New York, 1917, Lecture VIII.

Webb, C. C. J., *Religious Thought in England from 1850*, Oxford University Press, New York, 1933, pp. 83 ff.

THE IDEA OF CREATION

Joyce, George H., *Principles of Natural Theology*, Longmans, Green and Company, New York, 1934, Chap. XIV.

Matthews, W. R., *God in Christian Thought and Experience,* James Nisbet & Co., Ltd., London, 1930, Chap. X.

Pringle-Pattison, *The Idea of God,* Oxford, 1917, Chap. XVI.

Raven, Charles E., *The Creator Spirit;* A Survey of Christian Doctrine in the Light of Biology, Psychology and Mysticism. Harvard University Press, Cambridge, 1927.

OBJECTIVITY IN ETHICS

Lanz, Henry, *In Quest of Morals,* Stanford University Press, Stanford University, 1941.

Moore, G. E., *Ethics,* Henry Holt and Company, Chap. III and IV.

Moore, G. E., *Principia Ethica,* Cambridge University Press, London, 1903.

Rashdall, Hastings, *Is Conscience an Emotion?* Houghton Mifflin Company, Boston, 1914.

THE DEGRADATION OF ENERGY

Eddington, Sir A. S., *The Nature of the Physical World,* The Macmillan Company, New York, 1927, Chap. IV.

Inge, W. R., *God and the Astronomers,* Longmans, Green and Company, New York, 1933, especially Chap. II.

Royce, Josiah, *The Religious Aspect of Philosophy,* Houghton Mifflin Company, Boston, 1897, pp. 240 ff.

Urban, Wilbur, *The Intelligible Universe,* The Macmillan Company, New York, 1929, Chap. XII, "The New Götterdämmerung: Degradation and Value."

THE MEANING OF FREEDOM

Broad, C. D., *Determination, Indeterminism, and Libertarianism,* Cambridge University Press, London, 1934.

Compton, Arthur H., *The Freedom of Man,* Yale University Press, New Haven, 1935.

Everett, W. G., *Moral Values,* Henry Holt and Company, 1918, Chap. XII.

Hartmann, Nicolai, *Ethics* (Eng. trans.), The Macmillan Company, New York, 1932, Vol. III, pp. 80 ff.

Hocking, William E., *The Self, Its Body and Freedom,* Yale University Press, New Haven, 1930.

Sorley, W. R., *Moral Values and the Idea of God*, Cambridge University Press, London, 1918, Chap. XVII.

THE RELIGIOUS SIGNIFICANCE OF HISTORY

Mackay, John A., *A Preface to Christian Theology*, The Macmillan Company, New York, 1941, Chap. IV.

Taylor, A. E., *The Faith of a Moralist*, The Macmillan Company, New York, 1930, Vol. II, Chap. III.

Temple, William, *Nature, Man and God*, The Macmillan Company, New York, 1934, Chap. XVII.

Wood, H. G., *Christianity and the Nature of History*, Cambridge University Press, London, 1934, Chap. I, II, III, IV.

INSPIRATION AND REVELATION

Dodd, C. H., *The Authority of the Bible*, Harper & Brothers, New York, 1929, especially Chap. I-V.

Emmet, C. W., "The Psychology of Inspiration: How God Teaches," Chap. VI of *The Spirit*, edited by B. H. Streeter, The Macmillan Company, New York, 1921.

Rashdall, Hastings, *Philosophy and Religion*, Charles Scribner's Sons, New York, 1910, Lecture V.

Scott, E. F., *The New Testament Idea of Revelation*, Charles Scribner's Sons, New York, 1935.

Tennant, F. R., *Philosophical Theology*, Cambridge University Press, London, 1930, Vol. II, Chap. VIII.

THE NEED OF INSTITUTIONAL RELIGION

Barry, F. R., *The Relevance of Christianity*, James Nisbet & Co., Ltd., London, 1933, Chap. II and XI.

Hügel, Baron Friedrich von, *The Reality of God*, J. M. Dent & Sons, Ltd., London, 1931, Chap. XIII.

Niebuhr, H. Richard and others, *The Church Against the World*, Willett, Clark & Company, Chicago, 1935.

Taylor, A. E., *The Faith of a Moralist*, The Macmillan Company, New York, 1930, Vol. II, Chap. VI.

THE NATURE OF MAN

Berdyaev, Nicholas, *The Fate of Man in the Modern World*, Morehouse-Gorham Company, Milwaukee, 1935.

Calhoun, Robert L., *What is Man?* Association Press, New York, 1939.

Driesch, Hans, *Man and the Universe* (Eng. trans.), Allen & Unwin, Ltd., London, 1929.

More, Paul Elmer, *On Being Human,* Princeton University Press, Princeton, 1936, especially Chap. I.

Niebuhr, Reinhold, *The Nature and Destiny of Man,* Charles Scribner's Sons, New York, 1941.

Seth, Andrew, *Man's Place in the Cosmos,* Charles Scribner's Sons, New York, 1897.

Sherrington, Charles, *Man on His Nature,* Cambridge University Press, London, 1940.

THE POSSIBILITY OF MIRACLES

Gore, Charles, *The Reconstruction of Belief,* John Murray, London, 1926, Chap. VII.

Rashdall, Hastings, "The Ultimate Basis of Theism," *Contentio Veritatis,* E. P. Dutton & Company, Inc., New York, 1902, Chap. I.

Tennant, F. R., *Miracle and Its Philosophical Presuppositions,* Cambridge University Press, London, 1925.

THE RELIGIOUS SIGNIFICANCE
OF THE
CONCEPT OF PERSONALITY

Brightman, Edgar S., *A Philosophy of Religion,* Prentice-Hall, Inc., New York, 1940, Chap. XI.

Illingworth, J. R., *Personality Human and Divine,* The Macmillan Company, New York, 1894.

Smyth, Newman, *The Meaning of Personal Life,* Charles Scribner's Sons, New York, 1916.

Temple, William, *Mens Creatrix,* The Macmillan Company, New York, 1917, Chap. VIII.

Webb, C. C. J., *Divine Personality and Human Life,* The Macmillan Company, New York, 1920.

THE PERSONALITY OF GOD

Horton, Walter M., *God,* Association Press, New York, 1937.

Illingworth, J. R., *Personality, Human and Divine,* The Macmillan Company, New York, 1894.

Matthews, W. R., *Studies in Christian Philosophy,* The Macmillan Company, New York, Lecture V.

Oman, John, *Grace and Personality,* Cambridge University Press, London, 1919.

Webb, C. C. J., *God and Personality,* The Macmillan Company, New York, 1918.

PROGRESS IN RELIGION

Dawson, Christopher, *Progress and Religion,* Sheed & Ward, Inc., New York, 1937.

Dodd, C. H., *The Authority of the Bible,* Harper & Brothers, 1929, Chap. XII and XIII.

Galloway, George, *The Principles of Religious Development,* The Macmillan Company, New York, 1909.

Gore, Charles, *The Reconstruction of Belief,* John Murray, London, 1926, Book III, Chap. VII, "The Tests of Legitimate Development."

Hügel, Baron Friedrich von, *Essays and Addresses on the Philosophy of Religion,* E. P. Dutton & Company, Inc., New York, 1924, Chap. III.

Wood, H. G., *Christianity and the Nature of History,* Cambridge University Press, London, 1934, Chap. V.

THE PLACE OF REASON IN RELIGION

Balfour, A. J., *The Foundations of Belief,* Longmans, Green and Company, New York, 1933, Part III, Chap. II. First printed, 1895.

Brunner, Emil, *The Philosophy of Religion from the Standpoint of Protestant Theology,* Charles Scribner's Sons, New York, 1937, pp. 79-98.

Lunn, Arnold, *The Flight from Reason,* Dial Press, Inc., New York, 1931.

Newman, John Henry, "The Usurpations of Reason," in *Fifteen Sermons Preached before the University of Oxford,* Longmans, Green and Company, New York, New Impression, 1909.

Whitehead, A. N., *The Function of Reason,* Princeton University Press, Princeton, 1929.

Wieman, Henry N., *The Wrestle of Religion with Truth,* The Macmillan Company, New York, 1927.

THE NATURE OF RELIGION

Bosanquet, Bernard, *What Religion Is,* The Macmillan Company, New York, 1920.

Brightman, Edgar S., *A Philosophy of Religion,* Prentice-Hall, Inc., New York, 1940, Chap. II and III.

Moore, Edward C., *The Nature of Religion,* The Macmillan Company, New York, 1936.

Webb, C. C. J., *Religion and Theism,* especially Chap. I.

Wieman, Henry N., *The Wrestle of Religion with Truth,* The Macmillan Company, New York, 1927, Chap. VIII.

THE REALITY OF SIN

Niebuhr, Reinhold, *The Nature and Destiny of Man,* Charles Scribner's Sons, New York, 1941, Chap. VII-IX.

Taylor, A. E., *The Faith of a Moralist,* The Macmillan Company, New York, 1931, Vol. I, Chap. V, "Moral Evil and Sin."

Tennant, F. R., *The Concept of Sin,* Cambridge University Press, London, 1912.

TELEOLOGY

Henderson, Lawrence J., *The Order of Nature,* Harvard University Press, Cambridge, 1917.

Matthews, W. R., *The Purpose of God,* James Nisbet & Co., Ltd., London, 1935.

Montague, W. P., *Belief Unbound,* Yale University Press, New Haven, 1930, pp. 70-84.

Pringle-Pattison, *The Idea of God,* in the Light of Recent Philosophy, Oxford University Press, New York, 1917, Lecture XVII.

Sorley, W. R., *Moral Values and the Idea of God,* Cambridge University Press, London, 1918, Chap. XVI.

Tennant, F. R., *Philosophical Theology,* Cambridge University Press, London, 1930, Vol. II, Chap. IV.

THE RELIGIOUS SIGNIFICANCE OF TIME

Hartshorne, Charles, *Man's Vision of God and the Logic of Theism,* Willett, Clark & Company, Chicago, 1941.

Matthews, W. R., *God in Christian Thought and Experience,* James Nisbet & Co., Ltd., London, 1930, Chap. XII.

Pringle-Pattison, A. S., *The Idea of God,* in the Light of Recent Philosophy, Oxford University Press, New York, 1917, Lectures XVIII and XIX.

Taylor, A. E., *The Faith of a Moralist,* The Macmillan Company, New York, 1930, Vol. I, Chap. III.

Wood, H. G., *Christianity and the Nature of History,* Cambridge University Press, London, 1934, Chap. VI.

CLASSICAL THEISTIC ARGUMENTS

Bouquet, A. C., *A Study of the Ordinary Arguments for the Existence and Nature of God,* W. Heffer & Sons, Ltd., Cambridge, England, 1932.

Galloway, George, *The Philosophy of Religion,* Charles Scribner's Sons, New York, 1922, pp. 381-394.

Gore, Charles, *The Reconstruction of Belief,* John Murray, London, 1926, Book I, Chap. III.

Joyce, George H., *Principles of Natural Theology,* Longmans, Green and Company, New York, 1934, Chap. III-VII.

Plato, *Laws,* Book X.

MODERN THEISTIC ARGUMENTS

Martineau, James, *A Study of Religion, Its Sources and Contents,* The Macmillan Company, New York, 1888, Book II, Chap. II.

Rashdall, Hastings, "The Ultimate Basis of Theism," *Contentio Veritatis,* E. P. Dutton & Company, New York, 1902, Chap. I.

Sorley, W. R., *Moral Value and the Idea of God,* Cambridge University Press, London, 1918, especially Chap. XII.

Taylor, A. E., "The Vindication of a Religion," *Essays Catholic and Critical,* edited by E. G. Selwyn, The Macmillan Company, New York, Chap. III.

Wilson, John Cook, *Statement and Inference,* Vol. II, pp. 835 ff., "Rational Grounds for Belief in God."

THE RELIGIOUS SIGNIFICANCE OF TRAGEDY

Alexander, Hartley B., *God and Man's Destiny,* Oxford University Press, New York, 1936, Chap. II.

Bradley, A. C., *Shakespearean Tragedy,* The Macmillan Company, New York, 1904.

Krutch, Joseph Wood, *The Modern Temper,* Harcourt, Brace and Company, New York, 1929.

Royce, Josiah, *The Problem of Christianity,* The Macmillan Company, New York, 1913, Vol. I.

Temple, William, *Mens Creatrix,* The Macmillan Company, New York, 1917, Chap. XI.

Unamuno y Jugo, Miguelde, *The Tragic Sense of Life in Men and in Peoples,* The Macmillan Company, New York, 1921.

INDEX OF NAMES

Adams, Henry, 156
Alexander, H. B., 58
Alexander, S., 271
Amos, 121, 124
Anaximander, 90-91, 95
Anaximenes, 90
Andrewes, Lancelot, 119, 297-298
Aquinas, Thomas, 158 n., 292
Aristophanes, 91
Aristotle, 5, 76-77, 87, 96, 134, 143, 151
Arnold, Matthew, 10, 18
Atkins, Gaius Glenn, 207 n.
Augustine, St., 119, 207, 235

Bach, J. S., 184
Bacon, Francis, 234
Baillie, John, 258
Balfour, Arthur J., 53, 56, 58, 97, 103, 137, 181, 186, 190-193, 261, 271
Barclay, Robert, 71, 200
Barnes, E. W., 155, 160, 279
Barth, Karl, 203
Bavink, Bernard, 270 n.
Bennett, C. A., 65 n., 132, 209, 255, 309
Bennett, John, 284, 291-292, 296
Bergson, Henri, 271
Blake, William, 11
Blanshard, Brand, 115-116
Boas, George, 30 n.
Bogoslovsky, Boris, 256 n.
Bosanquet, Bernard, 229
Bradley, A. C., 187-188
Bradley, F. H., 20, 286
Bridges, Robert, 56
Brightman, E. S., 3, 291, 296
Buddha, Gautama, 216
Buffon, 234
Bunyan, John, 18

Burns, Robert, 11
Butler, Joseph, 35, 36, 41, 226, 229, 230, 308
Byrd, Richard E., 179

Cadbury, Henry J., 128 n., 218
Carroll, Lewis, 33
Case, S. J., 219 n.
Chase, Stuart, 28 n.
Clifford, W. K., 169, 170
Clutton-Brock, Arthur, 11
Cohen, Morris R., 40 n.
Coleridge, S. T., 24, 188, 190
Comte, Auguste, 101
Conant, James B., 68
Copeland, E. B., 244
Cyrus the Great, 126

Dante, 184
Darwin, Charles, 95, 231, 238, 245
Democritus, 91
De Morgan, Augustus, 35
Diderot, 239
Disraeli, Benjamin, 224
Dodd, C. H., 219

Eddington, A. S., 155, 309
Elijah, 123
Eliot, T. S., 65
Evans, Marian, 250 n.
Ezekiel, 127

Farnsworth, Paul R., 180 n.
Feuerbach, Ludwig, 249-250, 254
Fox, George, 12 n., 209
Fränkel, Hermann, 90 n.
Francis of Assisi, 19
Frederick the Great, 224 n.
Freud, Sigmund, 251 ff.
Froude, William, 80

Geddes, Patrick, 236, 240 n.
Gilson, Etienne, 133, 292, 298
Gore, Charles, 117, 234
Guest, Edgar, 182

Henderson, L. J., 152-153, 239
Hitler, A., 244-245
Hocking, W. E., 88 n., 239-240
Homer, 184
Hooker, Richard, 25, 230
Hosea, 124
Hügel, Friedrich von, 131, 148, 217, 280, 283-284
Hulme, T. E., 189 n.
Hume, David, 32, 33, 51, 159, 282
Huxley, Thomas, 62-63, 98 n., 169, 170, 216, 240, 243

Inge, W. R., 157, 211
Isaiah, 124-126

Jacks, L. P., 286, 289, 290
James, Henry, 311 n.
James, William, 117, 199, 210, 311 n., 317-318
Johnson, Samuel, 37-38, 66, 175
Jones, Ernest, 253
Jones, Rufus M., 196, 209, 314-315
Joseph, H. W. B., 37, 44, 60, 74, 109, 146 n.
Joyce, G. H., 158 n.
Jung, C. G., 254

Kant, Immanuel, 36, 158 n., 168, 170, 173, 177-178, 182, 192, 315-319
Keats, John, 184
Keynes, J. Maynard, 47, 48
Kingsley, Charles, 169
Korzybski, Alfred, 114

Laird, John, 23 n.
Lamarck, J. B. de, 234
Lanz, Henry, 165 n.
Laplace, P. S. de, 160, 270
Leibnitz, G. W., 282
Leighton, Joseph A., 67, 159 n.
Leuba, James, 199, 251
Leucippus, 91
Lincoln, Abraham, 225

Lovejoy, A. O., 27, 54, 72, 111, 113, 226, 272-273, 288
Lucretius, 316
Luther, Martin, 171
Lyman, E. W., 18

Mackay, John, 221
MacLeish, Archibald, 183
Masterman, C. F. G., 301-302
Matthews, W. R., 136, 163, 165, 166
McTaggart, J. M. E., 319
McWilliams, J. A., 155
Meyerson, Emile, 155
Micah, 124-125
Mill, John Stuart, 43
Milliken, Robert A., 72, 275 n.
Milton, John, 185
Mivart, S. J., 236
Montague, W. P., 23, 31, 72, 180, 182, 268, 280, 291, 310
Moore, G. E., 10, 168 n.
More, Paul Elmer, 135-136, 162-163, 171-172
Morgan, C. L., 271, 272-273

Nagel, Ernest, 40 n.
Napoleon, 264
Newman, J. H., 37, 80-81, 171, 201, 207, 209, 223-224, 230, 280
Newton, Isaac, 47, 185
Nye, Helena, 213 n.

Oman, John, 299-300

Paley, William, 237
Pascal, Blaise, 55, 81, 118, 120, 132, 134, 201-202, 209, 257, 259
Paul, St., 51, 202, 223, 307
Pearson, Karl, 204, 206
Phidias, 184
Plato, 91-92, 133, 158 n., 168, 291, 293, 313-319
Poincaré, Henri, 74 n.
Pratt, James Bissett, 8, 97-98

Quick, O. C., 17

Rashdall, Hastings, 289-290
Rauschenbusch, Walter, 17
Raven, Charles E., 206-207

Rembrandt, 184
Romanes, G. J., 19, 63, 212, 217
Ross, G. A. Johnston, 137
Royce, Josiah, 156, 264, 313
Russell, Bertrand, 156
Russell, O. F., 28

Sabatier, Auguste, 71
Santayana, George, 18
Schopenhauer, Arthur, 4 n.
Schurman, J. G., 241
Schweitzer, Albert, 133, 303
Seth, Andrew, 98 n., 160, 161 n.
Shakespeare, William, 183
Shelley, P. B., 12
Sisson, C. J., 26
Smuts, Jan, 273
Socrates, 91-92, 104, 316, 317
Söderblom, Nathan, 137
Somervell, T. H., 278 n.
Spencer, Herbert, 161, 233
Sperry, Willard L., 207 n.
Stebbing, L. Susan, 47, 49
Stephen the Martyr, 223

Taylor, A. E., 114, 158, 165, 170,
    177, 194, 311-312, 315, 319
Temple, Frederick, 235
Temple, William, 8, 9, 53, 54, 123,
    145, 147, 150, 151, 152, 170, 176,
    185, 188, 235, 241, 242, 276, 287-
    288, 293, 297

Tennant, F. R., 275
Tennyson, Alfred, 180, 188
Thales, 90
Thompson, Francis, 188, 203, 258
Toynbee, Alfred, 226 n.
Turner, A. C., 300-301

Velasquez, 184
Voltaire, 81, 288

Wallace, Alfred Russel, 98 n., 149,
    232-233
Walton, Izaak, 26
Ward, James, 97
Webb, C. C. J., 14, 136, 251
Webster, David L., 45
Westermarck, E., 166, 168
Whale, J. S., 17
Whitebread, A. N., 17, 161, 238 n.,
    248, 266, 272
Whittier, J. G., 19 n., 320
Wilson, William, 301
Wood, H. G., 131, 135, 215, 218-
    219, 224
Wordsworth, William, 6, 193

Xenophanes, 133
Xenophon, 91

Zinsser, Hans, 267, 269
Zoroaster, 125

INDEX OF SUBJECTS

Aesthetic argument, 194
Aesthetic experience, 119, 179 ff., 242, 245-246
Agnosticism, 62 ff.
Agreement of reports, 210-211
Amateurs, 79 ff.
Analogy, 47 ff., 205
Animal creation, 299
Anthropomorphism, 135-137
Art, 6, 183 ff.
Atoms, 46, 68
Augustness of ought, 169 ff.
Authority, 67 ff., 94-95, 215-217

Beauty, 179 ff., 245-246
Behaviorism, 100, 108, 111, 174-175
Belief, 23 ff.
Book of Job, 13, 293-294
Book of Jonah, 127, 258
Buddhism, 130

Carnot Principle, 154 ff.
Categorical imperative, 170
Catholic theology, 292, 296
Causation, 60, 99, 176
Chance, 174, 240-242, 265
Characteristic features of religion, 9, 10
Child spirit, 81
Childlike faith, 293-294, 320
Choice, 297
Christian Science, 283
Christianity, 128-129
Classical logic, 30, 75
Classics, 119-120
Communication, 185
Confucianism, 130
Conscience, 161 ff.
Consensus argument, 216
Cosmological argument, 158

Cross, The, 259, 299
Cumulative evidence, 41, 42

Darwinism, 149, 230 ff.
Deduction, 39, 40
Definitions of religion, 14-15
Determinism, 99
Difficulties, 229
Discipline, 77
Dualism, 283

Emergent evolution, 272-273
Empirical evidence for immortality, 310-312
Environment, 238-239
Epiphenomenalism, 277
Error, 31
Evil, 280 ff.
Evolution, 95, 148 ff., 230 ff.
Expectancy, 255, 260
Experience in religion, 197 ff.
Experts, 69, 79
Explanation, 146 ff.
Extrapolation, 38

Fact, 60
Fair sampling, 38
Finitude of God, 289 ff.
Freedom, 172 ff.
Friends, Society of, 71
Fruits of religion, 15-19, 211 ff.
Fundamentalists, 236

Genetic fallacy, 96, 256
Goodness, 104 ff.
Great tradition, 92
Greek philosophy, 90 f., 133

Heisenberg principle, 265 n.
Hinduism, 130
Historical development, 220 ff.

Historicity of Jesus, 218-219
History, 113 ff., 215 ff.
Humility, 13
Hypothesis, 138, 143

Illusion of evil, 286-287
Immortality, 307 ff.
Indeterminism, 173
Individuality, 308, 309
Inference, 196-197
Ingersoll Lectures, 307 n.
Israel, Religion of, 121 ff.

Jews, 224
Judaism, 124 ff.
Judeo-Christian stream, 129

Kinship of Mind and Nature, 146,
  151
Knowledge, 51 ff., 202
Knowledge and Faith, 58

Living God, 132, 137
Logic, 75 ff.
Love, 12, 135
Loyalty, 12

Man's uniqueness, 3-4, 162
Meaning of history, 277
Meaningless propositions, 28
Mechanism, 99, 266 ff.
Metaphysical thirst, 4
Milesian thought, 90-91
Mind, 150
Miracle, 250, 263-264, 276
Mohammedanism, 130
Monism, 98-99
Monotheism, 122
Moral evil, 295-301
Moral experience, 160 ff., 242-245
Moral philosophers, 5

Naïve spiritualism, 87 ff.
National socialism, 244
Natural beauty, 185-186
Natural evil, 301-302
Natural law, 261 ff.
Natural selection, 95, 149, 230 ff.
Naturalism, contemporary, 93 ff.,
  97 ff.

Naturalism, naïve, 89 ff.
Naturalistic fallacy, 10
Nazi movement, 16
New psychology, 248-249
Novelty, 273

Objectivity, 164 ff.
Omnipotence, 300-301
Ontological argument, 32
Optimism, 288-289

Perception, 199-201
Personal equation, 72 ff.
Personality, 134, 202, 299
Philosophy, 7
Philosophy and religion, 7 ff.
Philosophy of religion, 8
Poetry and religion, 10-12
Positivism, 101-102
Pragmatism, 27-28, 211
Praise and blame, 172-173
Prayer, 262, 263, 276-279
Primitive religion, 88
Probability, 35-36
Progress, 120 ff.
Projection hypothesis, 249
Proof, 37
Prophecy, 124 ff.
Providence, 223-224, 264-265, 276-
  277
Psychical research, 311-312
Psychology, 248 ff.
Purpose, 146 f., 267 ff., 297

Quaker journals, 207

Realism, 59 ff.
Regularity of nature, 57
Responsibility, 172-173
Resurrection, The, 312
Reverence, 14

Saints, 81
Sanity, 209
Science, 144 ff.
Scientific method, 7, 43 ff., 73-75, 94
Second law of thermodynamics,
  154 ff.
Sexual selection, 186, 245-246

Shintoism, 130
Solitariness, 15
Spiritual life, 4 ff.
Square of opposition, 30
Statistical laws, 270-271
Subjectivism, 59-61, 100-101, 167, 181, 204
Supernatural, 98
Survival value, 244 ff.
Syllogism, 40
Synagogue, 126-127

Taoism, 130
Taste, 181-183
Tautology, 31, 40

Teleology, 152 f., 237
Testimony of Christ, 218
Tests of veracity, 266 ff.
Theodicy, 282
Theologians, 81
Time, 113-114, 226
Tragedy, 260
Truth, 25 ff., 105 ff., 170

Variation, 239-240
Verification, 43 ff., 138-139, 177

Weight of evidence, 307
Wish thinking, 248 ff.
Worship, 193